Rakes, Highwaymen, and Pirates

Rakes, Highwaymen, and Pirates

The Making of the Modern Gentleman in the Eighteenth Century

ERIN MACKIE

The Johns Hopkins University Press

Baltimore

© 2009 The Johns Hopkins University Press
All rights reserved. Published 2009
Printed in the United States of America on acid-free paper
2 4 6 8 9 7 5 3 1

The Johns Hopkins University Press
2715 North Charles Street
Baltimore, Maryland 21218-4363
www.press.jhu.edu

Library of Congress Cataloging-in-Publication Data
Mackie, Erin Skye, 1959–
Rakes, highwaymen, and pirates : the making of the modern gentleman in
the eighteenth century / Erin Mackie.
p. cm.
Includes bibliographical references and index.
ISBN-13: 978-0-8018-9088-8 (acid-free paper)
ISBN-10: 0-8018-9088-8 (acid-free paper)
1. English literature—18th century—History and criticism. 2. Masculinity in
literature. 3. Literature and society—England—History—18th century.
4. Libertines in literature. 5. Adventure and adventurers in literature. 6. Burney,
Fanny, 1752–1840. Evelina. 7. Godwin, William, 1756–1836. Things as they are.
I. Title.
PR448.M37M33 2008
820.9′005—dc22   2008022422

A catalog record for this book is available from the British Library.

*Special discounts are available for bulk purchases of this book. For more information,
please contact Special Sales at 410-516-6936 or specialsales@press.jhu.edu.*

The Johns Hopkins University Press uses environmentally friendly book
materials, including recycled text paper that is composed of at least 30 percent
post-consumer waste, whenever possible. All of our book papers are acid-free,
and our jackets and covers are printed on paper with recycled content.

For my family,
past and present

CONTENTS

Acknowledgments   *ix*

1 Historicizing Masculinity: *The Criminal and the Gentleman*   1

2 Always Making Excuses: *The Rake and Criminality*   35

3 Romancing the Highwayman   71

4 Welcome the Outlaw: *Pirates, Maroons, and Caribbean Countercultures*   114

5 Privacy and Ideology: *Elite Male Crime in Burney's* Evelina *and Godwin's* Caleb Williams   149

Notes   *193*
Index   *225*

This book was begun in St. Louis, Missouri; the bulk of it was written in Christchurch, New Zealand; and the final manuscript was prepared in Syracuse, New York. My thanks, then, go out across the continents and hemispheres. At the University of Canterbury in New Zealand, Patrick Evans and Howard McNaughton made possible the period of leave during which I drafted the manuscript. The final stages of writing and revision have been supported generously by the Syracuse University English Department and the excellent work of my research assistant here, Elizabeth Porter.

Many individuals have made definitive contributions to this book. Beth Kowaleski-Wallace generously read my proposal, and her suggestions for the title revealed to me precisely how the book comes together conceptually. She has my warmest thanks. Robert Markley's attention to the proposal and early chapters of the book contributed to its greater depth and substance. Guinn Batten, always an inspiring and loyal champion of my endeavors, contributed to the conceptual framework of chapter 4; I feel ever grateful as the recipient of her enthusiasm and ideas. Laura Brown's reading also helped pull that chapter into clearer focus. Philip Armstrong shared tips about proposal writing and gave me excellent support and advice along the way. The witty, wise, and wonderful Alex Evans shared his expertise on men and helped me immensely as I thought through the more theoretical aspects of the history of masculinity and sexuality.

Portions of this book have appeared in *Cultural Critique, The Eighteenth Century: Theory and Interpretation,* and *Media History.* I stand in debt to the observations from readers for those journals. Michael Lonegro, humanities editor at the Johns Hopkins University Press, has been a pleasure to work with; his dependable and expert guidance through the publication process has rendered it painless.

The material, emotional, and spiritual support of friends and family have sustained me through the transitions across hemispheres and the work of writing this book. So all my love and gratitude, first, to my late mother, Benita Mackie, whose generosity supported me during the unpaid portion of my leave, and next, to all those closest to me: Palmer Mackie, James Mackie, Daisy Jones, Dan Jones, and, of course, Eddie and Sid, the most charming of guys. As I put these final touches on the manuscript, I recall with gratitude the steady and longstanding friendships of Celeste Fraser-Delgado, Guinn Batten, Alex Evans, Jed Mayer, Claire Hero, and Patrick Evans, and the more newly found companionship of Dennis Giacomo. Finally, my thanks go to my father, the late James Mackie, whose inventive, knowing, industrious, and often amusing approach to self-fashioning has enhanced my own understanding of how a person might become.

Rakes, Highwaymen, and Pirates

Historicizing Masculinity

The Criminal and the Gentleman

This study grows out of the observation that the modern polite English gentleman shares a history with those other celebrated but less respectable eighteenth-century masculine types: the rake, the highwayman, and the pirate. Following Norbert Elias's exposition of early modern codes of conduct, contemporary scholarship has elaborated and revised our understanding of the sociocultural, political, and economic matrices from which the polite modern gentleman has emerged.[1] Guided by codes of polite civility and restraint, eschewing personal violence for the arbitration of the law, oriented toward the family in an increasingly paternalistic role, purchasing his status as much, if not more, through the demonstration of moral virtues as through that of inherited honor, and gendered unequivocally as a male heterosexual, the modern English gentleman has been cited in contemporary masculinity studies as the first type of "hegemonic masculinity." In contemporary eighteenth-century scholarship, he is identified as the embodiment of the ideals emergent on the cultural negotiations following the political settlement of 1689.[2] The rake, the highwayman, and the pirate have not been examined fully in relation to these developments in the nature of authority, patriarchal power, honor, virtue, manners, and gendered subjectivity.[3] To do so is one object of this study, and by so doing, I intend to show the cultural negotiations attendant on the emergence of modern masculinity in a more integrated manner that accounts for both the gentleman and his outlaw contemporaries.

On both a macro- and a micro-level, literary history attests to the ways in which the discourses of masculine prestige and criminality were articulated together in the seventeenth and eighteenth centuries. The proliferation of conduct manuals and treatises on gentlemanly behavior and education in the seventeenth and eighteenth centuries occurred alongside a wave of popular criminal lives.[4]

Populated by rakes, rogues, highwaymen, and pirates, not only biographies but also plays, novels, and popular journalism engage through such figures the lively debate about masculine honor, prestige, and civility. All these texts share with the conduct literature a foundational concern with masculine behavior, how it develops for good or ill, what limits should be imposed upon it, what ideals guide its best, or worst, manifestations. The notion of the modern polite gentleman emerges in good part from the commonplace juxtaposition of the gentleman and the criminal described at one level by this literary history. This juxtaposition is largely cultural: the gentleman and the criminal are two kinds of male figures around which cluster seventeenth- and eighteenth-century preoccupations with authority, legitimacy, and masculinity. But this juxtaposition often takes more immediate and intimate discursive forms: from the seventeenth-century gallant highwayman to William Godwin's 1794 gothic hero-villain Falkland, the gentleman criminal is a male type of recurrent and enduring significance and prestige. Deriving their most immediate significance from their role in the substantiation of patriarchal power, forms of masculine prestige change over time with the shifting nature of patriarchy itself. That masculine prestige clings so tenaciously to illicit modes of conduct through three centuries speaks to the ways in which masculine power continues to rely on modes of privilege, aggression, and self-authorization that violate the moral, social, and legal dictates that constitute its own legitimacy.

While completely conventional to the period, this juxtaposition between the criminal and the gentleman is overlooked by contemporary scholarship, which usually divides its attention between the two types: ideas of the modern gentleman emerge from the history of manners, and those of the criminal from histories of dissent and labor.[5] By bringing these figures back together, this study synthesizes two major strands of sociocultural inquiry, one attentive to the emergence of modern notions of manners, civility, and taste among the elite, and the other to the tradition of radicalism and resistance among the laboring classes. Granted, the examinations of the rake and the gentleman highwayman presented here engage most heavily issues at the fore in the history of masculinity and manners, whereas the discussion of the pirate takes place more fully within the history of radicalism and dissent. What I seek to show is how both of these, the history of manners and of dissent, take modern shape around the same set of related seventeenth-century developments in the status of aristocratic ideology, especially its accompanying ethos of absolutism, and in the conceptualization of sex/gender.

This synthesis, then, is rooted in gender, specifically masculinity, a topic underexamined within both strands of scholarship. Concepts of masculinity in this period were tied to revised notions of sexual difference and, among the elite and aspiring elite, to codes of politeness and sociability. Transformations of the sex/ gender paradigm have been analyzed extensively by literary and cultural historians, especially those, such as Randolph Trumbach, concerned with the history of homosexuality and male subjectivity. The emergence of new codes of manners and civility from the sixteenth through the eighteenth centuries, likewise, has been expertly investigated by historians such as Anna Bryson and Robert Shoemaker.[6] Yet with one or two exceptions, attention to these matters of gender and conduct consistently overlooks the conventional juxtaposition between the gentleman and the criminal that is the guiding figure of this book.

One of the theses on which this study is grounded is that, within the modern paradigm of gender difference that specifies masculinity as a component of personal subjectivity, all these figures can be understood to share a gender identity in the modern sense, along with an accompanying set of gendered interests. Following from this, I argue that all of these figures may play a supportive role in the reformulation of patriarchy taking place in the seventeenth century. Identified within a polarized sex/gender system as *masculine* figures, the highwayman and pirate, the rake and the gentleman, all share a primary index of identity: their gender. As prestigious masculine figures, all are potential emulative models for everyone so gendered. But as Thomas King has emphasized in his recent study of gender and male subjectivity, this sort of participation in a shared *gender* category, "masculinity," is specifically modern and emergent only with the redistribution of sex/gender within a polarized system of complementary difference.[7] Accordingly, in the incarnations examined here, all these figures—the rake, the highwayman, the pirate, and the gentleman—share a historical status as *modern* masculine types.

Although there has been a recent wave of work on crime and criminality in England from the sixteenth through the eighteenth centuries, those social historians who focus on early modern crime usually do so as part of a larger project of writing the history of labor. Consequently, the most recent and most fruitful historical considerations of eighteenth-century criminality and society, such as those of Peter Linebaugh and Marcus Rediker, have largely excluded consideration of elite criminality necessary both to the examination of the rake and the highwayman and to the articulation of the exchange between high and low, licit and illicit, that guides my understanding of these figures and their cultural status.[8] Literary scholars such as Lennard Davis, Bryan Reynolds, and Hal Gladfelder are preoccupied with the generic modalities involved in the representation of criminality.[9] Lincoln Faller's account of criminal biographies seeks to understand how these narratives reflect contemporary attitudes toward morality, crime, and authority.[10] None of these studies pays attention to the place of the criminal types in the history of masculinity or in the history of manners. In contrast, a number of social historians examining early modern criminal violence and the duel do integrate their accounts within a larger history of manners and masculinity and are useful in this regard as I pursue my predominantly discursive account of masculine prestige and criminality.[11]

Bringing the rake, the highwayman, and the pirate back together with their contemporary, the modern gentleman, within an integrated history of masculinity, this study shows how the creation of an illicit space underwrites prestige and enshrines many of patriarchy's privileges. These figures are linked as products of the same sociocultural milieu and also by their similarity as masculine types that make culturally successful claims on prestige. More dramatically, especially in the case of the rake and the highwayman, unauthorized types often forward a claim to those very characteristics of gentility which the modern gentleman would monopolize, as with the iconic "gentleman highwayman." And while gentility is not often a quality claimed for the legendary pirates, an examination of the place of these seafaring outlaws alongside authorized powers illuminates the ways in which official culture retains investments (military, political, cultural) in forms of power it disowns. At the same time, it reveals the dependence, even complicity, of "transgressive" and "resistant" outlaw powers on the institutions and discourses against which they define their own autonomy. In chapter 4, I trace the development of this kind of constitutive complicity between authorized and outlaw powers among the early modern pirates of the Caribbean and three other West Indian groups: the early modern Maroons, the late modern rudies and yardies, and the late modern Rastafarians. Tracing the historical and cultural relations among all four groups highlights the ways in which the complicity between law and outlaw has been generated by a political and socioeconomic milieu where licensed powers exploit outlaw forces such as the pirates (as privateers), the Maroons (as bounty hunters), and the West Kingston rudie gangs (as security forces) that are at odds with overt ideologies of law and order. So while the pirate, unlike both the rake and the highwayman, is not involved with the modern gentleman through a shared claim to gentility, his relation to authorized institutions and powers is analogous to that of those other illicit types. That is, in every case these relations are shaped not only by overlapping claims but also, within the cultural symbolic field, by interdependence, often complicity, and a common ideological purpose: to support the claims of patriarchal power. It is this commonality, I believe, that ultimately supports the purchase of all these figures on cultural prestige. And this commonality is underscored by the ways in which all four of these figures—the gentleman, the rake, the pirate, and the highwayman—participate in forms of prestige absolutely denied to the gender-compromised figures of the molly and the fop.

Thus, in distinction to the claim that sociologist R. W. Connell has made for the modern gentleman as the first modern hegemonic masculine figure, I do not see him *alone* as the figure of hegemonic masculinity. Instead, I view him as one among a set of culturally prestigious masculine types—notably the rake, the highwayman, and the pirate—through which hegemony is secured.[12] As historian John Tosh observes, masculinity has to do with "upholding patriarchal power rather than a particular class order"; it may work across class lines and across different configurations of types and characteristics.[13] Hegemonic masculinity, then, as I see it here, comprises both licit and illicit modes of masculinity that serve to consolidate the legitimacy of patriarchy.[14] So the cultural history of masculinity needs to take into account unauthorized as well as legitimate forms, not only the polite gentleman but also the rake, the highwayman, and the pirate, and to understand them together. Likewise, the literary-cultural history of these figures and the texts they inhabit cannot make full sense outside of the field of patriarchy and masculinity within which they are established. Unauthorized forms of masculinity such as those embodied by the rake, the highwayman, and the pirate continue over three hundred-odd years to enjoy cultural prestige and significance in both the popular and the scholarly imagination. This book attends to the cultural and discursive means of the cultural negotiation between the licit and illicit, the gentleman and his outlaw brothers. My examinations of the three criminal types concentrates on how and why they attain and preserve their prestige, and thus on the means by which dominant culture gains access to powers and structures of authority that, in order to sanction its own legitimacy, it officially renounces.

Forms of masculine power and prestige change over time with the shifting nature of patriarchy. As has been widely recognized, the modern civil gentleman emerges to make his claim on patriarchal power from a set of historical changes that can be seen to coalesce around the Whig settlement of 1689.[15] The changes that affect the relative authority of different masculine types and traits are tied into the larger sociopolitical upheavals of the seventeenth century. Most basically, these might be viewed as a set of related crises of authority in politics, religion, knowledge, and the social order. The civil wars beginning in 1642, the execution of Charles I in 1649, the institution of Cromwell's commonwealth, the Restoration of Charles II in 1660, and the continuance of dynastic crisis, exacerbated by James II's ascension to the throne in 1685 and his flight in 1688—these are the bare political bones of events that signal changes in the conception, exercise, and representation of authority. Michael McKeon outlines the historical changes in patriarchy during this period: "In the Hanoverian Settlement of 1689, England's rulers agreed that dynastic inheritance, and the patriarchalist principles on which it is based, may be overruled." This is part of the more general and ongoing "early modern disenchantment with aristocratic ideology."[16] While this disenchantment is vividly registered by earlier events, the 1689 settlement institutionalizes a government authorized outside of, and in some defiance of, aristocratic ideology with its claims of inherited worth and its insistence on patrilineal primogeniture.

The events of the seventeenth century unsettle the old style of patriarchy, what McKeon calls "patriarchalist patriarchy," as it operates domestically as well as politically, and lead to the development of a revised form of "modern patriarchy." This updated institution is marked in the family, as in the political arena, by the increasingly contractual and legal articulation of its authority and the elaboration of individual rights and interests of members of the family other than its head.[17] The features attendant on this revision most relevant to my concern with the modern gentleman include: the insufficiency of inherited honors to secure worth; the greater reliance on juridical means to claim and protect authority; and the articulation of rights and interests of individuals within the family and the consequent realignment of the rights of the patriarchal head of that family in relation to its other members. With the eclipse of aristocratic ideology and its categorical investment in inherited status, the claims of class affiliations rise in importance.[18] The significance of one's place in a vertical chain of inherited rank diminishes; relations with one's social equals across a set of recognized commonalities of interests and cultural norms increases in its value as a means of securing personal authority and prestige.

What this means for the modern gentleman is not that he in any way relinquishes authority, but that he secures that authority by altering the ground of its legitimacy and the mode of its representation. He thus should ensure his own and his family's worth and honor through education and the personal cultivation of virtues and abilities; he ought to exercise a greater self-restraint, depending not on violence but on legal redress to protect his honor and authority; he needs to enter into negotiation with members of his family rather than rule through autocratic dictate; further to this, in order to secure the loyalty of his household, he should represent his authority as paternal benevolence. Sensitive to the importance of cultivating cohesive, class-based social relations, he should shape his emotions, attachments, and conduct within the parameters of polite civility. This mode of polite manners ideally provides a way to socially register and communicate personal virtue as benevolence, sense, taste, affection, and sympathy. Personal worth gravitates from the contingencies of wealth and status inward to an ethical-aesthetic realm variously manifest as taste, sensibility, and virtue. This is the arena of internal subjectivity in which the idea of the self as an identity grafted inalterably onto gender takes root and gathers sociocultural weight as a locus of absolute authenticity.

A substantial body of scholarship, including McKeon's, suggests that the emergence of modern patriarchy was accompanied by the paradigm of sexual difference with its articulation of modern gendered subjectivity. The medical models for the notion of sex defined in two incommensurable entities have been forwarded by Thomas Laqueur. The sociocultural contexts of this model, especially its relation to status and class, form part of McKeon's theme. The ways in which such a model naturalizes gender as sex and thus simultaneously reorients sexuality from hierarchical to differential relations have been developed by scholars of sexuality such as Alan Bray, Randolph Trumbach, and Thomas King.[19] King's analysis notes how the shift to the modern, subjectively invested mode of sexual difference simultaneously involved the categorical shift from status- to class-based claims to sociocultural dominance: "To the extent that gender polarity and heterosocial and heteroerotic desires defined the social difference of the gentry [against status claims and a court-based aristocracy], establishing themselves as the dominant class in the eighteenth century . . . , sexuality must be linked as well to the emergence of class."[20] This model of polarized sexual difference was accompanied by a revised concept of relations between men and women that were increasingly idealized as complementary relations between opposites rather than hierarchically as a relation between dominant (male) and subordinate (female). The perfected nature of these relations between the sexes, like sex/gender itself, is understood as fundamentally affective and personal, a sympathy of sensibility realized in unions that have as their aim, not the unification of estates that furthers a corporate interest, but of one private individual to her complementary counterpart. This is modern romance and is examined in chapter 5 in relation to Frances Burney's *Evelina*.

Perhaps most fundamentally, the paradigm of sexual difference locates gender within an individual's innate character, his or her subjectivity; it makes gender a personal, private matter fixed inwardly. So successfully has this model been naturalized that now we may need reminding both that there are external determinates of gender and that our commonsense understanding of sex/gender is itself a product of history, not nature. The modern ubiquity of this understanding of gendered sex is what necessitates the contemporary sociologist's injunction to twentieth-century readers to look outside personal subjectivity for the structure of gender relations: "Masculinity is not just an idea in the head, or a personal identity. It is also extended in the world, merged in organized social relations."[21] It is during this period in the seventeenth and eighteenth centuries that masculinity *becomes* "an idea in the head . . . a personal identity." The older, hierarchical model of the sex/gender system, without a distinction between male and female as absolute difference, relied more exclusively, and perhaps less anxiously, on "organized social relations" for the production of gender. So it is not until gender is thus naturalized in subjectivity that we can even speak of "masculinity" and "femininity" in the modern sense; for first and foremost, these characteristics are experienced as personal identity. It perhaps is in its recognition of this historical dimension of *gender as personal identity* that Connell's assertion that the eighteenth-century English gentleman represents the first type of hegemonic masculinity remains most valuable.

As we see in the discussion of rakish performativity in the following chapter, when masculinity is attached to a naturalized, "inborn" subjectivity, the performative, socially contingent means of securing masculine prestige either might fall into disrepute as inauthentic or, as mere play-acting, serve as an alibi for misconduct. Furthermore, the easy "bisexuality" of the Restoration rake is no longer available within a model that defines sexual relations within a paradigm of complementary difference rather than along a scale of hierarchical gradations in which an adolescent boy might occupy a homologous relation to a woman.[22] Sexuality becomes attached ineluctably to personal, gendered identity: "Gender differences were presumed . . . to be founded on an ineradicable difference of experience: men did not know what it was like to desire men." Those men who did desire other men, then, acquired a distinct identity, that of the effeminate molly; this is the "third sex." As Trumbach notes, this alteration in the relation of sexuality to gender and to personal identity brings in its train a change in masculine codes of honor, in what counts as defamation. Whereas there is evidence that in earlier periods male authority was not so heavily based on the overt expression of sexuality and instead tended to find support in sexual self-control, within the newer paradigm "it was no slander to say that a man was debauched or a whore-monger—it was proof of his masculinity—and such cases disappeared from the courts, but adult men could not tolerate a charge that they were sodomites."[23]

However, any too overt and extravagant expression of sexual profligacy, at least among the genteel, stands at odds with the strictures of self-restraint, moral conformity, politeness, and decency: the gentleman risks devolving into the libertine rake. Yet on the other hand, without some signs of assertive, successful (hetero)sexuality, the expression of masculinity remains incomplete: the gentleman might be taken for a fop, or worse. More crucially, modern masculinity emerges with the notion of inward, inalienable sexual identity so that the expression of one substantiates the other. The status of the much-indulged rake, both among his contemporaries and among historical and literary scholars, depends heavily on this modern emphasis on sexuality as a confirmation of masculinity.[24] The narrative of the reformed rake, in which all the sexual energies necessary to full masculinity are manifest extravagantly but then assimilated smoothly into the polite self-discipline of the gentleman, grows out of this contradiction between prestige, or honor, as politeness, on the one hand, and as sexual self-assertion on the other. Quite unlike their Restoration forefathers, the iconic rakish figures of eighteenth-century culture are emphatically heterosexual: Steele's pitiable rake in *Tatler* 27; John Gay's celebrity highwayman, Macheath; the lively and conflicted young man who takes on the pleasures of the metropolis in Boswell's *London Journal;* even Samuel Richardson's iniquitous Lovelace, who does not count sodomy among his plenitude of offenses. So while the eighteenth-century rake embodies residual nostalgic cultural associations with the pre-1689 world, within the paradigm of sexual difference his character is updated in ways that preserve the energies of his sexuality even as they reorient these around an exclusive heterosexuality. In this manner, the rake, like modern patriarchy itself, retains prestige by shifting the ground of its orientation and representation; for although admonished for his transgression of the codes of civility that ensure social cohesion, the rake's sexual profligacy can be appreciated as an expression of the very kind of heterosexual masculinity that is supportive of modern patriarchy. As this instance suggests, the tensions between cultural prestige and criminality so evident in such types as the rake, the highwayman, and the pirate provide opportunities to trace both changes in the understanding and representation of gender and continuities in the powers accessed by patriarchal authority.

The Cultural Politics of Nostalgia

The discrediting of aristocratic ideology that brings with it the reformulation of patriarchy, while increasingly evident in official culture and its institutions, was never uniform or complete. In relation to England's political culture, adherents to the exiled Stuarts and the principle of inviolable dynastic succession continued to challenge the Hanoverian settlement as witnessed most dramatically in the

Jacobite rebellions of 1715 and 1745.[25] Even where, as we see below in Daniel Defoe's *Colonel Jack* and his *The Compleat English Gentleman*, the insufficiency of inherited honors to secure virtue is an insistent principle, the prestige of rank and title is always recognized. So in relation to the development of codes of manners and taste, cultural arbiters such as Joseph Addison and Richard Steele sought not to discard ideals of refinement associated with the aristocratic elite but to reorient them toward what we would call aesthetic standards unmoored from any specific status milieu. Most significantly, perhaps, modern codes of civility and taste addressed the excesses of elite as well as the limitations of bourgeois culture. Aimed at both, they comprised a set of norms that determined modes of discourse and behavior for all gentlemen, aristocratic or otherwise. One much-discussed arena for the exercise of these modern forms of gentility is the polite public sphere associated in eighteenth-century English cultural history with the coffeehouse and the popular journals read and discussed there.[26] Although ostensibly transcendent of political as well as of class and status identities, the new standards of politeness, associated in the early eighteenth century especially with Shaftesbury, Addison, and Steele, were articulated in line with identifiable, emphatically Whiggish political and cultural ideologies. Such ideologies, in turn, found articulation around ideals of sex and gender relations. Advocate of the notion of complementary relations between the two "naturally" distinct sexes, *The Spectator* models in the private affective sphere "an ethics of mutuality between same and other" as relevant in the public arena as in the private.[27]

These ideologies associated with the polite public sphere, often identified with eighteenth-century cultural hegemony, maintained their authority only through often competitive negotiation with conflicting perspectives and arenas of identification.[28] While to some extent the modern, ultimately class- rather than status-oriented discourse of civility transformed aristocratic culture and manners, the power and prestige of rank and title continuously threatened to trump the dictates of taste, virtue, and good sense. In her history of the culture of "the middling sort" in the eighteenth century, Margaret Hunt isolates the seductive power of rank as a major obstacle to the successful promotion of "new, nonaristocratic definitions of 'manliness.'"[29] The claims of aristocratic masculinity are made most insistently and conventionally by the prestige secured through sexual prowess. A tradition of licentious court culture and of anti-court critique going back to the early seventeenth century secured the association between illicit sexuality and aristocratic culture; after 1689, the consolidation of anti-aristocratic sentiment forged an even stronger link between aristocracy and libertinism.[30] Even where, as in Addison and Steele, the more severe dictates of Puritanism are disowned, modern politeness maintained its adherence to conventional religious standards of sexual morality as well as to the discourses of prudent expenditure, understood both as sexual and economic output. As Hunt notes, these strictures conflict with "the widely accepted linkage between sexual potency and manhood," all the more so within a model of sexual difference that insists on the realization of masculinity through heterosexuality.[31] In a study of the institutions of eighteenth-century heterosexuality, Trumbach argues that this contradiction between the official ideology of marital chastity and the pressure on men to secure their masculinity through sexual activity expresses itself in the nearly ubiquitous resort to prostitution. Almost universally discountenanced, prostitution was almost completely licensed in the eighteenth century to service the requirements of heterosexual masculinity.[32]

An analogous contradiction, I believe, informs the cultural ambivalence surrounding the illicit, yet prestigious figures I examine here. A great part of their attraction as well as a significant component of their illegitimacy lies in the ways in which they figure modes of masculine license that, officially at least, have been disowned by the new dispensation of modern patriarchy. Because of transformations in the bases and representation of masculinity, this license is often, though not always, understood sexually. Because of anti-aristocratic cultural traditions confirmed by the settlement of 1689, this gendered sexual license registered socially as aristocratic. More exclusively than any other character, the rake embodies this elite license and the politics of nostalgia in which it is embedded. As I argue in the next chapter, in the Restoration, the rake's orientation to the aristocratic license he exploits is already self-reflective and nostalgic. Perhaps more immediately than any other texts, Rochester's poems manifest the intensely skeptical self-consciousness with which a libertine rake might address his persona. By the mid-eighteenth century, Richardson's Lovelace appears in *Clarissa* as a distinctly atavistic character, shrouded in all the menace and glamour of the libertine culture identified with the court of Charles II.[33] Thus, Elaine McGirr argues that Richardson uses his rake to ground a loyalist Hanoverian response to the failed 1745 Jacobite uprising. Slain in a duel, Lovelace, avatar of aristocratic ideology, finally falls in defeat, a casualty of Richardson's cultural battle against "Stuart pretensions" to absolutist dynastic rights of sovereignty.[34]

The nostalgic allure and the prestige of the rake, the highwayman, and the pirate, then, resides in their purchase on that very kind of absolute authority which had been supplanted by the revisions of patriarchy outlined above. There are two modern features of this kind of absolute license: first it represents, in a concept recently forwarded by McKeon, a kind of absolutism "devolved" into

the sovereignty of the individual; and second, embodied as such by outlaw figures, it is criminalized and so appropriated into official culture through gestures
of disavowal.[35] My study attends to the ways in which this devolved absolutism
of the subject takes different, ethically polarized forms: the absolutist sovereign
individual (the rake, highwayman, pirate) and the absolute sentimental subject
(Evelina, Lord Orville, Sir Charles Grandison). Whereas the modern sentimental
subject secures his or her authority through the validation, perhaps paradoxical,
of the sovereignty of other subjects, the modern criminal individual does not,
but rather he continues to understand social relations as hierarchical rather than
reciprocal and to support his dominance by drawing on modes of authority associated with a discountenanced, indeed criminalized, aristocratic ethos.

The distance of disavowal established between legitimate culture and its outlaw forms goes far toward the production of the glamour and prestige of these
modern criminals. Such distancing draws ethical, temporal, and sociocultural
distinctions that, on the one hand, cordon off the criminal as a misfit "other" and,
on the other hand, thus safely labeled, allow him back into cultural circulation
in heavily stylized and reified forms. All these modes of distance may be summoned to support the various types of nostalgic glamour and ethical immunity
enjoyed by these unauthorized types. The rake performs his outrages to claim a
kind of fully approved license already becoming outdated by the later seventeenth
century. The mid-eighteenth-century Lovelace is emphatically anachronistic and
all the more romantic for his association with the milieu of elite Restoration
culture, its naughty sophistication and decadent elegance. The gallant highwayman, as brought forward into the eighteenth century by John Gay's Macheath
and then into the nineteenth by William Harrison Ainsworth's Dick Turpin, is
originally a cavalier figure entrenched in the royalist struggles of the mid-seventeenth century. The ways in which Macheath nostalgically figures forth the
aristocratic ideology of honor and customary modes of social relation displaced
by the bottom-line mentality of the Peachums of the world have long been remarked.[36] The pirates as well emerge from this seventeenth-century world, specifically the arena of New World imperialism. While the pirates no less than
the highwayman or the rake nostalgically figure a type of personal sovereignty
operating above the law, their glamour is based as well on geographical distance,
on their allure as outlandish denizens of a floating world. In all three figures,
the very feature of their character that is most outdated and most illicit—their
commitment to the exercise of personal will self-licensed as absolute authority—
enjoys, as an aspect of this anachronism, the glamour of nostalgia. One modern
role for such characters, then, is to serve masculinist fantasies of unchecked self-

assertion permissible because romanticized through their removal from ethical accountability, historical actuality, and, in the instance of the pirates, a common national-cultural identity.

A Villain of Higher Degree: *Colonel Jack* and *The Compleat English Gentleman*

The commonplace contiguity between the gentleman and the criminal produced within the critique of aristocratic ideology presented a social and moral dilemma with which eighteenth-century writers wrestle as they produce models of ideal masculinity. A brief excursion across Defoe's conduct cum education treatise, *The Compleat English Gentleman* (ca. 1728/29), and his fictional autobiography of the pickpocket turned gentleman planter, *Colonel Jack* (1722), can illustrate how the proximate discourses of criminality and of manners operate in ideologically matched ways across two disparate genres and thus outline some of the terrain of this study. Both texts are preoccupied with the definition of the gentleman: his manners, morals, and education; his national-cultural, political, social, and professional identities.[37] Both repeatedly return to the stubbornly tenacious imbrications of the criminal and the gentleman conventional within early eighteenth-century culture. Going against the grain of convention, Defoe protests throughout *The Compleat English Gentleman* that "it is a great mistake to say that a profligate, vicious life is consistent with a compleat gentleman" (234). *Colonel Jack's* first concern is to unhinge the popular concept of the gentleman thief; *The Compleat English Gentleman's* primary task is to discredit a dissolute elite countenanced by the claims that status-linked prestige posed against the demands of religious and juridical law. The relative weight of status, or degree, against all the counterweights of moral and social probity is an ongoing preoccupation with those concerned with the formulation of gentlemanly codes of conduct. Status-based claims against the obligations of law were conventional both among the elite and on the street, and Defoe combats them at both levels.

It is widely noted that the major dilemma faced by courtesy and conduct writing lies in the propensity for the external, stylistic, and performative modes of conduct to come unmoored from their internal morally authenticating base. Unhelpfully, the English word "manners" ambivalently comprises both formalized codes of behavior, as in "etiquette," and authenticating codes of morality, as in "mores."[38] This ambiguity in the term "manners" informs a parallel one in the term "gentleman": "Since at least the time of Chaucer, there has been a distinction between the social meaning of the word [gentleman] and the moral [meaning]."[39] The discourse of manners is concerned with establishing the harmonious conformity between the individual, subjective, and moral on the one hand, and the social, objective, and behavioral on the other; the modern gentleman should embody this conformity from the inside out. In his *Compleat English Gentleman*, Defoe tropes the manners/morals split as one between the mere frippery of degree and the authenticating, ethical, and subjective bases of true honor. Gentlemen cannot be fashioned by manners alone. Their education cannot be achieved "by dressing them up like Actors upon a Stage, adorning worthless and degenerate Heads with Laurels and Bays, that they may act the Conquerors who never drew a Sword" (21).

In both of these texts, Defoe annexes this fracture between manners and morals to the related discontinuity between inherited honors and virtue produced by the skeptical critique of aristocratic ideology. For those like Defoe who participated in this critique, the discourse of manners provides an alternative way of aligning internal and sociocultural value that the birth/worth paradigm can no longer stabilize. It does so by revising the terms of authenticating value. The birth/worth paradigm seeks to ground virtue in inborn status; the discourse of manners posits status more as a historical accident in the realm of the external and contingent. The value of manners, then, is secured not in status but in moral virtue, internal to the authentic ground of subjectivity rather than inborn through the temporal chain of inheritance. In the place of authenticating status, the discourse of manners posits authenticating virtue.

Thus, unsecured by authenticating virtue, claims to value made merely on the strength of inherited rank are fallacious. In both his conduct treatise and his fictional autobiography, Defoe explores the import and implications of this fallacy through the discourses of criminality. In the *Compleat English Gentleman*, Defoe conducts an impassioned rhetorical campaign against the effects of ignorance, anti-intellectualism, and complacency within an elite that assumes the sufficiency of inherited degree to underwrite gentility. He presents the resulting failures of elite education as a list of criminal charges: "1. Here's a violence upon the free will of a person; for the child has certainly a right of option, and the father has no just authority to deprive him of it. 2. Here's a violence upon Nature, which I call an insultt on heaven. . . . Here is a kind of rape committed upon the genius of the child" (148). The presence of what Defoe sees as a sanctioned criminal class within the elite is an ongoing lament: "Why shall not a gentleman forfeit his rank and be suppos'd degenerate when he dishonours his blood by . . . crime, such for example as a generall contempt of all morall virtue, a total degenerasy of manners, and in a word an avowed practice of all degrees of scandal and crime?"

(28). While fully appreciative of the fact of prestige that accompanies inherited status, Defoe refuses the substance of status claims in any isolation from those of merit. He even posits that status can itself be rendered null through a course of criminality: "The blood of a gentleman poison'd and tainted with crime is lost, and ought to be no more valued" (26). Reflecting similar sentiments about status in his parallel world of the street, the young guttersnipe in *Colonel Jack* observes that the so-called gentleman highwayman is nothing better than a "Villain of a higher Degree than a Pick-Pocket" (62).

In *Colonel Jack*, Defoe poses the inherited versus acquired honors problem with the narrative postulate that Jack, though bred a guttersnipe, is born a gentleman's bastard and thus may claim an "original . . . as high as any Bodies" (3).[40] *Colonel Jack*, then, recapitulates the "birth versus worth" debate that McKeon has articulated as it develops through the novelistic discourses of the seventeenth and eighteenth centuries.[41] While the circumstance of his genteel origin remains foregrounded in Jack's consciousness, it by no means provides him with a model to guide his self-fashioning. Jack is aware that he is a gentleman's son, but this awareness brings no understanding of what being a gentleman actually involves. The accident of Jack's birth, however, does define two conditions relevant to his quest for gentility. First, as represented in the text, mere birth does not convey any understanding, let alone any instantiation, of merit and honor; all that being born a gentleman can bestow is the empty fact of its occurrence. Second, the alienation of birth from worth, here figured as Jack's illegitimacy and parental abandonment, is thus figured as an effect of elite misconduct, here the crime of adulterous relations. Both of these conditions militate against an easy reading of *Colonel Jack* as a kind of updated romance wherein the inborn gentility of the misplaced hero finally is revealed and affirmed. Although Jack slowly begins to piece together what he thinks a gentleman is and is not, this process is gradual, laborious, and full of apparent contradiction. It is only through the long career of his life that Jack acquires, bit by bit, by trial and error, the knowledge and mastery of a code of gentlemanly conduct secured by authentic value. *Colonel Jack*, the fictional criminal autobiography, then, might be seen as a kind of early *Bildungsroman* of the English gentleman. Jack's understanding of what a gentleman might be only begins to take firm root with his awareness of what a criminal he has been. Fittingly, the catalyst of these recognitions is Jack's interaction with a gentleman highwayman transported as an indentured servant to his estate, where he is enlisted as tutor.

Just as in *The Compleat English Gentleman* Defoe marks and excludes from honor a sanctioned elite criminal class, so in *Colonel Jack* the narrative quickly forwards and discards the claims to honor of a sanctioned underclass of criminals. According to Michael Shinagel, *Colonel Jack* responds directly to the contemporary plethora of criminal biographies that debased the gentlemanly ideal with their elevation of the heroic criminal character. With his "almost reverential regard for the ideal of the gentleman," Defoe tries to "check this trend."[42] As Defoe's protagonist begins his exploration of various claims to masculine prestige, those of the gentleman highwayman are the first to be introduced and disqualified. This comes about when Will, the rogue character under whom young Jack serves as a sort of apprentice thief, tries to entice Jack into an older, more seasoned gang by unfolding the fantasy familiar from criminal biography: "I'll bring you into a brave Gang . . . where you shall see we shall be all Gentlemen" (59). But Jack soon defines his own notions of a gentleman against Will's: "*Will* it seems understood that Word in quite a differing manner from me; for his Gentleman was nothing more or less than a Gentleman Thief, a Villain of a higher degree than a Pick-pocket. . . . But my Gentleman that I had my Eye upon, was another thing quite, tho' I cou'd not really tell how to describe it neither" (62). The criminal hierarchy in which the highwayman occupies a higher degree than the pickpocket is modeled on the aristocratic status hierarchy; a commonplace of criminal biography and popular cultural discourse, the notion is exploited to satiric effect by John Gay six years later in *The Beggar's Opera* (1728).

Born a bastard, though of "origins" that "may be as high as any Bodies," Jack becomes a street urchin, a thief, a soldier, a deserter, an indentured servant, an overseer, a plantation owner, a merchant, a soldier again, a Jacobite, a black marketeer, and ultimately perhaps something of a gentleman. There is a variousness bordering on incoherence in the modes of gentlemanly conduct and character that Jack identifies and adopts. Jack's career as a gentleman, like his life overall, is "a Checquer Work" (3). Just as James Boswell adopts and discards a number of often contradictory, sometimes criminal masculine types as he strives to establish his character in the *London Journal* discussed in chapter 3, so does Colonel Jack move through a similarly various repertoire of models. This registers, as does Boswell's *London Journal*, a sociocultural arena in which a number of different ethical codes contend for the last word on masculine gentility. It also conforms to the insistence on the acquired, experiential bases of genteel merit that attends Defoe's arguments for elite education in *The Compleat English Gentleman*.

We have already reviewed the challenges posed in the seventeenth century to aristocratic ideology with its identification of honor as status, and to the hierarchical notion of gender by the paradigm of sexual difference. The activation in the eighteenth century of these alterations in standards of prestige on the one

hand, and in the constitution of gendered subjectivity on the other, did not uniformly replace the older hierarchical models of status and sex but rather emerged
alongside them, producing a field of proliferated possibilities. The cultivation of
masculine prestige might follow a number of available avenues: through birth
and inherited honors (status); through wealth (class); through the cultivation of
polite manners; through the pursuit of fashion; through the assertion of national-
cultural and cultural-ethnic identity; through valorous martial accomplishment;
through religious and moral cultivation; through successful sexual self-assertion;
through literary and cultural accomplishment. It is within such a mushrooming
of possibilities that Colonel Jack picks his own way and that this study of masculine prestige and criminality follows.

Jack's early confrontation with gentlemanly possibility begins with his rejection of the notion of the gentleman highwayman. Later in the text, a central
episode highlights the confrontation between two dominant ideologies of proper
masculine conduct: one based on the elite code of gentlemanly honor, secured by
the duel; and the other on the counter authority of the law, secured by the state
and its magistrates. Taking place at the culmination of Jack's self-cultivation in
the mode of a French gallant, this episode occurs when he is confronted with a
bill by a creditor of his former wife. As is the case throughout the narrative, in
this episode the identification of so-called "gentlemanly" qualities and characters
as criminal serves as a way that Defoe sifts through licit and illicit claims on
gentility.

Jack, or "Jacques," as he now likes to be known, has acquired the polish of a
gentleman in France and returned to London where he passes "for a Foreigner,
and a Frenchman" (185). His acquisition of the charms of French gallantry aid
him in the courtship of his first wife. Up to this point he had been "a meer Boy in
the Affair of Love, and knew the least of what belong'd to a Woman, of any Man in
Europe." In France he learns how to make conversation, play cards, and dance; he
becomes "accomplish'd . . . with every thing that was needful" to develop socially
and sexually "from a Boy" into a "Gentleman" (186, 191). He marries, but the wife
turns out to be a spendthrift and a wanton, a "wild untam'd Colt, perfectly loose";
Jack divorces her in the ecclesiastic court but is dogged by her debts (193).

One day a "Gentleman well Dress'd" comes to his lodging and demands pay-
ment for a thirty-pound bill drawn by Jack's ex-wife. Jack refuses to pay it. An
altercation ensues about decorum, first of presenting a bill, and then of receiving
a challenge. In this, Jack, as the merchant gentleman invested in the authority
of the law, stands firm against the "gentleman-thug" who attempts to pervert a
matter of contract into a contest of honor and settle it through the anti-juridical,

elite mode of contestation, the duel (199–201).⁴³ In the duel, the preservation of honor and the commission of crime come together to articulate the explicit contradiction between judicial law and what Jack's opponent calls "Gentleman's Law" (201). The law or code of honor obligates a gentleman to accept a challenge; the law of the land forbids it. Participation in a duel implicitly acknowledges the priority of the "Gentleman's Law" above that of the magistrates and so asserts the sovereignty of the participants outside the judicial system and finally outside the authority of the monarch.

With great tenacity, the duel continues current long after the more general sociocultural discreditation of aristocratic ideology. More than any other institution, the duel indicates that the type of sovereign personal will typical of the gentleman criminal remains entrenched. Anti-dueling laws had little or no effect; only an ongoing campaign of anti-dueling sentiment finally helps to dampen the very short fuses of a male elite who relied on this means of deadly self-preservation. Shoemaker notes how the deliquescence of the duel required a shift in men's subjective orientation to their own honor and its representation. This occurs through a change in manners, "an increasing intolerance of violence, new internalized understandings of elite honour, and the adoption of 'polite' and sentimental norms governing masculine conduct."⁴⁴ Campaigns against duels are campaigns not merely against an absurd, retrograde, self-destructive custom, but against the authority of a highly prestigious arena of identification to claim the ultimate power over life and death. In her study of opposition to the duel, Donna T. Andrew elaborates the nature of the threat it presented: "By thus claiming the rights of independent sovereignty, the duellist defied and threatened the continuance of both the law and the state."⁴⁵ Participation in a duel silently declares one's absolute allegiance to a cultural code impervious to judicial control. Rooted in the preservation of personal prestige, the duel, according to its adherents, trumps all other sociopolitical institutions in the determination of honor.

So the gentleman-thug taunts Jack: "They say, you are a Gentleman, and they call you Colonel; now if you are a Gentleman, I accept your Challenge Sir." Jack denies he has offered any challenge and suggests that the man seek his "satisfaction at Law." This unleashes a torrent of abuse: "Law! Says he, Law! Gentleman's Law is my Law; in short, Sir, you shall pay me, or Fight me" (201). Jack who "had forgot the main Article" of all his education in French gallantry, that is, "how to use a Sword," since he "had been perfectly unacquainted with Quarrels of this Nature," is saved from violence by the entrance of a constable, who determines the quarrel in Jack's favor. The matter must be settled before the magistrates. The law, not the duel, prevails. This episode insists, against much elite convention, that the so-called Gentleman's Law is criminal and that the outcome of all Jack's (or Jacques') pursuit of French gallantry is vanity and vexation. In a single stroke, Defoe disqualifies the claims made by the code of honor and the whole world of fashion and the beau monde it regulates; gentlemanly prestige must be sought elsewhere.[46]

Recently, George Boulukos has identified the acquisition of whiteness as one of the status features that Jack acquires during his time in Maryland and Virginia, first as an indentured servant, then as an overseer, and finally as a plantation owner. Just as notions of masculinity and of the gentleman are fairly fluid and unfixed in Jack's social landscape, so at this time are those of "race" and "ethnicity."[47] In *Colonel Jack*, then, Defoe brings together "the still inchoate category of race" and translates it into the field of status, a mark of social prestige consequential on the New World plantation just as French language and manners are in Europe. Yet while Boulukos sees whiteness operating here "as a ready means to, or replacement for gentility," I see it as just another possible way to code prestige that Colonel Jack encounters, a mode newly emergent in the Americas.[48] Since Jack goes on, thoroughly confirmed in his whiteness, to also pursue classical and biblical learning, further advancement in a martial career, a brief stint as a Jacobite, a run as a black marketeer in the Spanish Americas, and an interlude in those territories as a kind of elite colonial, I cannot see whiteness as operating as a replacement for other modes of gentility, nor as in itself a sufficient means to gentility. Nonetheless, the inclusion of whiteness in Jack's repertoire of status features signals a dramatic and, as is often the case with Defoe, prescient moment in the history of modern hegemonic masculinity.

Settled on his plantation and reflecting upon the qualities that make men "Rich and Great, and [give] them a Fame, as well as a Figure in the World," Jack begins "to love Books" (157). Immediately upon the articulation of these aspirations to learning, fame, and figure, "Fate" presents Jack with a tutor in the shape of a transported gentleman scholar cum gentleman highwayman sent as an indentured servant to his plantation (157). The tutor teaches Jack the gentleman's lingua franca, Latin, and provides him with a revised, more explicitly criminalized sense of his own past identity. This understanding, in turn, supplies Jack with a definition of honor that might secure his concept of a gentleman. "I had been an Offender as well as [had the tutor]," reflects Jack, "tho' not altogether in the same Degree, but I knew nothing of the Penitence; neither had I look'd back upon any thing as a Crime: but as a Life dishonourable, and not like a Gentleman" (162). While Jack has long realized that his life as a thief was "not like a Gentleman" and was "dishonourable," until his highwayman tutor introduces him to the fully criminal nature of his misdeeds, he has had no fixed referent for either "honor" or its embodied form "gentleman."

Jack's reasoning that his past deeds were "dishonourable, and not like a Gentleman" proves tautological. As noted, conceptions of what characteristics are "like a Gentleman" flourish in such conflicting proliferation that the concept "gentleman" cannot in itself secure the significance of the term "honor." Furthermore, although, removing the negatives, the syntax here connects "honor" to "gentleman," this relation is purely conjunctive, a juxtaposition, not hierarchical, a cause. But when Jack gains an understanding of his past deeds as crimes, he finally does secure a referent for their evaluation, one congruent with his earlier realization that the highwayman is not a gentleman: the deeds were criminal and *therefore* dishonorable and not like a gentleman. Here Defoe turns about the commonplace juxtaposition of the gentleman and the criminal in order to define them against one another and to fix a true understanding of what a gentleman is, or is not, in the moral consciousness of crime. The code of honor, Defoe thus suggests, is not an autonomous self-governing system, but it is dependent for its value on a higher moral code that identifies dishonor with crime. This conforms to the arguments Defoe forwards in *The Compleat English Gentleman* as he insists that illicit conduct annihilates honor in ways not recoverable through the claims of inherited rank—the mere fact of the elite status one might be born with, as is Jack.

When Jack returns to Europe, he continues his quest for gentility and again becomes embroiled in crime, this time of a treasonous, capital nature. Fulfilling his earlier fantasy of "being a Gentleman Officer," he joins the Old Pretender's army (105, 207). Enlisted in the Jacobite cause, he becomes actively involved in the 1715 rebellion and only narrowly eludes capture at the battle of Preston. His outlaw status as a rebel traitor dogs him for the rest of the narrative. He immediately flees England for the Americas, but even there becomes alarmed that he might be recognized by his fellow rebels when they arrive as transported felons on his plantation. In order to escape possible detection, he launches into a convoluted and protracted course of trade and negotiations through the Spanish Caribbean, enjoys the refined hospitality of his Spanish merchant host, and finally makes his way through Cadiz back to London, where he is joined by his wife. Although finally released by the Royal General Pardon, Jack's involvement with the rebellion stands as the most grievously criminal act of his life. Led into it by his thirst for martial honor, this episode in Jack's life invalidates the heroic, aristocratic ethos that engenders it. George I's pardon becomes, in turn, occasion for an encomium on the Hanoverian regime (276). It is not so much, as David

Blewett has argued, that "Defoe uses Jacobitism to emphasize those aspects of his hero's character which ironically undercut his progress to gentility" by revealing him for the deluded upstart he is, as that Defoe presents, in order to deny, the proposition that the Jacobite is a gentleman, just as he presents in order to eliminate the proposition that the highwayman is a gentleman.[49] Both Jacobite and highwayman are criminals, and *therefore* not gentlemen. Bookending Jack's career, the gentleman highwayman and the gentleman Jacobite, then, represent the two most criminal types of prestigious masculinity that Jack encounters as he pursues his aspirations of gentility.[50]

In *Colonel Jack,* Defoe approaches the education of the gentleman from the lower, and in *The Compleat English Gentleman* from the upper, realms of the social order; both texts are governed by the same ideology of conduct and, as they grapple with the same set of problems, reach largely the same conclusions. The modern gentleman comes to us not solely through the conduct and education treatise and its discourse of manners but also through the fictional criminal autobiography and its narrative negotiations. The critique Defoe launches in these two texts is relevant to all the types of criminalized masculine prestige examined in this study. Indeed, from almost any perspective but that which they authorize for themselves, what are those notorious courtly rakes Rochester, Buckingham, and Dorset, or that infamous literary libertine Lovelace, but villains of a higher degree?

Stereotype and Myth

Even where, as with Richardson's Lovelace, they are further developed as what we call literary characters, all the figures addressed by this study are stereotypes. While courtesy and conduct writers work largely through the elaboration of ethical traits and codes of behavior, the texts I deal with handle issues of masculine conduct and honor more through their manipulation of social types. Not absolute, these distinctions are a matter of emphases. Seventeenth-century "character writing," elaborated from the Theophrastan model, records a veritable cornucopia of contemporary social stereotypes, and these sit side by side with more traditional ethical types. Thus *The English Theophrastus, or, the Manners of the Age* (1702) includes the Beau, the Country Squire, Servants, Authors, Wits, and Critics as well as sketches of Avarice, Courage, Hypocrisy, Gentility, and Rashness.[51] Evaluation and representation of conduct and character clearly took both forms simultaneously, and this earlier genre of character writing is apparent in the critical, moral, novelistic, and pictorial discourses of the eighteenth century.[52] The prominence of masculine social stereotypes as admonitory or emulative models for personal character is familiar to any reader of *The Tatler* and *The Spectator,* for instance, where ideals of masculine conduct are presented through portrayals of the fop, the rake, the pretty fellow, the smart fellow, the beau, the man of sense, and so on.[53]

In her examination of early novelistic character writing, eighteenth-century scholar Deidre Lynch notes how it registers that culture's "investment in the eloquence of the material surface," its "idealization of what was graphically self-evident."[54] Participating in the same mimetic and commercial logic realized in the printing presses that produced it, character writing becomes enmeshed in tensions between the general and the particular: "The printed characters of writing were freighted with assurances about the legibility and, in their uniform replication, about the coherence of the social body. These assurances . . . were in tension with . . . an understanding of character as . . . the peculiar feature that distinguished one thing from another."[55] Literary historian J. W. Smeed links the seventeenth-century proliferation of new character types to the demand for novelty characteristic of a burgeoning commercial market in print.[56] Thus fixed in stylized and reproducible form, contemporary forms of individual or even cohort distinction are made both generic and widely imitable. Imitation of scripted social types from the page or the stage in turn leads to modes of identification between individual subjects and the sociocultural types. This problem vexes Addison and Steele as they seek to "erect a model of character that is at once founded on criteria outside of mere . . . external sociocultural conventions, and yet also able to be represented and recognized within those conventions."[57] At this period, then, the distinctions between "stereotype" and "character," between what is typical and generic and what is individual and distinctive, are only just coming into view. This is all by way of saying that talking about stereotypes *is* talking about character.

The sociocultural power of such types is assumed by critics such as Addison and Steele, both as they produce positive types for emulation and as they condemn negative types they see proliferating in popular culture and in the popular imagination. The stage provided a particularly powerful platform for the promotion of popular types. In chapter 3, I look at one example of how a popular stage type, the gentleman highwayman Macheath, works within the imagination of one distinct individual, James Boswell. *The London Journal* records the internalization of this fictional character in Boswell's personal subjectivity in ways that maintain both its stereotypical generality and its specific relevance to Boswell's own psyche and circumstance. So we see how the public and culturally conventional may be integrated with the private and psychically specific, how reading character becomes inseparable from reading stereotypes. Employing the analysis of conventionalized types in her exposition of seventeenth-century codes of civility, Bryson insists that "each stereotype suggests a social world and the meanings which inform that world"; conversely, each stereotype, as in Boswell's case, suggests a subjective world and its meanings, desires, and emotions.[58] It would be naïve to so fully believe in the autonomy of internal subjectivity as to suppose it immune from culture and so from what is mimetic and generic. Indeed, as I have argued elsewhere, the very notion of autonomous, internal subjectivity is generated within an acute awareness of the absence of such immunity and of the threats that (bad) culture can have on the self.[59] People are always copying their true selves.

My use of the term "culturally mythic type" means to register, first of all, the special intensity of meaning these types exercise in both sociocultural and subjective worlds. Emphatically, this term bears no relation to any psychological, psychoanalytic, or structuralist elaboration of the notion of myth. The mythic figures here are fully historical, sociocultural, and ideological types. Yet I do exclude from my use of the term the common negative connotation of unreality that sometimes accompanies both "myth" and "ideology." As Graham Holderness asserts in his elaboration of the Shakespeare myth: "Myth is . . . a real and powerful form of human consciousness, holding some significant place within a culture."[60]

Usefully, Roland Barthes' outline of the signifying logic of the second-order nature produced by modern bourgeois cultural myths insists on their ideological function. Yet Barthes' focus is on one historically and culturally distinct form of myth; my mythic outlaw figures might well participate in the contemporary kind of naturalization of the historical with which he is concerned, but such participation is not my primary concern here.[61] Rather, I use my culturally mythic figures to trace discursive negotiations engaged in preserving, even while disowning, certain forms of masculine authority and prestige within the new patriarchal dispensation of the later seventeenth century. Their capacity to accommodate this ideological contradiction and, even more, the degree to which their status as culturally mythic characters depends on that accommodation, distinguishes the rake, the pirate, and the highwayman from the polite modern gentleman with whom, nonetheless, they are enlisted, if more surreptitiously, in cultural work on behalf of patriarchal power. Insofar as he indicts the modern gentleman as *not* free of this criminalizing contradiction, William Godwin's depiction in *Caleb Williams* produces that type as well as an ideological myth.

In her elaboration of the eighteenth-century myth of passive womanhood,

Ellen Pollak discusses the relation between ideology and myth. Myth is not an unmediated equivalent of ideology; rather, myth refers to "the representational forms that ideology takes." These forms manufacture "the social fictions that evolve at once to cover and to enable" an ideology's effects. The propositions forwarded by these kinds of cultural myths are frequently contradictory; thus, Pollak cites the prevalence within a single gender ideology of the two antithetical female types: the sexually insatiable woman of pure matter and the spiritually idealized woman of pure spirit.[62] Like Pollak, I am concerned with the ideology of gender in the eighteenth century, though with the myths it weaves around masculine rather than feminine figures. One central contradiction described by my culturally mythic outlaw figures lies in the way they serve to maintain the prestige and currency of forms of masculine authority and power discredited within the new paternalistic form of patriarchy. Most usually, this contradiction is written onto the surface features of these types, who are at once unauthorized, often even criminal, and prestigious, sometimes even genteel. During the period of their emergence, these figures rather baldly register anxieties about the loss incurred within the emergent, more contractual and mediated, modes of patriarchal power and the fantasies of recuperation that accompany this loss.

Looking at the mythical status of Robinson Crusoe, Frankenstein, and Dracula in European culture, literary scholar John Bender formulates a process of modern myth making that works through the formal features of novelistic realism and its accompanying epistemologies.[63] Examining narratives that encapsulate modern experiences with gender, urbanism, capitalism and finance, the New World, and the nonhuman, eighteenth-century scholar Laura Brown defines a set of modern fables: "Stories without a text, imaginative events without an author . . . built from the concrete materials of modern European experience . . . they pervade and surpass the various movements, forms, genres, and modes of eighteenth-century English print culture."[64] Although differing in their relative investments in textuality, especially in the formal features of realism, both Bender and Brown usefully conceptualize the detachability of narrative and character from text, and thus the autonomy and mobility that are features of the iconic outlaw figures I examine here. Outlaw figures such as the rake, the pirate, and the highwayman likewise pervade a broad range of English print culture and may be difficult to pin down to any single text or genre. Indeed, in order to trace the kind of cultural work that they do, an examination of their figuration within multiple generic conventions can be indispensable, as we see especially in the case of the highwayman examined in chapter 3.

In his study of criminal narrative, Lincoln Faller uses a concept of myth he traces from that developed by the cultural anthropologist Stanislaus Malinowski. According to this formulation, myth is "a narrative . . . told in satisfaction of religious wants, moral cravings . . . practical requirements." In line with this heavily personal, ethical, and utilitarian notion of myth, Faller divides criminal narratives, along with their mythic functions, into two categories. One type of narrative, "a species of spiritual biography," aims for the realistic depiction of particularly horrendous crimes such as familial murder and the greater elaboration of criminal consciousness in order to turn the tale toward distinctly moral and so "happier" outcomes. Horrible crimes are perpetrated, but they are punished; psychopathic serial killers do exist, but they can repent. The other type of narrative specified by Faller "imitated the picaresque novel." Its mythic function is to provide readers "escape from a variety of real-world concerns, not the least of which was the increasingly troublesome business of hanging men for merely crimes against property."[65]

Confined as it is to the production of moral reassurance, Faller's first species of cultural myth seems not to take into account much of culture at all. While the second variety, that of the mythic picaresque, does note the capacity of such narratives to register dissent from contemporary sociopolitical conditions, Faller never integrates his exposition of this capacity within a fuller historical-political narrative. Faller's notion of myth remains limited in its conception and operation to the arena of personal moral and psychological effect.

Furthermore, Faller expresses disappointment with what he sees as the depleting and depersonalizing tendencies of popular criminal narrative. So in his summation of his chapter on the renowned gallant highwayman James Hind, he says: "All that was published between his capture and execution . . . served in the long run only to reinforce an image that, however much it shimmered and threatened to disappear, never quite gave place to the actual man. Hind lingered on in the popular imagination like so many other thieves: eviscerate, scattered to pieces, the chiefest part of him taken down secretly and buried" (20).[66] Confined to a single genre of criminal discourse and a curtailed register of significance, Faller's study sacrifices access to that richer range of texts and cultural discourses that remember and compose the highwayman in more ideologically substantial and historically preservative forms. In contrast, this study suggests that the "chiefest part" of the romantic highwayman and of his outlaw brothers lives on for centuries in culturally mythic figures unconfined by, though always responsive to, genre and legible as sorts of cultural palimpsests copied in scripts that trace continuity even as they shift with history.[67]

What Lies Ahead

While each of the four following chapters is founded in the history of patriarchy, masculinity, and manners sketched here, each adapts its methodology, textual selection, and chronological range to the specific character addressed. For while all these unauthorized figures share an initial orientation within this history, the most salient issues figured by their subsequent developments vary. These chapters, then, each do different things with the outlaws they discuss. Chapter 2, "Always Making Excuses: The Rake and Criminality," is organized around the questions of how and why the often egregious criminality of the rake is so often overlooked both by his contemporaries and by subsequent critical and scholarly evaluations. At issue here as well is how criminality and masculine prestige can operate in relation to notions of subjective authenticity and performativity. The chapter concludes with Richardson's Lovelace while intimating that the apologies for rakish misconduct it describes remain current into the present, as attested by the proverbial colloquialism "Boys will be boys."

Chapter 3, "Romancing the Highwayman," while sustaining attention to the ways in which the social stereotype works in the performance of personal subjectivity, attends to some of the more specifically generic and formal features at play in the evolution of the modern romantic highwayman. This examination begins with the seventeenth-century cavalier highwaymen and concludes with William Harrison Ainsworth's early nineteenth-century depiction of Dick Turpin. For it is in Ainsworth's incarnation that the highwayman is bequeathed, fully romanticized, to mass culture and to the heritage industry. In chapter 4, "Welcome the Outlaw: Pirates, Maroons, and Caribbean Countercultures," I bring my discussion of iconic outlaws into the West Indies and the arenas of African diasporic, colonial, and postcolonial studies. By comparing two pairs of outlaw types in a chronologically chiasmic fashion—the early modern pirate and the late modern rudie, or yardie, on the one hand, and the early modern Maroons and the late modern Rastafarians, on the other—I also bring the study well into the twentieth century. The Maroons shared a geography and history with the pirates of the Caribbean; and both sustained organized opposition to, as well as complicity with, the two central institutions of the colonial machine: plantation slavery and the navy. By attending as well to the rudies and the Rastafarians, contemporary West Indian heirs of the pirates and the Maroons, I hope to facilitate a better understanding of how culture works in the historical relations between early and late modernity.

Returning to England and to the late eighteenth century, the final chapter,

"Privacy and Ideology: Elite Male Crime in Burney's *Evelina* and Godwin's *Caleb Williams*," examines the role of criminality in sentimental and political discourses. Thus the book ends with case studies of two well-known novels in order to integrate the two dominant concerns that shape this study as a whole: the first foregrounds the role of discourses of masculine prestige and criminality in the reform of manners; the second, their role in the articulation of radicalism and dissent. In both Burney's and Godwin's novels, discourses of criminality are paired in conventional ways with those of manners and ideal gentility in order to produce reformative arenas of relation and awareness. Focusing on Burney's representation of elite male criminality and of its counterpoint, ideal gentlemanly sensibility, this chapter revisits the guiding figures and concepts of the study in ways that reveal their implications for *feminine* subjectivity and sociocultural power. I argue that the novel undertakes a reassessment of the nature and effects of such criminality from a point of view that articulates damage and reparation, not through juridical or religious discourse, but through the private discourse of sensibility. Embodying the virtues enshrined in this discourse, Lord Orville distributes them within patriarchal authority, reconfigured here as benevolent paternalism. As a model of modern masculine subjectivity, Orville represents the perfect gentleman, not as a feminized (like the fop), but as a privatized individual. Finally, the revisions of patriarchal power in *Evelina* depend upon the absolute authority of the sentimental subject that successfully challenges absolutist claims to domination made by figures of faulty masculinity such as the rake, the unreconstructed patriarch, and the fop.

Utilizing the conventional eighteenth-century juxtaposition of the gentleman and the criminal, Godwin's *Caleb Williams* (1794) reorients the concepts and themes isolated by this study from the context of seventeenth-century revolutionary England to that of contemporary revolutionary France. Godwin's novel draws on the characteristic eighteenth-century discourses of masculine prestige and criminality in order to show how both function across a range of social and experiential arenas: in aristocratic ideology, its chivalric discourses and its institutions of patronage and absolute honor; in the legal system and its penal institutions; in the sociopolitical hierarchies supported by government; and in that realm of emotional interiority realized here most vividly as an arena of terror and guilt, exultation and dominance, veneration and abjection (the Gothic). Exposing the subject formed within these institutions ("things as they are") as an ideological deformation, Godwin's novel discountenances the kind of redemptive sentimental subject forwarded both by Richardson and Burney. Armed with the fictions of this subject, Godwin, in *Caleb Williams*, indicts the criminal character of ideology and locates any possible recognition of justice in a political awakening possible only outside the discourses of the novel itself.

Coda: The Exception of Jonathan Wild and Jack Sheppard

Readers familiar with eighteenth-century literature and culture will remark the absence from this study of two of the period's most infamous criminals, the racketeer and thief-taker Jonathan Wild and the petty thief and celebrated escape artist Jack Sheppard. Paired in the popular imagination, these two figures intersect biographically: both emerged from the London criminal underworld of the first decades of the eighteenth century, and they knew one another; indeed, it was on Wild's information that Sheppard and his companion Elizabeth Lyon were incarcerated. Sheppard was executed in November 1724, and Wild followed him in May 1725. Their characters and tales are interwoven symbolically as well. As the modern editor of their early lives remarks: "There was a natural and dramatic rivalry between Sheppard and Wild, which quickly caught the popular imagination ... the incorrigible young escapist pitted against the grim relentless thief-taker ... a duel between ... rebellion and authority, youth and age."[68] A mesmerized and sympathetic throng of 30,000 turned out for Sheppard's execution, sealing his claim to the underclass celebrity that reemerges in iconic form a century later with William Harrison Ainsworth and George Cruickshank's massively popular *Jack Sheppard* (1839). Six months later, Wild, befuddled with laudanum, staggering and incoherent, was pelted with rubbish at Tyburn and confirmed in popular contempt for all time.

On the one hand, the omission here of this legendary pair may seem to require little discussion: neither is a pirate, rake, or highwayman; nor do either make any claim on revised forms of gender and civility that shape the modern gentleman. Yet some reflection on these figures helps throw into sharper relief the specificity of the criminal characters this study *does* address, for a comparison of Wild and Sheppard with the three figures examined here underscores the exceptional qualities of nostalgic prestige embodied by the latter. Whereas the rake, the pirate, and the highwayman all take definitive shape from the changes in authority, absolutism, and gender rooted in the seventeenth century, Wild and Sheppard emerge from later situations, institutions, and conflicts: in Wild's case, the sophistication of business administration and the commercialization of politics underway in the eighteenth century; and in Sheppard's, the social dislocation and working-class unrest, first of the 1720s and then, more dramatically, of the industrialized 1830s. Sheppard and Wild, then, do not share with the rake, the highwayman, and the pirate an orientation to the nexus of sociopolitical and cultural developments that I outline here. Theirs is a different set of moments and concerns.

Criminal businessman rather than gentleman criminal, Wild seems to have been universally reviled both within the criminal subculture he exploited and, finally, by the legitimate world he first accommodated but finally scandalized. Never is Wild celebrated, even ambivalently, as a rogue hero. In John Gay's *Beggar's Opera*, Wild inspires Peachum, that petty, cold-blooded, avaricious brute of the bottom line. In his political satire, *The Life of Mr Jonathan Wild, the Great* (1743), Henry Fielding pursues the conceit of Wild as a Walpolean Great Man so relentlessly that his censure overreaches the usual inversions of the mock-heroic mode to extend into a kind of "double reversal" that topples not merely the insatiable, parasitic Wild/Walpole but also the very standard of heroic greatness invoked as foil for the fathomless corruption of its protagonist.[69] Unlike Gay's comic opera and Fielding's mock-heroic biography, the early life of Wild attributed to Daniel Defoe presents this ruthless entrepreneur in less rhetorically layered terms and emphasizes at once Wild's industrious, methodical application to business and his vile exploitation of the most disenfranchised and vulnerable.

Defoe aptly characterizes Wild's vocation as "the thieving trade."[70] Wild systematizes crime into a well-oiled machine operated according to regularized procedures of business administration. Fascinated with the organization Wild set up for receiving and restoring stolen goods, Defoe lingers for about ten pages over the techniques and procedures that maintain it.[71] Wild's diligent management— of people, of property, of accounts—weaves a tight web of neatly organized crime: "He openly kept his counting-house, or office, like a man of business, and had his books to enter everything in with the utmost exactness and regularity."[72] With his methodical "exactness and regularity" and his extensive network of more-and-less-willing staff, Wild's operation might be viewed as an early small-scale instance of bureaucratized evil; historians have confirmed more than 120 of his victims, thieves he employed and then betrayed to execution.[73] Defoe reserves the highest pitch of his condemnation for Wild's seduction and corruption of the homeless youth who swarmed the London streets. Wild, it seems, was an eighteenth-century Fagin. Cannily perverting the institution of apprenticeship, Wild preyed on the dislocated, often starving children of the streets, promising them sustenance and a place in the business. Defoe refers to several documents recording how Wild "on pretence of providing for them, and employing them" took on children "strolling about the streets in misery and poverty," trained them and had them executed: "Horrid wickedness! His charity has been to breed them up to be thieves; and still more horrid! several of these, his own foster-children, he has himself caused afterwards to be apprehended and hanged for the very crimes which he first taught them how to commit."[74]

Whereas Gay and Fielding emphasize the ways in which Wild's methods mirror in the low life the corruption of politics and ethics in the legitimate world, Defoe's narrative highlights Wild's more viscerally horrific violation of all human, social, and familial bonds ("his own foster-children"). These systematic exterminations within the underworld that supported him earned Wild the ignominy and contempt that followed him well beyond the grave. Taken together, Wild's pathological reduction of every social, familial, judicial, and occupational institution and value to naked monetary terms speaks most directly to eighteenth-century anxieties attendant on the post-1690s commercialization of what seemed to contemporaries almost every sphere of existence. His "management" of his "staff," especially of the young "apprentices" he bred up himself to the "trade," realizes in near-demonic terms the potential bankruptcy of all customary bonds within a modern world obligated only to financial gain.

In contrast with Wild, Sheppard enjoyed an unprecedented popularity at the time of his execution and held a steady place as a popular hero throughout the century. As contemporary newspaper accounts and early lives of Sheppard attest, his fame rested not on any exceptional prowess as a thief, but rather on his uncanny handiness as an escape artist. It is as a kind of eighteenth-century Harry Houdini that Sheppard is celebrated. However, as the wayward apprentice breaking from prison and as the sympathetic victim of the diabolical Wild, Sheppard's exploits participate in the realm of popular underclass culture, where they are symbolically tinted with shades of resistance to oppression and near-magical emancipation.

Sheppard three times escaped from Newgate prison, most famously from the "Tower," a maximum security hold where he was chained, arms and legs stapled to the floor. Squeezing his wrists out of their irons, he broke his leg fetters with his bare hands, made a breach in the room's chimney, took the iron flue bar, and climbed up the chimney to the "Red Room," a cell reserved for elite prisoners, empty at the time. Using the flue bar, he then broke the lock off the ironclad door and made his way into the prison chapel and through the massive outer door of the prison. Once outside, Sheppard climbed further up, scaling a wall until he reached the very top of the prison and from there jumped down over the London rooftops. Yet, as Linebaugh emphasizes, Sheppard's final breakout was posthumous. At his execution there were day-long "running skirmishes and subtle stratagems for the control of his corpse." These matches between the anatomists who would dissect the bodies of the executed and the mob who would bury the bodies were customary. Sheppard's execution and the retrieval of his body, however, witnessed an almost unparalleled popular involvement and the vanquishing of the anatomists a populist triumph.[75]

Sheppard, as Linebaugh argues, occupies a place in class politics nascently emergent in the early eighteenth century around the "weaver's riots, the recomposition by immigration of the working population, the political repressions of the second decade [i.e., the Black Act], the new enclosed structures of coercion and discipline."[76] Sheppard's mob appeal, then, can be understood as largely generated by his identity with this working population. Trained as a carpenter, Sheppard was technically skilled at the making and unmaking of locks and doors; he opportunistically and brilliantly improvised a toolbox from found objects. These artisanal skills, combined with intense bodily strength, gymnastic ability, and sheer nerviness lie at the core of his triumphant escapes: "Sheppard's fantastic abilities as escaper were no mystery. They came from his outstanding skills as a carpenter and builder, learned during his six-year apprenticeship, but also inherited from his father and his grandfather (both carpenters)."[77]

A figure of fascination across class strata in the eighteenth century, Sheppard was famously visited by notables John Thornhill, who painted his portrait; William Hogarth; and John Gay. Some critics surmise that Sheppard provided the model for Gay's Macheath, as did Wild for his Peachum in *The Beggar's Opera*. However, I believe the traces of Sheppard in Macheath delineate only Sheppard's substitution by the more established stereotypical gallant highwayman, whose persona and prestige take shape, not within artisanal and apprentice culture, but, as I discuss in chapter 3, around the social and political reversals of the seventeenth century. The seventeenth-century gallant highwayman, given iconic shape by Gay's Macheath, is a nostalgic figure closely coupled with the Stuart cause and the mode of Cavalier masculinity associated with its adherents. The eighteenth-century escape artist Sheppard is a modern figure most intimately affiliated with disaffection and unrest within an industrialized working-class culture not formed until a hundred years after his death. In characteristically conservative fashion, Gay's indictment of the corruption generated by the Walpolean political machine pits its villain, Peachum, not against the ambiguous and relatively inchoate escape artist Sheppard, but against the nostalgic mock-heroic gallant highwayman, Macheath, whose character brings with it ready-made those inversions of authority that structure the entire production. Most importantly perhaps, as Isaac Kramnick and Michael Denning have argued, Macheath is affiliated with the traditional elite whose reliance on the "paternalism, customs, ancient rights, a discretionary system of law" is challenged by the Peachums of the emergent commercial society.[78] In order to articulate the terms of his conservative critique most effectively, then, Gay rewrites the popular Wild/Sheppard criminal duo, replacing the apprentice escape artist with the traditional and nostalgic highwayman, Macheath.

While there was a modest efflorescence of Sheppard texts around the time of his own life and execution, the full cultural potential of this modern working-class hero is not realized until labor unrest is more sharply defined by the saturation of industrialization and the populist demands of the Chartist movement. In his publication of *A Narrative of all the Robberies and Escapes of John Sheppard* (1724), John Applebee had prefaced the text with an engraving showing in eight frames the stages of Sheppard's escape. In his illustrations for Ainsworth's novel, Cruickshank drew very closely on Applebee's original illustrations; the 1839 prints were sold separately and, as the first artifacts in a deluge of mass cult Sheppard commodities, contributed to the iconic Sheppard legend.[79] Sheppard mania surges most strongly in 1839–40, ignited by the publication of Ainsworth and Cruikshank's illustrated novel and spreading irresistibly among "the young, 'masterless' men who constituted much of [London's] growing industrial labor force." As the social historian Matthew Buckley points out in his study of the mass appeal of the Jack Sheppard media event: "The wave of 'books, plays, and pictures,' seemed to produce not mere enthusiasm or admiration for Sheppard, but a specific, defining impulse among the city's most dislocated, volatile population 'to be another Jack Sheppard,' to mime his actions 'in real arnest' [*sic*] and, in a distinctly modern sense, take on his identity as the model of one's own."[80] Thus, in what may be the first instance of a modern media "copycat" crime, a London valet, B. F. Courvoisier, murdered his master, Lord William Russell, the idea coming to him "upon reading *Jack Sheppard*."[81]

In Ainsworth's novel, Sheppard's distinctly modern and urban identity is thrown into sharp relief by his pairing with a foster brother, Thames Darrell, who is orphaned and apprenticed to the same master, Mr. Wood. For while Wild makes a strong and villainous appearance, the Wild/Sheppard coupling characteristic of the earlier eighteenth-century accounts is replaced by Ainsworth with the Darrell/Sheppard fraternal pair positioned within the appropriated narrative of Hogarth's idle and industrious apprentice series.[82]

In Ainsworth's *Jack Sheppard*, Thames Darrell, the industrious apprentice, evolves into the romantic hero of melodrama, discovering by signs and tokens that he is actually "of the blood royal of France."[83] Invoking "an earlier generation's anxieties, fantasies and modes of truth," Darrell's elevation as the Marquis de Chatillon takes place in pre-Revolutionary France, even as, in the 1839 novel, it evokes, from a conservative perspective, all those Revolutionary-era preoccupations with criminally corrupt aristocracy, interrupted inheritance, and the disruption and resumption of valid modes of authority.[84] Appropriately, Darrell is consistently portrayed in Cruickshank's and in later illustrations as a formally dressed, bewigged eighteenth-century gentleman. Loyal, productive, compliant, Darrell always is recognizable, morally and stylistically, for the nobleman he finally turns out to be. In contrast, Sheppard appears wigless, with closely shorn hair in a mode identifiable by contemporaries as both modern and urban working class.[85]

While Ainsworth's Sheppard starts off very like Darrell as a foster-child apprentice with some claim to aristocratic birth, the narrative quickly builds up the contrast between the two in conformity with the Industrious and Idle Apprentice script. Darrell achieves integration within the domestic sphere of his master and foster father, Mr. Wood, and elevation within the family romance of the narrative; Sheppard defaces the domestic realm and is excluded from any positive familial identity. Sheppard's father, in Ainsworth's rendition a "Notorious Housebreaker," is an executed felon, and his mother is a pathetic drunk who ends her days in Bedlam. The first pages of the novel predict that "little Jack," like his father before him, "will never die in his bed."[86] Both his parents dead before his own execution, Sheppard has no family within which he might be recognized or restored. Indeed, with such a mother and a father, Sheppard emerges not so much from a family as from its dissolution.

Whereas his foster brother, Darrell, receiving the melodramatic reward of his loyal industry, evolves into his French title and Lancashire estates from his fully productive and integrated role within the Wood household, Sheppard never achieves domestic integration as an apprentice. While he is meant to be working, Sheppard instead wiles away the time daydreaming of "giving old Wood the slip" and going on the highway, as he carves the verses of a song celebrating the highwayman Claude Duval into the beams of the workroom. Alongside these verses, in emphatically enormous block letters, Sheppard inscribes his own name. He is then "cuffed" by Mr. Wood for defacing the walls.[87] Recalcitrant in response to this labor discipline, Sheppard intimidates his master into leniency: "I won't be struck for nothing. . . . I wouldn't advise you to lay hands on me again."[88]

This early scene introduces Sheppard in his domestic, quasi-familial role as Wood's apprentice and presages Sheppard's fate, not only his narrative fate as the idle apprentice born to be hanged but also his cultural fate as the rebellious apprentice whose name affiliates him, not with a family, but with a constellation of legendary outlaws celebrated in popular print and song. Ainsworth's narrative highlights Sheppard's refusal of labor discipline, productivity, and domestic fili-ation, insisting on his election, instead, of a celebrity achieved through noncom-pliance, economic parasitism, familial and social alienation, and public notoriety. While Ainsworth's novel writes Sheppard's biography as an overly determined "tragedy," unequivocal in its insistence on the wages of sin, his casting Shep-pard as the Idle Apprentice brings to the fore, if in eighteenth-century costume, those issues of social dislocation, alienation, and labor unrest so resonant with the urban populace of young "masterless men" in the industrial age. Finally, Ainsworth's Sheppard, more than simply articulating gestures of defiance and attitudes of independence, also enacts, as we can see in this early scene, the very modes of desire and identification made available by the mass culture of celebrity that such young men would replicate in their own emulation of the famous Jack Sheppard.

CHAPTER TWO

Always Making Excuses

The Rake and Criminality

Style and Subjectivity

The rake's elite social status and reputation for dazzling erotic and stylistic prowess has often overshadowed his grubbier, more overtly violent and criminal features. In distinction to the highwayman and the pirate, the rake's criminality is frequently not named as such, and his cultural prestige seems perpetually guaranteed by his elite social status. The rake, then, differs from the other two figures examined in this book precisely because his outlaw status is often overlooked even as his elite prestige is assumed. The modes of this oversight constitute a dominant theme of the present chapter.

As an examination of representations from Rochester's rambler to Richardson's Lovelace shows, the persistence of the rake's prestige depends on three intertwined modes of apology made on his behalf. First, there is the celebratory defense of the rake inspired by his stylistic, that is, aesthetic and performative, mastery. Then there are apologies for his misconduct based on appeals to the irresistible pressures of his innate character, as with Steele's sentimentally noble rake. Finally, there are excuses made for him that appeal to the *merely* performative and thus ultimately inconsequential status of this behavior, as in John Gay's *The Mohocks*. The first mode of apology often characterizes the rake's self-defense as well as his appreciative reception in modern scholarship. Such a defense implies the dominance of a performative rather than essentialized notion of subjectivity; the rake's prestige resides in the culturally confirmed success of his social performance rather than in fixed qualities of some internal self.

The second and third modes of apology reveal a shift from a primarily performative toward a more essentialized notion of subjectivity and thus of the ground on which the rake's prestige can be fixed. For social action can only be *merely* performative where there is some notion of another more authentic site of identity. Accordingly, these two apologies often appear together, as in *Tatler* 27, where Steele excuses the *authentic* rake as a victim of his own exuberant innate spirit and dismisses any threat or competition posed by his base imitators as merely derivative and therefore inconsequential. Yet, likewise, there often seems an overlap of the first defense of the rake on the strength of his stylistic mastery with the third, which excuses his actions as merely performative and so not impeachably "real." Thus in John Gay's *The Mohocks*, the entertainment value of the young hooligans is fully affirmed even as their threat is completely disarmed; after all, they are only "frolicking." Yet we can still make a distinction between the two: the former endorses the rake's aesthetic and performative prestige *despite* his admitted criminal transgressions; the latter exploits the performative status of his actions, their status as mere play, as an *alibi for* those transgressions. The first defense fully sustains the status of performance as a mode of powerful social action; the third tends to locate performance in a realm of dramatic play separate from real life and actual consequence.

Yet as we see both in seventeenth- and eighteenth-century defenses of the rake and in contemporary scholarly work, although they can be distinguished conceptually, all three modes of apology might overlap rhetorically. Even in Steele's portrait of the sentimental rake, surely the most dependent of all on a concept of innate, gendered subjectivity, there remains a celebratory appreciation of the exuberant manliness of the rake's personal style. Indeed, this rakish style of manliness is preserved from sociohistorical contingency as Steele fixes it as a feature of innate and ideal masculine subjectivity. Ultimately, then, my examination of the rake notes the ways in which performative and innate notions of authentic character might inform and support one another and even, as in the case of Steele's sentimental rake, undergo a kind of dialectical transformation by means of which style becomes subjectivity—all in aid of preserving a kind of masculine prestige complicit with criminality.

The cultural significance and tenacity of all three mythic outlaw figures lie in their capacity to embody problems of masculine authority and authenticity endemic to modernity. In this chapter, I focus on what the rake can show us about how criminality and masculine prestige operate in relation to notions of subjective authenticity and performativity. For at issue with developing concepts of masculine authority is the nature both of legitimate authority and of the ground of subjectivity that can support it. Even as this period witnessed revolutions in the conceptualization and institutionalization of political and sociocultural authority, so too did it see the emergence of revised, and heavily gendered, understandings of human subjectivity. The rake's progress from the mid-seventeenth through the mid-eighteenth centuries charts shifts in the values that address this interwoven problem of authority and subjectivity: from court-based prestige to civic respectability; from the affirmation of the sovereign's privilege to the celebration of the sovereign individual; from hierarchical to oppositional models of sexual difference; from character as the expression of performative mastery to character as the expression of subjective integrity.

The rake's sociocultural competition with the fop receives attention here for at least three reasons. First, it provides a prominent instance of the sustained contest for prestige between different masculine types. Second, the close competition between these two ultimately reveals that both rake and fop contend for prestige in performative and thus socially contingent ways that are discountenanced by masculine ideals founded in emergent notions of innate gendered subjectivity and embodied in the modern polite gentleman. Significantly, the vulnerability of these sorts of performative claims on distinction is exposed not only in the satire on the ludicrously affected fop but also in the skepticism with which a rake such as Rochester contemplates his own place in the world. Third, and related to this last, the superior stylistic mastery that distinguishes the rake from the fop, if only barely and from his own perspective, is the very same thing that, in the literary and historical record, distinguishes the rake from the common criminal.

As the bases of masculine authority and prestige shift, they take with them much of the ground on which elite license staked its claim. The rake's outlaw status, then, is generated by what remains to him after the assault on his prestige by emerging reconfigurations of the polite gentleman and the foundational notions of subjective authenticity that underwrite them. And what remains is a kind of allure both outdated in its association with the pre-1688 Stuart world and updated in its revision around privileges authorized more immediately by gender than by status. For while society may no longer so overtly defend status and class privilege, the privilege of outlaw masculinities is preserved where gendered exceptionalism cashes in on the prestige value handed down through a history of status elitism. Boys will be boys still; their high jinks, their trespasses against decency and civility, even against the law, are countenanced by conventions of (previously aristocratic) masculine privilege established in the early modern period.

As I emphasize throughout, the glamour of the rake and his outlaw brothers is fabulous and residual, colored by a nostalgia for a kind of fully approved license already becoming outdated by the late seventeenth century, and yet one that through the centuries has retained its currency in fantasies of masculinity.

So in the early nineteenth century, the English essayist Charles Lamb comments on the idealized denizens of the rakish beau monde: "They break through no laws, or conscientious restraints. They know of none. They have got out of Christendom into . . . the Utopia of gallantry, where pleasure is duty, and the manners perfect freedom."[1] In the twentieth century, mythic outlaw types such as the pirate, the rake, and the gentleman highwayman enjoy a distinguished place in literary and historical studies appreciative of their stylistically masterful brand of individuality and apparent independence from social conventions.[2] In part, the dream for this particular brand of liberty has its origins in notions of absolute individual sovereignty that arose even as absolutism came under assault in the political sphere. A law unto himself, the outlaw rake asserts the ultimate aristocratic privilege of sovereign will and thus, in Rochester's words, as a "peerless peer," the right to lord it over everyone.[3]

Perhaps paradoxically, this assertion of aristocratic privilege above the law generates both the criminality and the glamour of modern outlaws, just as it produced both the indictments against and the nostalgic allure of the Stuarts. As I note in chapter 1, the specific sociopolitical and cultural developments from which these figures emerge in their modern forms are those that precede and concentrate around the Restoration and then the Whig settlement of 1689. Indeed, the notorious "frolics" of those "savage nobles" at the court of Charles II set a standard of fashionable masculinity that, though under steady assault from social and cultural reform, retained potent cultural currency after 1689 and through the next century.[4] So in the 1690s, following what had become the laughably predictable formula for rakish high jinks, Jonathan Swift in *A Tale of a Tub* mocks the three brothers' aspirations to stylish hooliganism. Although initially untutored in the ways of the big city, they quickly began to improve in the good Qualities of the Town:

> They Writ, and Raillyed, and Rhymed, and Sung, and Said, and Said Nothing; They Drank, and Fought, and Whor'd, and Slept, and Swore, and took Snuff: They went to new Plays on the first Night, haunted the *Chocolate*-Houses, beat the Watch, lay on Bulks, and got Claps: They bilkt Hackney-Coachmen, ran into Debt with Shopkeepers, and lay with their Wives: They killed Bayliffs, kick'd Fidlers down Stairs, eat at *Locket*'s, loyterd at *Will*'s.[5]

Juxtaposed so that each indicts the other, here is the entirely commonplace contiguity of the criminal (whoring, fighting, swearing, committing adultery, cheating, incurring debt, killing, and kicking) and the fashionable (rhyming, taking snuff, attending plays, frequenting chic restaurants and coffeehouses like

Locket's and Will's). This correspondence between the illicit and the illustrious, the criminal and the gentleman, shaped the ethos of the Restoration court, where figures such as Charles Sedley, Earl of Dorset ("already famous in the 1660s for manslaughter, incitement to riot, and cultural patronage") and George Villiers, Duke of Buckingham (blamed by Bishop Burnet for Charles II's "ill principles and bad morals") led the Merry Gang of courtiers immersed "in violence, promiscuity, invective and theatrical excess."[6] After his heyday in the 1660s and 70s, the rake came under increasing, and to a significant extent effective, assault through the rest of the seventeenth and the eighteenth centuries. Challenged by a more domesticated, restrained, privatized, and polite masculine ideal, the kind of illicit and extravagant masculinity embodied by the Restoration rakes loses its easy purchase on the title of "gentleman," but at the same time effects a stylized, even glamorized consolidation of criminality and prestige characteristic of outlaw forms of masculinity that continue to compete successfully for sociocultural status into the present and are the subject of this book.

Civility, Criminality, and Rakish Nostalgia

The Restoration libertine rake has been scrupulously examined by literary and social historians attentive to shifts in codes of conduct and in the paradigms that structure sexual difference in the late seventeenth and early eighteenth centuries.[7] By all accounts, this period witnessed the emerging dominance of a new code of civility that invalidated much of the conduct that previously had defined the prestigious (aristocratic) male.[8] Most often, these narratives highlight the atavistic character of the rake as he violently resists the new civility; almost never do they account for his continued hold on prestige in this fresh social climate. This new code of civility required from all "gentlemen" a degree of consideration, respect, decency, and restraint at odds with the assertion of those extravagant forms of status-linked privilege most jealously preserved and zealously performed by the libertine rake. So, according to Anna Bryson, the rake can be defined by his "anti-civility," by the self-consciously outrageous opposition he posed to this new code of gentlemanly conduct.[9] Defined in negative reaction against a standard of civility the dominance of which, at the same time, is assumed, the rake is in effect mummified and removed from the living narrative of manners, criminality, and masculinity in which he persisted and continued to play a culturally central role in the ways I outline here.

The development of new modes of civility revises the relationship between crime and masculinity in the history of violence in eighteenth-century England.

As documented by the social historian Robert Shoemaker, there was throughout the eighteenth century a steady decline in murder and manslaughter that reflects a change in male behavior brought on, in great part, by "the changing role played by violence in constructions of masculinity."[10] This more general decline in the prestige and thus the incidence of personal violence might well be viewed in relation to the decline in elite criminality documented from the sixteenth century on. As new standards of civility start to take hold in the upper echelons of English society, the role of violence in the preservation and performance of prestige diminishes, and this has a kind of "trickle down" effect as people aspire to the standards set by their betters.[11]

Two features of this trend seem especially significant: first, that a change in *manners* is convincingly forwarded as the cause for this decline in violent crime; and second, that despite this change, a small coterie of elite males who aggressively flouted the new codes of civility enjoyed a disproportionate and, sociohistorically speaking, anomalous share of cultural currency and social success. For while elite criminality had been and continued to be on the wane throughout the early modern period, the Restoration court witnessed, as Sharpe notes, "an upsurge in upper-class debauchery."[12] It is this upsurge that interests me here; for just as the rake is an exception in the history of civility, so he is in the parallel history of violent crime.[13]

From one angle, the outrages perpetuated by the Restoration rake seem merely to continue the well-established tradition of aristocratic extravagance and violence. What, after all, is really new about rakish violence, rakish crime? For centuries, elite masculinity in England had been performed through personal violence and sometimes even organized crime, through habitual and insistent claims on that license which defined immunity from legal, social, and religious laws. As historian Lawrence Stone remarks, "In the sixteenth and seventeenth centuries tempers were short and weapons to hand. The behaviour of the propertied classes, like that of the poor, was characterized by the ferocity, childishness, and lack of self-control of the Homeric age."[14] However, the diehard rake perpetuates elite criminality with a difference. It is not simply a matter of a coterie of aristocratic males continuing to behave as their fathers and grandfathers did before them; there is much self-consciousness, even staginess in their outrage. So Bryson notes how violence and sexual license are pursued, not merely as a matter of traditional course, but with the "will to outrage others, rather than simply enjoy excess. Libertine codes of conduct depended on the positive elaboration of grossly 'uncivil' modes of behavior and on the open transgression of some of the forms of 'civil' nobility."[15]

Leaving aside the problem of whether such "simple," unmediated enjoyment can account for elite license at any period, from my perspective what is really new here about the rake's transgression is that it is nostalgic: in order to assert a sovereignty whose restoration was never secure, it evokes a period when masculine aristocratic will seemed to enjoy greater customary license.[16] As it does so, outlaw rakish masculinity articulates fissures between past and present that structure the modern self-reflexivity (Bryson's greater self-consciousness) of its nostalgic gesture and throws into relief the fault lines within the body of the nobility that generate the ironic, skeptical self-consciousness of the restored Stuart court culture. It is from this moment in the 1660s and 70s, then, that criminality becomes a distinctively nostalgic and self-conscious aspect of masculine prestige. The rake retains this relationship between masculinity and criminality, nostalgia and self-consciousness in English culture well into the 1740s when Richardson's Lovelace draws on classical heroic example and Restoration heroic drama as he expatiates with comically inflated grandiosity on his own imperious transgressions.

So with the cachet of its court associations augmented by the allure of nostalgia, rakish transgression gets colored with a glamour that often equivocates its ethical status. That is, it becomes possible for certain styles of criminality to make claims on alternative value systems all the more romantic for being increasingly obsolete. For while extravagant transgression and violence certainly can signify nothing more complex than brute masculine dominance, in this period they become heavily inflected through aristocratic ideology's lost dreams of heroic glory.[17] I would suggest that this upsurge in upper-class lawlessness registers the absence of the authority by which a "peerless peer" could establish himself. For finally, the only "peerless peer" is the king, and the fragility of his authority had been exposed by the execution of Charles I on January 30, 1649, for the capital crime of treason, and confounded by the criminal failure of his libertine son, Charles II, to reclaim it.

During this period, then, the libertine rake takes shape as the agent of a nostalgic modern masculine fantasy, one that supported Charles II's own promiscuous habits. So in lines that satirically forward the impossible conditions of this fantastic lost golden age, John Dryden articulates the prolific propagation attending England's succession crisis:

In pious times, ere priestcraft did begin,
Before polygamy was made a sin;
When man on many multipli'd his kind,
Ere one to one was cursedly confin'd;

When nature prompted, and no law deni'd
Promiscuous use of concubine and bride;
Then Israel's monarch, after Heaven's own heart,
His vigorous warmth did variously impart
To wives and slaves, as wide as his command
Scatter'd his Maker's image through the land. (1–10)[18]

Such "promiscuous use of concubine and bride" becomes a hallmark of rakish life and fantasy, often articulated, as here, in biblical language that temporally distances and textually legitimates sexual offense, and often through the Turkish figure of the harem that culturally distances such transgressions and conventionalizes them within an established, if foreign, institution. Lord Baltimore, for instance, notoriously kept a "modest harem of eight houris."[19] Musing on his ideal marital situation, Lovelace summons a fantasy painted in biblical colors like these opening lines of Dryden's poem. His wife would be "*Lady Easy*" to all his pleasures, cheerfully gratifying him with a constant supply of concubines and so following hallowed precedent: "Thus of old did the contending wives of the honest patriarchs; each recommending her handmaid to her lord, as she thought it would oblige him."[20] Such fantasies of hyperbolic sexual prowess often seem to accompany circumstances where actual potency and legitimate procreation are under threat. Thus Lord Baltimore was reputed to be impotent, unable to satisfy one woman, "let alone the needs of a harem."[21] The whole duration (about 1,500 pages) of *Clarissa* witnesses Lovelace engaged in sex only once and with a woman who is not only unwilling to gratify him but also unconscious and so unable to. Furthermore, according to Judith Wilt, Lovelace's performance in this instance is uncertain at best.[22] Lovelace cannot secure one wife, let alone a wife and a parcel of willing handmaidens. Such fantasies of performance finally speak only of its failure.[23] Both Dryden and Richardson cannily supply the compensatory psychosexual rationales that accompany the failures they narrate. Dryden's poem invokes the language of a biblical golden age in order to reflect ironically on Charles II's shaky status as England's "patriarch" by pointing up his nonproduction of an heir and his surplus production of bastards, including the rebel Monmouth. Throughout the period, then, masculine libertine fantasies represent both the claims of elite privilege and the failures of its powers.

Boys Will Be Boys: Criminality, Prestige, and Performance

Both "rakes" and "crimes" are masculine phenomena; there is no *feminine* analogue for the rake. Indeed, as William Hogarth's two narrative series, *The Harlot's Progress* and *The Rake's Progress,* witness, the rake's counterpart is not a "female rake" but the harlot.[24] Due to her insufficient assimilation to notions of sexual difference, the harlot, as Kathryn Norberg points out, is not hyperbolically but deficiently feminine.[25] So in Oliver Goldsmith's *She Stoops to Conquer,* Marlow associates the whore's sexual dynamism with his own masculine potency and remarks of such women to Hastings, "They are of *us* you know."[26] Likewise, Rita Goldberg notes how the puritanical rake Robert Lovelace differentiates "angelic" from "fallen" women in ways that erode gender difference: "Fallen women become . . . so much like him that femaleness is no longer their most conspicuous feature."[27] Rake and harlot, then, have an inverse relation to gender: as a harlot, a woman's femininity is diminished; whereas as a rake, a man's masculinity is enhanced. Harlots are sexual criminals, and crime, sexual and otherwise, in the seventeenth and eighteenth centuries as now, is overwhelmingly a masculine province.[28] This identity between bad behavior and masculinity resounds in the idiomatic apology, "Boys will be boys," where gender becomes the tautological explanation of its own (unruly) character and thus, as in Marlow's statement, provides a way for whores to be boys as well. For if illicit behavior, sexual and otherwise, is irreducibly masculine, then so are even its female participants.[29]

Because of its exploitation of sexual discourses and the erotic inflections of political discourse at the Restoration court, and because of its inheritance of the aristocratic heroic ethos of competitive martial prowess, the brand of criminality associated with the rake is heavily invested in masculinity. With his every frolic, the rake sets in contest his prowess, his potency, and, by implication, the potency and authority of the elite order of masculinity on which his personal prestige ultimately depends. In extravagant fashion, then, the rake's masculinity asserts criminality as a status privilege; at the same time, it asserts the elite status of this criminal brand of masculinity.[30] Those sorts of criminality that are strongly linked to ideals of masculinity, then, are specific, as are the ideals to which they relate: rakish criminality is linked through nostalgic compensation to aristocratic ideals of peerless privilege and through competition to emerging ideals of the polite gentleman.

The rake's reliance on prestige garnered through social performance can be illustrated by his competitive relation to his doppelganger, the fop. Even as the fop and the rake are often presented as competitive and, in relation to styles of masculinity, contrasting figures, the modes in which this competition is staged point to their shared reliance on performative, socially contingent claims to status. In this they stand paired together in contrast to the modern polite gentleman whose dominance is consolidated, not through visual displays and performances of mastery, but through moral and affective capacities that, like his masculinity itself, are essentialized and internalized as part of his inalienable subjectivity.

Both the rake and the fop are often portrayed, right up through the twentieth century, as embodiments of faulty sorts of masculinity and thus set as foils for the greater luster of the new polite gentleman. Representations of the fop, on the one hand, record a precious, narcissistic, affectedly refined sort of bad masculinity, or "queerness"; those of the rake, on the other hand, portray a ruthless, sometimes violent, predatory, dangerously antisocial sort. Yet, as Thomas King argues, the rake and the fop are matched as dual instances of a residual, court-based, "pederastic" erotic economy and as types of subjectivity deficient in "privacy."[31] The fop cheerfully constitutes his self through performance in the visual field and refuses an inward subjectivity consisting in "sense, feeling, reason, taste, consciousness."[32] Like the rake, the fop rejects the modes of politeness expressive of this subjectivity and the gendered, complementary sexual economy articulated through it. While the rake violates complementary sexual difference by remaining devoted to "erotic practices . . . organized according to the aim of penetration rather than by desire for a particular gendered object," the fop's refusal is more visual and autoerotic: "Whereas the polite recognized and granted each other legitimacy . . . through a mutual regard, fops could get by with a mirror."[33]

The intimacy of this complementary relation between the rake and the fop is staged, for example, in George Etherege's *Man of Mode, or, Sir Fopling Flutter,* where Dorimant (a character widely believed to be based on Rochester) contends for a social dominance won, in the action of the play, through invalidating Fopling's status as his rival. Dorimant would have his status as "Man of Mode" stand outside any relation, even competitive, to "Sir Fopling Flutter"; that it does not wholly do so is one of the chief ironic insights of the play.

The fopling's proximity threatens the rake because the fop figures all those flawed forms of imitation, emulation, and affectation that the rake so strenuously disavows in his bid for nonpareil social mastery. The rake's purported advantage lies in his fluency in, and his performance and mastery of, those modes of sociocultural discourse that the fop seems only to parrot and ape. In Etherege's world, the fop is simply a failed rake; consequently, Fopling threatens Dorimant by revealing the vulnerabilities of his own status. If Medley affirmed and the world adopted Harriet's opinion that Dorimant, just like Fopling himself, was apish and "affected," his advantage could soon evaporate.[34]

Historically, both the rake and the fop are superceded by the newly developing polite gentleman. The fop suffers a perhaps more ignominious decline than the rake. By virtue of a recoding of his effeminacy as definitive not simply of his social but also of his sexual status, the fop becomes a victim of the newly gendered form of masculinity consolidated "by displacing the demonized publicity of aristocratic bodies onto a male body figured as outside privacy: the theatrical, effeminate, and finally queer male body."[35] Within the emergent regime of polarized sexual difference and its conventions of complementary sexual relations, the rake is both demonized and glamorized; his violations are more often figured as Satanic and dangerous than as pathetic and ludicrous, as is the case with the fop. By the eighteenth century, while the fop remains irreducibly "queer," the rake most often has become exclusively heterosexual. So by virtue of a sexual prowess that has been recoded as an expression of masculinity, the rake retains his prestige and, as we can see in Richardson's Lovelace, as late as the 1740s is still asserting his status-linked position above the laws of social convention and common human decency. Moreover, Richardson is still having to caution his readers against the seductions of his Lovelace, whose diabolical facility with language threatens, like Dorimant's, to "tempt the angels to a second fall."[36]

As we look at how the specifically criminal aspects of the rake's masculinity have been represented, especially by twentieth-century literary and social historians, we find that the rake's performative mastery, his style, consistently wins him an exemption from the ranks of the common criminal. But this exemption is insecure, for it relies on performative (and so imitable) and competitive (and so socially contingent) means that render the rake's mastery vulnerable to rivalry and to contingent sociocultural judgment. Moreover, as we can see in Rochester's poetry, the rake's vulnerability to competitive emulative displacement is exposed not only through contests with fops and would-be rakes but also through his competition with the ideals of aristocratic martial honor staged in his mock-heroic deflation of his own "important mischiefs" that, by means of this juxtaposition, become tainted with the flavor of obnoxious, mean delinquency. Indeed, these texts discover the vulnerability of the "real" rake both to the debasing emulation of his foppish inferiors and to his own degraded (mock-heroic) exploitation of the forms of martial honor; they reveal the frailty of the rake's claims to a status rendered contingent and insubstantial by the degradation of inherited honors with which he himself was complicit.

The status of rakish "criminality" remains largely unresolved: even when it involved homicide, rape, murder, sodomy, assault, libel, perjury, vandalism, and so on, it has often passed, well into the twentieth century, as a species of youthful exuberance, or "frolic." Boys, after all, will be boys. The exceptionalism of elite criminality was a real social fact.[37] Gentlemen of a certain status were rarely charged and almost never convicted for legal trespasses; these gentlemen were the law and so unlikely to condemn their own. So it is with good reason that both Lovelace and Clarissa assume that even if the capital charge of rape were brought against Lovelace, the interest of his family would be sufficient "to obtain his pardon" (1253).[38]

The status of rakish masculinity rescues its transgressions from relegation to the ranks of ordinary crimes and, instead, transforms them back into signs of the very prestige that guarantees the status-linked exception in the first place. As the literary historian John Harold Wilson writes in his *Court Wits of the Restoration*, "Granted that the Wits were a raffish fraternity, who fought duels, made love not wisely but too much, and engaged in riots and debauches, yet they were not devils of indecency. Too much has been made of their private lives; they have been pictured consistently as elegant loafers, spendthrifts, rakes, and wastrels."[39] Far from seeing these "riots and debauches" as "crimes," Wilson wants to downplay the libertine status of these courtiers in order to lift them up onto the literary stage as wits. Similarly, Sharpe refers to the upsurge in "upper-class *debauchery*" rather than in upper-class *crime,* even as he cites it as a break in the downward trend of elite criminality. This exceptionalism pervades contemporary scholarship which, as does Bryson, views rakish transgression as "anti-civility" rather than criminality or, as the literary critic Michael Neill does, elevates it above garden-variety criminality into a process of subversive overcoming that he dubs "this exercise in the criminal sublime."[40] These features of the juridical and scholarly history, each producing its own kind of immunity for the rake, have ensured as well that the proximity between the rake and other explicitly criminal characters, such as the pirate and the highwayman, remains underexamined in the academic and scholarly record, despite the shift in codes of conduct that would seem to relegate the rake to the outlaw underworld.[41]

Those historians who do focus on early modern crime usually do so as part of a larger project of writing the history of the laboring classes, so the most sophisticated considerations of eighteenth-century criminality and society, such as those of Peter Linebaugh and Marcus Rediker, have largely excluded consideration of elite criminality. Likewise, in his emphasis on the sociocultural history of the working class, Geoffrey Pearson sidesteps the phenomena of upper-class

violence and cites as precursor of the modern hooligan only the unruly apprentices of the seventeenth and eighteenth centuries. Ultimately, what secures this
historical relation is not the similar nature of the behavior exhibited by modern
hooligans and early modern apprentices, but what Pearson sees as their shared,
or at least analogous, class positions. Only "those crimes that are associated with
the materially disadvantaged underclass" can provide "the continuing thread"
between the nineteenth- and twentieth-century hooligans and their early modern forerunners.[42] Accordingly, Pearson excludes "respectable" crime perpetrated
by middle- and upper-class professionals from his survey, even as he notes its
prevalence. He excludes as well the upper-class hooligans of the seventeenth and
eighteenth centuries.

Two points raised by Pearson's approach are relevant here. First, the relative
prominence of certain classes of crime is ideologically, that is, culturally, produced, often independently of the events (facts) of occurrence or conviction. Although white-collar crime may be every bit as prevalent and every bit as socially
expensive as hooliganism, it does not incite the same kind of "moral panic" or
attract the same popular fascination. Second—and this knots a kink in Pearson's
"continuing thread"—early modern rakes, I contend, do qualify as precursors to
later hooligans, yet their prominence in the history of respectable fears comes
from their position, not in the underclass, but in the upper class. In the seventeenth and early eighteenth centuries, the widely publicized, violently criminal,
and greatly feared hooligans, sometimes banded together as Scowrers and then
Mohocks, are most frequently, even stereotypically, from the elite classes. Their
omission by Pearson, certainly predictable in a study of criminal subcultures
grounded in the historical sociology of labor, obscures the important presence of
the resilient strand of respectable fears that, especially pre-1800, attached more
strongly to the moral and sociopolitical failures of the elite than to any threats
from below.[43]

Such historiographic exceptionalism that excludes the elite from its consideration of certain classes of criminality, such as hooliganism, accurately analyzes the
record of legal reprisal: victims of severe punishment (execution, disfigurement,
transportation) in the Restoration and eighteenth century were overwhelmingly
from the ranks of the laboring poor. Nonetheless, such a record perpetuates an
association between class and crime that overlooks the tradition of elite criminality winked at by the legal justice system.

Conversely, the record of elite criminality seems always already to enjoy the
more culturally and socially inflected readings that historians such as Linebaugh
and Rediker bring to that of demotic crime. Thus, elite crime is rarely "crime-

crime," but usually seems to qualify as "social crime" of an oddly retrogressive sort, claiming not a pre-political consciousness of unfolding conditions but a kind of pre-modern privilege rooted in residual conditions. Rather than being seen, as is the case with more conventional "social criminals," as "premature revolutionaries or reformers, forerunners of popular movements," elite criminals are represented as raffish representatives of a glamorous high life, the exquisite pleasures and absolute freedoms of which are being doomed to obsolescence by the compromises and civilities of modernity.[44] Just as the status of the demotic criminal colors his actions with sociological significance—not so much vandalism as revolt—so that of the elite criminal has colored his with stylistic consequence—not so much assault and battery as elegant frolic.

This sublimation of criminal violence into elegance is first and foremost rhetorical and performative.[45] In the literary historical record, the signs of status as style again and again redeem the rake from his place in the criminal subculture, even when he most seems to affect the scandalous emulation of it. Thus again, what distinguishes the rake from the (mere) criminal is the same thing that distinguishes him from the fop: his superior stylistic mastery. As James Turner, one of the few scholars to consider the dialectic between high and low in the milieu of Restoration "riot," says of Rochester's literary pose: "The 'extravagance' of the wit and the 'handsomeness' of the contrivance are supposed to outweigh the 'ill,' to heighten the abject gesture and transform it into the *je ne sais quoi,* the charming and inimitable artifact."[46] Turner is interested in the exchanges between high and low, between rakish frolics and apprentice riots; accordingly, he codes as "low" the gross "uncivility," or criminality, that Rochester's poem recounts. However, this analysis might lose sight of the extent to which the "handsome ills" referred to here in Rochester's *The Disabled Debauchee,* are the stereotypically *elite,* rakish crimes of sodomy, drunkenness, fornication, assault, and vandalism:

> I'll tell of whores attacked, their lords at home;
> Bawds' quarters beaten up, and fortress won;
> Windows demolished, watches overcome;
> And handsome ills by my contrivance done. (33–36)[47]

Although, as Turner chronicles fastidiously, there is significant discursive commerce between rebellious apprentices and the rakes who frolicked about the court of "that riot-prince" Charles II, the particular set of transgressions recorded here do not, from a sociological perspective, conjoin "high and low behavior," nor, from a discursive perspective, do they even conjoin low behavior and high language; rather, they *match* elite criminal behavior to the language of the heroic through which that behavior is sublimated into the sign of masculine prestige. That Rochester writes sardonically in mock-heroic can be read, not as a heightening of the abject gesture (the "handsome ills"), but as a knowing deflation of the claims of status as style through which such elevation routinely occurred in his culture and in his own psyche.

Rochester's mock-heroic figures establish a comparison between the martial prowess on which his own aristocratic prestige is founded and the libertine prowess that depends on this status-linked association for its own immunity from incrimination as merely sordid, and perhaps actionable, offense. Yet especially as it is *in itself* a (mock-)heroic rhetoric and thus associated with martial *contest*, this rhetoric also establishes in that comparison an ironic and skeptical *competition* between traditional—at this point nostalgic—notions of aristocratic honor and their contemporary articulation as the frolics of the libertine courtier. I read this irony as one that works to discredit both terms: the heroic here is little else but the outworn bombast that panders as degraded euphemism to the rake's "important mischiefs."

The concept of ennobling competition that is so central to the establishment of relative status *within* the aristocracy is debased by the burlesque in *The Disabled Debauchee*. In his *Ramble in St. James's Park*, Rochester confronts its further degradation as he extends the contest beyond the pale of the elite and implicates the rake persona in compromising competition with those contemptible "knights o' th' elbow and the slur" that he finds frolicking with his mistress.[48] Here the rake reviles the "abortive imitation" of the would-be blades and challenges the threat that such base imitators pose to his own prestige (57). The situation in St. James's Park, then, might seem to pose the question: Is there such thing as an "authentic" rake? And if so, in what does this authenticity and thus his authority reside? Does the "real" rake have any purchase on an authenticity that can secure distinction from the emulative incursions of his imitators?

But the kind of rhetorical, socially contingent distinctions that the rake depends upon seem fragile at best in this world of phantasmagoric discursive and social perversions. The poem records a realm where all social and discursive decorum has broken down. The relation between words and things consists in dissonance and juxtaposition, as in the opening lines that record a "grave discourse, / Of who Fucks who, and who does worse" (1–2). Nature itself is inverted by perverse rhetoric: "Each imitative Branch does Twine, / In Some lov'd fold of Aretine" (21–22). The perversion of the natural order in this royal park remarks the parallel deformation of the sociopolitical order at a court ruled by a monarch who, like his rambling courtier, cannot secure the terms of his own status. In the poem, the three imitative rakes seek prestige by gaining greater proximity to the court, following a chain of sexual associations that links from Corinna to her rambling courtier and so to Charles himself.[49] The metonymy of desire traces the trajectory of authority; authentic prestige derives from the sovereign power of that "peerless peer." Authenticity, then, has nothing to do here with an inner-directed movement toward one's true subjectivity and everything to do with an outward drive toward the court and King. The rambler's superiority rests in his closer proximity to the monarch and in his consequent status as an object of emulation. Consequently, the distinctions with which the poem is concerned are not those between real and the fake rakes, between authentic and imitative value, but those between degrees of imitation, between first-, second-, and third-generation copies. Yet in *St. James's Park* the assurance of even this distinction remains skeptically, even savagely, undermined by the rhetoric of the poem that goes to extravagant lengths to impugn the corruption of the model of sovereign authority that would secure it.

Prestige authorized by court and king stands on broken security; Charles's own authority, as Duane Colthorp remarks in this context, has been radically compromised by his engagement *in* competitive sociosexual rivalry, the value *of* which he cannot fix or secure.[50] Unsecured, the phallus passes from king to courtier to "Whitehall blade," in a circulation tending toward the ever greater depreciation of its value within the ever more dispersed and debased chain of sexual associations in which it is implicated. The "frolics" of the "peerless peer" Charles II render sovereign privilege insecure and those, such as Rochester, whose positions depend on it, fraught with anxiety about their own sociosexual status. In the world of *St. James's Park*, the court generates exchanges that depreciate the very regime of value within which they operate. This situation has its monetary analogue in the financial insecurity of Charles II's rule that reached its nadir in 1672 with the closing of the Exchequer and the subsequent bankruptcy of the Crown's creditors. Rochester, like most who were reliant on income from the court, found his emolument in constant arrears and was at one point reduced to pawning his silver in order to sustain himself through an illness.[51] The security of the rambler's claim on court-based prestige is about as reliable as Rochester's claim on court-granted income. Stretched to the point of implosion, sovereign value offers no safeguard against bankruptcy in either the financial or the sociocultural realm.

Within the terms of Rochester's poem, the sovereign phallus is displaced further, beyond the sociosexual rivalry in which it is complicit; for the trajectory of desire in St. James's Park (site and text) may be traced outside court and king to the pornographic text that seems the true author of this world in which the very trees stand erect in imitation "of some lov'd fold of Aretine." So while the "Whitehall Blades" busily copy the court mode set by Charles II and his taste for "Banstead Mutton," with its early mention of Aretino's *Postures,* the poem suggests a more primary model for the erotic performances at court that are themselves imitations of a text and as such neither original nor authoritative (45–52). In the world of *St. James's Park,* both discourse and court generate exchanges that finally threaten to dissolve into the mere simulacra of a printed and pornographic text.

While the emulative intimacy between the rake and his imitators like the "Whitehall blades" pinpoints the set of perils and privileges the rake faces through circumscription within the beau monde, that between the rake and the criminal highlights those that await him on the meaner London streets. In gangs such as the Hectors, the Scowrers, the Ballers, and the Mohocks, men identified as rakes banded together in the pursuit of violent criminal activities often designed in ways that exploited and mirrored traditional codes of honor.[52] At court, in town, and on private estates, men of fashion, identified as aristocrats and members of the gentry, banded together in pursuits scarcely distinguishable from those of common hooligans.

Both because of the ways that the exceptionalism of elite criminality is supported by the historiographic and literary-critical record and because of the often exclusive focus on the rake's sexuality within that record, there has been little attention to the criminal commonalities between elite rakes and vulgar hooligans. Thus Harold Weber concludes that the Restoration rake is a hero whose "most distinctive, and therefore most important characteristic is his sexuality."[53] But Weber's view of the Restoration rake as a conquering Don Juan, while drawing attention to the ways in which sexuality is an important medium of the rake's will-to-power, suffers from a few distortions. First, it smacks of a certain triumphalism that, I believe, collapses under the weight of the skeptical exposure and deflation of rakish prowess that we find in Wycherley, Etherege, and Rochester, for example.[54] That the rake's prestige and thus his power is itself subject to the sociopolitical order it would dominate becomes one of the conventional ironies of these texts. Second, Weber's thesis seems invested in a privatizing, individuating psychologism that underestimates the public and political nature of sexual discourse in this period. Finally and predictably, it fails to attend to those other, not explicitly sexual, though no less rakish, exploits that produce masculine prestige through a course of semi-organized, violent hooliganism.

Interestingly, attention to these other spheres of rakish self-assertion reveals many of the same problems with authenticity and imitation that we find him confronting in the sociosexual realm. No less than the formulaic emulation of status-seekers in elite society, the equally formulaic exploits of hooligans in the streets of London produce a conformity and equivalence of self-representation—here through criminal violence—that threatens ·the exclusivity central to the rake's prestige. In the 1693 *The Rake: or, The Libertine's Religion*, the speaker exhorts his comrades to join him in some nonpareil criminal assault on person or property:

> Come, let us leave this Smoaky House,
> And at next *Tavern* take a large *Carouse;*
> A large *Carouse* to spur us on,
> To do what never yet was done,
> By *Antient Hector,* or by *Modern Rake.*

This however, is more easily said than done, for all the forms of vandalism and assault that are expressively rakish are also hackneyed with overuse:

> *Frightening of Cullies,* and *Bumbasting Whores,*
> *Wringing off Knockers,* and from *Posts and Doors,*
> *Rubbing out Milk-Maids,* and some other *Scores,*
> *Scowring the Watch,* or *Roaring in the Streets,*
> *Lamp-blacking Signs,* with divers other Feats,
> Are low Mechanick Actions, most unfit
> For *Us,* the *Sons of Fancy, Sense* and *Wit.* (5–6)[55]

Significantly, no sufficiently outrageous deed is hit upon, and bereft of significant gestures, this rake turns instead to conscience and reform.

This little ephemeral poem obliquely registers the position of rakish prestige in relation to the overt criminality through which it was pursued. It reveals an absence of intrinsically heroic and exceptional crime exclusive to the authentic rake and immune from imitative debasement. The problem of what in a moral-social register is emulation, and in a rhetorical-performative one is imitation, is central to those seventeenth-century discourses that articulate hierarchies of libertine prestige. They are key as well to later narratives of the rake's downfall and/or reclamation, such as Hogarth's in his series *The Rake's Progress* and Steele's in his discussion of the rake in *The Tatler,* that seek to establish a ground of subjective authenticity on which the rake's discipline and reform might be accomplished.

The perverse proclivity of contemporaries to imitate and to elevate problematically antisocial social types to exemplary status is a constant theme in the rake narratives of the eighteenth century. So the progress of Hogarth's Rakewell toward criminal insanity follows a path of "mimicry, imitation, and masking" of

bad exemplars.[56] Hogarth's rake, the jumped-up son of a merchant, like the affected blades in Rochester's world, imitates what seems always already to be a
heavily reified set of stylized attitudes, behaviors, and appearances that announce
claims on masculine prestige. The social and psychic alienation this produces is
graphically narrated in the final prints of the series, in which Rakewell lands first
in prison and then in Bedlam. This is "abortive imitation" of a sort, but the failure is moral—social and psychic—rather than stylistic and performative. There
is no way to be a successful rake here, no matched pair of the triumphant and
failed libertine as we find with the good and bad apprentices in the *Industry and
Idleness* series. Yet the narrative of alienation here suggests, if only by its loss, a
truer, more virtuous self whose trajectory can be glimpsed in the mirror projected
by the vicious courses of the rake's ruinous advance. This self and its lost possibilities registers only as a shadow cast by each step of Rakewell's progress of
rakish desire.

In contrast to Hogarth's, Steele's picture of the rake draws heavily on an explicit
distinction between true and imitation rake in ways that at first seem congruent
with those of Rochester's rambler. In *Tatler* 27, Steele's authentic rake emerges
like some Restoration rake redux, distinguished by superabundance and extravagance: "His Desires run away with him through the Strength and Force of a lively
Imagination." Cursed with an embarrassment of affective riches, "his Faults proceed not from Choice or Inclination but from Strong Passions and Appetites; he
commits Faults out of the Redundance of his good Qualities."[57] Inspired by the
greater gust of irresistible impulse, the real rake is distinguished from all those
Pretty Fellows and Fops who "roar, fight and stab" artificially by "Study" and
"Application." However, this distinction is not, as it is in Rochester, stylistic and
rhetorical, one between, on the one hand, a successful performance unmarked
by the signs of its own production and, on the other, an abortive one laboring
under the traces of its fabrication. It rests rather on a more fundamental difference between being and acting that excludes the performative wholesale from
any claim on rakish prestige or, indeed, on any sort of masculine authority.

Here then, we find the eighteenth-century presence of what twentieth-century
sociologist Pierre Bourdieu has analyzed as the modern bourgeois distinction between two different modes of cultural prestige: one that emerges "naturally," unmarked by signs of acquisition, and the other, less prestigious sort, which is artificially achieved by studied application.[58] In Steele, as in Bourdieu, these different
modes of relation to the stuff of cultural status supply the distinction between the
gentleman of taste and the pedant. Significantly, in Steele, they also supply the
distinction between the authentic rake and his sorry imitators. Finally, according

to this formulation that secures the authentic rake's claims on cultural status, the rake as a diamond in the rough, a gentleman in the making is reassimilated into the legitimate social order on the strength, not of his inherited status, but of his intrinsic, natural character. This distinction between authentic and spurious is between what is intrinsic and inalienable on the one hand, and what is superficial and merely an act on the other. The rake's prestige no more than the gentleman's honor can be secured through performance. Predictably, then, Steele debunks the practice of dueling, which, after all, worked on the assumption "that honour could be won or lost by the performance of a single act."[59]

Although recognizing that the rake's pleasures are unlawful and his courses irrational, Steele does not so much undermine the macho charisma of the rake as essentialize it in deep subjectivity. He then affirms the personal integrity of the rake beyond the terms available in the Restoration, for it is precisely through his affirmation of the true rake's authenticity, sentimentalized now as a resistless, inborn affective disposition, that Steele is able to neutralize the challenge he poses. Asserting the exclusivity of rakish prestige, Steele seeks to limit the social threat posed by the proliferation of roaring, stabbing, and fighting rake manqués; predicting the rake's inevitable reform, he further disarms the menace. This reform, as befits Steele's habitual progressivism, awaits only the fullness of time. The reformed rake narrative simply joins the notion of natural-born character with that of progressive history to write a redemptive biography wherein change works to actualize subjectivity in the happiest of ways.

With a dissimulation, such as Dorimant's in Etherege's *The Man of Mode,* which seeks to veil any dependence on the forms of mediation (linguistic, sartorial, social) that it exploits, the Restoration rake comes close to affirming an authenticity independent of such forms and thus of looking very like Steele's authentic rake. But as he asserts his supremacy and invulnerability, the Restoration rake acts as an absolutist rather than as a liberal individualist. As we have seen, within the terms of the radically skeptical and rhetorical performativity that affords him such extensive purchase on the media of competitive self-representation, the Restoration rake is vexed in any claims he might make to a personal authenticity that could stand beyond and thus underwrite the self-authorization he so baldly asserts.

In ways that evade such threats of social contingency, Steele maintains the exclusivity of rakish prestige by turning it inside out, making it a matter of involuntary expression rather than of formidable performance. Reduced to the slave of his own passions and the dupe of his own "good Qualities," Steele's rake should inspire sympathy rather than awe. All those powers, once expressive of heroic will, are reduced to objects of benevolent compassion: "The most agreeable of all bad Characters. . . . A Rake is a Man always to be pitied; and if he lives is one Day certainly reclaim'd; for his Faults proceed not from Choice of Inclination but from strong Passions and Appetites, which are in Youth too violent for the Curb of Reason, good Sense, good Manners, and good Nature."[60]

The survival into late modernity of such a seemingly nostalgic and outmoded fantasy of fully licensed masculine will is facilitated by its assimilation into precisely that kind of essentialized masculinity that underwrites Steele's apology for the rake in *Tatler* 27. For here, established on the foundation of a natural and irresistible subjectivity, rakish prestige, even as its exclusivity is preserved within a model of temperamental exceptionalism, becomes more socioculturally mobile as it becomes first and foremost a function of gender (which everyone has) rather than of elite status. Boys will be boys: gender rather than status provides the validation of delinquency. The full light of modernity might not reveal a greater number of truly authentic rakes, but it does show how the sociocultural positions in which we might find them are greatly expanded, and thus how licensed claims of outlaw masculinity proliferate beyond the bounds of status and class. There may be a historical irony in the way Steele's reformative sentimentalization of the rake provides such a transportable and palatable rationalization of outlaw masculinity even as it seeks to limit it by cancelling the currency its performative emulation.

Rakes at Play: The Mohocks

Steele's *Tatler* paper witnesses an important preservative transformation in the representation of the ground of rakish prestige. Later *Tatler* and *Spectator* papers remain preoccupied with masculine social types, and there the rake emerges in two discrete figures: that of Will Honeycomb, aging relict of Restoration high life, predictably married and reformed at last; and, more significantly, that of the Mohocks who terrorized the streets of London in the spring of 1712. These elite hooligans appear both in *The Spectator* and in John Gay's unperformed farce, *The Mohocks*. In *Tatler* 27, Steele's solution to the rake problem exploits an anti-performative distinction between real and imitation rakes and in doing so translates rakish masculinity from its perilous supremacy in a contingent social world into the fixed, and fixedly gendered, ground of essential subjectivity. Here the authentic rake is excused as a victim of his own, ultimately redemptive, natural character. But this concept of subjectivity that divides mere imitative performance from authentic character-defining action can also be employed to excuse those who are merely acting up. In what follows, I examine the relation of the Mohocks to Steele's earlier apology for the authentic sentimental rake in *Tatler* 27, and, more broadly, to the way criminal masculinity sits alongside social prestige in the cultural myth of the rake, especially as it persists through the alibi of mere performance.

This distinction between the rake and the Mohock draws on an implicit division between the explicitly criminal and the more benignly libertine and reassuringly faded aspects of the rake figure. While Will Honeycomb's laurels surely rest on his execution of violent pranks closely akin to those of the Mohocks in 1712, these are figured as deeds belonging to the bygone era of Honeycomb's rakish youth. In the present, Honeycomb, a safely domesticated incarnation of Rochester's disabled debauchee, only recounts and does not repeat the glories of "whores attacked, their lords at home; / Bawds' quarters beaten up, and fortress won / Windows demolished, watches overcome" and all the rest of his "handsome ills" (lines 33–36). Age and the settlement of 1689, we understand, have put to rest the more violent impulses of the Restoration and its progeny. By *Spectator* 530 (November 7, 1712) Will is happily married and utterly reformed: "I shall endeavour to live hereafter suitable to a Man in my Station, as a prudent Head of a Family, a good Husband, a careful Father (when it shall so happen), and as Your most Sincere Friend." We can be certain of Will Honeycomb's success; a reformed rake, after all, makes the best husband.

Yet the spring before Honeycomb's glorious restoration to matrimony and sense, a rash of violence attributed to a set of young upper-class men called the Mohocks broke out on the streets of London. As social historian Daniel Statt recounts, the Mohock, defined by his gratuitous and brutal physical assaults, embodies the violent criminality of the rake in isolation from his more winning ways as a sexual libertine. Going against the grain of conventional assumptions supported both by popular cultural myth and by historical and literary scholarship, Statt's work on the Mohock scare of 1712 emphasizes the contiguity of these two facets of the character: the Mohock and the rake, sociologically speaking, are the same person. Statt's point is that the criminal personal assaults perpetrated by these Mohocks are fully typical of rakes, who are more often remembered in their more "appealing" stylistic guises as youthful humorists and sexual libertines.[61] In ways that substantiate the tenor of Statt's claims and show how instantaneously the cultural aesthetic work of representation takes effect, both the contemporary accounts of the Mohocks in the *Spectator* papers and John Gay's two-act farce built around them transform the vile criminality of these youthful assailants by highly stylized parody and satiric irony. Ultimately, the Mohocks' riots are excused as a species of genteel, youthful frolic.

The Mohocks dominate three *Spectator* papers published between March 12 and April 8, 1712. All three reports come in the form of letters received. Mirroring *The Spectator*'s own agenda of reform, two of these letters on the Mohocks join in a generalized satiric offensive against late-night roistering and whoring.

The first report is straightforward, disapproving, and concerned; it comes in *Spectator* 324 as a letter from a civic-minded gentleman calling on Mr. Spectator to censure this "club" of hooligans in print before more "thoughtless Youngsters" would join in "out of a false notion of Bravery, and an immoderate Fondness to be distinguished for Fellows of Fire." Offering information that might prove useful for Mr. Spectator's proposed "History of Clubs," his letter outlines the Mohock club's jargon and rituals, giving the cant names of their various modes of assault: "tipping the Lion," "the Dancing-Masters," "the Tumblers." Operating as euphemisms as well as insider language, these glibly contrived phrases suggest that the Mohocks' assaults were facetiously stylized even as they were committed. The letter elaborates, in order to deflate, the heroic, exotic ton of the Mohocks' rituals and self-representation: "The President is stiled *Emperor of the Mohocks*; and his Arms are a *Turkish* Crescent, which his Imperial Majesty bears at present in a very extraordinary Manner engraven upon his Forehead. . . . To put the Watch to a total Rout, and mortify some of those inoffensive Militia, is reckon'd a *Coup d'eclat*." This letter at once deflates the Mohocks' pretensions and diminishes the criminality of their members. They are at once ridiculous, if deplorable, and largely guiltless of anything worse than the reckless vain gloriousness of youth.

The second account, on March 21, again in a letter, offers to correct an omission of the first: "You have particularly specified the ingenious Performances of the Lion-Tippers, the Dancing-Masters, and the Tumblers: But as you acknowledge you had not then a perfect History of the whole Club, you might very easily omit one of the most notable Species of it, the Sweaters" (*Spectator* 332). Having reported his findings on "sweating," the author confesses that he had his run-in with the Mohocks while he was trolling the midnight streets for whores. In this letter he offers his own experience as a warning to all who might similarly lay themselves open to risk. The letter, then, is not merely informative but admonitory, a moral caution to all those "treating with Night-Walkers" on the London streets.

The Mohocks make a final appearance on April 8 in *Spectator* 347, which contains two documents prefaced by Mr. Spectator's sceptical caveat that he doubts whether these are "Genuine and Authentic." The first piece is a letter from "Taw Waw Eben Zan Kaladar, Emperor of the Mohocks," and the second, accompanying it, is the "Manifesto" of that club. Written as a mock royal edict, this manifesto denies all reports of "tumultuous and irregular Proceedings" attributed to the Mohocks. No bona fide Mohock, claims their Emperor, would assault any innocent, sober, and unoffending citizen. He confirms the club's rule-governed conduct and its disciplined commitment to social reform: "We have nothing more at our Imperial Heart than the Reformation of the Cities of *London* and *Westminster*." Concerned for their welfare, the Emperor exhorts "all Husbands, House-keepers, and Masters of families . . . not only to repair themselves to their respective Habitations at early and seasonable Hours; but also to keep their Wives and daughters, Sons, Servants and Apprentices from appearing in the Streets." As defined here, the Mohocks' ends complement Mr. Spectator's own, if indeed their means rely on more corporeal methods of persuasion.

These documents make a joke of the Mohocks and turn that joke against anyone who is out late and up to no good. Gay is sometimes rumoured as the author of the "Manifesto" printed in *Spectator* 347, and his farce, *The Mohocks*, follows the details of all three *Spectator* papers closely.[62] Gay's joke there turns against both the juvenile posturing of the gentleman Mohocks and the bumbling panic of the citizen watchmen. In ways that foreshadow the rhetorically topsy-turvy world of *The Beggar's Opera*, Gay's Mohocks speak a high-flown faux-heroic language. "Thus far our Riots with Success are crown'd / Have found no stop, or what they found o'ercame," proclaims the Mohock "Abaddon," echoing the opening lines of Dryden's *Tyrannick Love*.[63] In language redolent of the heroics of the last age, with their stagy mock-demoniacs, the Mohocks, like Will Honeycomb, are quite preposterously anachronistic. They are nothing but young gentlemen dressed up to play at being wicked; thus, they plead to the justices: "We are gentleman, Sirs, 'twas only an innocent Frolic" (2.3.159–60). This farce, then, represents the Mohocks as harmless youthful humorists; its entertainment value derives wholly from their theatrical shenanigans. The worst thing Gay's Mohocks actually *do* is force the watchmen to trade costumes with them, an act that itself only underlines the purely staged nature of their character as violent ruffians.

Whereas Will Honeycomb and Steele's sentimental rake are ultimately redeemed by the reformed rake narrative in which the rake's innate character unfolds through a progressive history, in Gay's farce the Mohocks are reprieved by the status of their criminal behavior as mere play-acting (frolicking) and their own social standing as "gentlemen." In the first, more sober and condemnatory *Spectator* paper, the Mohocks' crimes are extenuated in much the same way that they are in *Tatler* 27, as the unfortunate byproduct of misdirected youthful spirits. In all these cases, the particularly reprehensible, often criminal behavior of these characters is distanced from both temporal and moral immediacy. Will Honeycomb and the Mohocks are cultural anachronisms; their transgressions wear the livery of the past age. Attention to the moral content of the Mohocks' actions often is overwhelmed by attraction to their stylistic guise, and this is based on outdated heroic modes. When, as in Steele's apology, any true rake must by definition be a potentially reformed rake, his sins, in a sense, are always already in the past.

In this chapter I have remarked the division, apparent in the *Spectator* and commonplace in later representations, of the rake character into two types—the criminal, explicitly malevolent type we would call an antisocial delinquent, and the more benignly libertine, appealing sort of young man of undisciplined high spirits. I suggest that this distinction collapses not only under the weight of historical analysis, such as Statt's, which indicts the rake as no better than the Mohock, but also, and more immediately, under the weight of contemporary representations that exonerate the Mohock as no worse than the rake.

Finally, I want to underline the link between apologies for criminal masculinity that rely on appeals to innate subjectivity, as with Steele's sentimentally noble rake, and those that depend on appeals to the merely performative and thus ultimately inconsequential status of this behaviour. As we have seen in *Tatler* 27, the bases of both of these exonerations are available to Steele, though in his zeal to preserve and defend the rake's prestige he also uses the standard of performativity to draw a hierarchical distinction between the authentic rake and his base imitators. In the *Spectator* papers on the Mohocks, both excuses are at play: these are just spirited young men expressing, in misdirected ways, their (commendable) thirst for glory; good boys at heart, they are only emulating bad examples, submitting momentarily to what we call "peer pressure." Gay's farce thematizes impersonation and claims it as an alibi. What is merely theatrical can hardly be criminal: "We are gentlemen, Sirs, 'twas only an innocent Frolick." From the antitheatrical perspective of Richardson, to whom we next turn, the rake's criminality is identified with, rather than defined against, his histrionic exploits.

The Rake on Trial: Lovelace

Rakish characters and actual libertine rakes continue to impose their frolics on culture and society throughout the century, and the apologetic formulas I outline here retain their currency right up to the present.[64] Yet no eighteenth-century rake has achieved the notoriety of Richardson's Lovelace, perhaps, after Rochester and his autobiographical ramblers, the most infamous of literary rakes, and certainly one who, in degree of rhetorical and psychological elaboration, remains unsurpassed. Much of this attention, as is typical with the rake, tends to attenuate rather than to spotlight Lovelace's criminality, strictly speaking.

Richardson's *Clarissa* follows through to full-blown tragedy the conventional seduction plot derailed in *Pamela* by Mr. B's reform. While the heroine's virtue and victimization are redoubtable, the villain protagonist Lovelace is articulated with such imaginative verve, emotional acuity, and sheer rhetorical vivacity that the moral condemnation of his character might be seen as equivocated by the aesthetic and psychological strength of its portrayal. As with Milton and his Satan, some readers have concluded that Richardson, wittingly or not, is really on the side of the devil. Moreover, like Milton's Satan, Lovelace's character is not merely drawn with consummate rhetorical skill and energy but is also defined by his own ambiguous mastery of the arts of representation and performance. As he lurks and plots and plays and plans, Lovelace brilliantly parades his motives, thoughts, and emotions in his letters, especially those to his friend Belford. Lovelace's approach to the Harlowe family; his correspondence with the conflicted Clarissa; his quarrel with her officious, doltish brother, James Harlowe; his seduction of Clarissa into an elopement; the brothel captivity and elaborate marriage pantomime; and finally the rape—all these are opened up through the sharply lit consciousness of both the heroine and her tormenter. The torturous decline of Clarissa that follows her rape may seem matched in psychological intensity by the overwrought agony of Lovelace as he struggles with his remorse and his pride. Lovelace is a three-dimensional predator, not amoral as much as morally and emotionally perverted; the richness of his representation in the novel offers abundant attractions to the reader who would be so seduced.

Predictably, then, Lovelace's status in literary-cultural studies remains unresolved; every species of apology and accusation seems to have been leveled at him. Thus, while Terry Eagleton sees Lovelace as a pathetic and destructive psychosexual basket case, he is celebrated by others as "a Byronic hero, Satanic vitalist or post-modernist artist."[65] Nor does criticism confine itself to the mere parameters of Lovelace's personal character. Lovelace, perhaps much like Clarissa herself, is a kind of cipher that marks, not an absence, but an almost limitless plenitude of psychological, philosophical, ethical, erotic, and literary-historical potential.[66] Like that of Clarissa, Lovelace's character figures in deeply subjective form a constellation of heavily gendered sociopolitical, moral, and rhetorical problems whose resolutions participate in the reconceptualization of gender, class, morals, and manners in the eighteenth century. As a literary character heavily invested in literary culture, Lovelace displays many of the ways in which the ideological investments at stake in *Clarissa* are negotiated in literary-cultural forms: the novel, the heroic drama, libertine erotic and satiric poetry, private letter writing.

Lovelace is the corrupt, unrepentant doyen of a regressive and discredited aristocracy keen to challenge the rising bourgeoisie; Lovelace is the envoy of the heroic drama that Richardson seeks to displace with his own novelistic discourse; Lovelace is the representative of a misogynist satiric tradition that Richardson would discredit with his epistolary advocacy of virtuous womanhood; Lovelace is the living contradiction produced by the philosophical investments of libertine ideology; Lovelace is the authorial proxy, stand-in for all that Richardson desires but dares not; Lovelace is the aesthetic individual; Lovelace is the Hobbist man; Lovelace is Proteus embodied, avatar of both Rochester and Milton's Satan; Lovelace is the supreme postmodernist, playing his endgame at the limits of meaning; Lovelace is the hybrid subject emerging with the increasing consolidation of juridical discourse.[67] Lovelace's hefty appetite for self-aggrandizement is well supplied by the sheer amount of attention garnered by his character and the range of conclusions he serves to confirm. These bestow on him a somewhat (anti-)heroic stature in the canon of English literature.

Yet while various, most readings of Lovelace support the arguments I make both about the ways rhetorical and aesthetic alibis work in the apologies for the rake and about the rake's rootedness in the matrix of seventeenth-century issues of authority, absolutism, and masculinity. Lovelace, attesting to the ongoing currency of these issues, is their eighteenth-century literary-cultural avatar. His fate in Richardson's text, I believe, insists both on the compelling attractions and energy of the libertine masculinity he embodies and on its narcissistic self-annihilation. As I point out in chapter 5, Richardson again takes up the problems of masculinity, authority, and prestige with his paragon hero in *Sir Charles Grandison*, and there he writes a character with a will as absolute as Lovelace's but one defined by its benevolence, sensibility, and virtue rather than by the heedless, often malevolent self-aggrandisement that marks Lovelace's. In the terms of this study, Lovelace stands as the arch-embodiment of everything that I have intimated here: a mid-eighteenth-century incarnation of one central type of masculinity in which criminality and prestige are ineluctably joined. Stereotypically, Lovelace is an elite male who depends on his social status and his stylistic prowess for immunity from the law and from social alienation. Affiliated with the aristocracy, as a rake he is engaged in a class-based competition with the polite bourgeois gentleman.[68]

As expected, Lovelace struggles with the two intertwined contradictions I have discussed in relation to prestige and performance: the libertine's reliance on authority for the confirmation of his unique independence from it and his dependence on sociocultural confirmation of his exemption from the conventions according to which such confirmation is distributed.[69] "Thee"-ing and "thou"-ing, spouting heroic drama, and perpetrating the misogyny scripted by a venerable satiric tradition, Lovelace is a cultural anachronism in 1748, heavily invested in the nostalgic ethos that I have argued characterizes the modern rake.[70]

So far, so predictable. Even comically so at times. Yet in relation to the representation of rakish criminality that is my subject here, what may be most notable—and most rhetorically risky—about Richardson's Lovelace is the extent to which his character is authenticated in ways designed not to justify but to damn him. Exploring at exhaustive length the representation of internal subjectivity only gestured toward by Steele, Richardson produces Lovelace's psyche not to redeem but to damn him. The risk, of course, is that Lovelace, like Milton's Satan, can be dangerously seductive and convincing, all the more so the closer we get to him. Richardson's second and third editions of *Clarissa*, accordingly, contain changes intended "to blacken Lovelace's character" in the hope of forestalling readers' sympathetic misreading.[71] So in distinction to other characters elaborated at comparable length through the intimate imaginings of epistolary discourse—characters such as Pamela, Clarissa, Harriet Byron, and Sir Charles Grandison—Lovelace's character is fully drawn in order to alienate rather than cultivate reader sympathy and attachment. If Richardson's virtuous characters engage in seemingly limitless self-regard, much like Lovelace himself, they do so in order to discipline, rather than to celebrate, their vanity and pride. Certainly, doing this engages rhetorical risks, since even sympathetic characters are thus necessarily engaged in some amount of self-authorization, that central feature of Lovelace's ethical failure. But recognizing the risks shared by these modes of self-reflective representation does not equivocate the accompanying realization of a not overly fine distinction between, on the one hand, the self-examination employed as a means of self-correction and self-preservation and, on the other, the self-inflation, even self-obsession that accompanies Lovelace's pathological predations on the selves of others.

So what we would call psychological and cognitive realization here produces much of the ground on which Lovelace is condemned and, as a moral, intellectual, and emotional subject, even undone. In post-Freudian terms, Lovelace is a wretched narcissist; in almost any one's terms, he is conflicted, self-defeating, and sick in spirit. As Eagleton says, Richardson's representation produces a new and fully modern inflection of the rake as a *pathological* subject. And certainly, what we so easily read as psychological pathology also conforms to conventional eighteenth-century notions of madness, moral disorder, and sick fancy.[72] So while, like Steele, providing his rake with an authenticating subjectivity, Richardson departs radically from Steele's progressive narrative of the reformed rake.[73] I have suggested that in Steele's rake we can trace a dialectical transformation of the performative style of the rake into the authentic substance of his character. Likewise, in Richardson's rake, there is a marked interrelation between performance and authentic character, but here this contributes to the dissolution rather than the redemption of that character's integrity. By all accounts, just like his Restoration forefathers (including Milton's Satan), Lovelace is a supreme performer, a dissembler, hypocrite, actor, liar par excellence.

But as Richardson shows how Lovelace casts himself in grandiose, paranoid, often sadistic fantasies, he reveals the extent to which Lovelace's power and status are confined to these self-gratifying, self-contained performances.[74] Lovelace's character as the imperious, triumphant rake is most fully realized only in these imaginary, fantastic scenes. The ground of redemptive authenticity—internal subjectivity, especially as the imagination and as sensibility (the moral-aesthetic self)—is displaced by these highly artificial, stylized performances; it can provide no rehabilitation of the subject, only the confirmation of its pathology. Modeling his performances of his self on a "strangely archaic" group of literary "knights-errant, rakes, knaves, and lovers," Lovelace is updated through modern novelistic discourse in ways that realize his subjectivity in order to shape it as the agent of its own undoing. "Lovelace," as Elaine McGirr recently has written, "must die."[75]

As part of the fabric of his pathology, Lovelace's crimes are often explicated in psychological and psychoanalytic terms that give full consequence to their gendered and sexualized nature.[76] Yet crime in *Clarissa* is presented not only in psychosexual but also in juridical terms that recently have been examined by John Zomchick.[77] Zomchick argues that the constitution of the modern individual proceeds in tandem with and informed by the emergent "juridical subject," a figure that "owes its coherence to a system of legal beliefs, principles, and practices, which attain frequent and clear visibility both in the society and the narratives of eighteenth-century England."[78] According to Zomchick, both Clarissa and Lovelace are "hybrid" figures. Clarissa is "a hybrid of juridical and patriarchal values." Lovelace's relation to juridical discourse is more mediated and complex. His "hybridity" consists in his status at once as "the site of the deliquescence of aristocratic ideals and the emergence of an anarchic version of individualism," in his affiliation "with both an heroic past and a transcendent future."[79]

I challenge the understanding of this characterological divide in such temporal terms as Zomchick posits. As I have shown earlier, in the rake this contradiction between allegiance to aristocratic ideals, to his own elite corporate body on the one hand, and devotion to an antisocial, "anarchic" individualism on the other, is conventional, an inheritance, like so much that is Lovelacian, from the Restoration. The rake's sovereign individualism, moreover, manifests one form of the "devolution of absolutism" attendant on the critique of aristocracy discussed in chapter 1. Typically, the rake is a personally anti-authoritarian individual who nonetheless grounds the privilege of his own imperious will in the elite authority he so frequently assaults. Lovelace's character, then, is riven by an ideological contradiction rather than a temporal divide. Consequently, Lovelace's rakish anarchic individualism need not be understood in terms of his (partial) formation as a "juridical subject" who straddles a kind of historical discursive divide between right as customary privilege (the aristocratic past) and right as legal sanction (the bourgeois, juridical future). The kind of immoral and asocial individualism that Lovelace the rake embodies need not be located in an emergent juridical discourse and oriented toward the future. Rather, it is the product of conflicts *within* the very "aristocratic value" system from which Zomchick distinguishes it, conflicts situated firmly in those past failures of dynastic aristocracy most dramatically enacted from 1649 to 1688.

Lovelace's relation to juridical discourse, then, is not one of partial incorporation but of imperious overcoming. So while seeing, with Zomchick, that Lovelace's imagination has "a pervasive juridical cast" and that Lovelace, as a "civil antinomian," often entangles himself in the legal discourses he so opposes, I do not think with him "that Lovelace's aristocratic values have been *altered* by a juridical fancy and sanctioned by a legalistic conscience" or that Lovelace's allegiances are "divided."[80] Rather, Lovelace's engagement with juridical discourse only confirms his allegiance to elite privilege; he enters into juridical figures and conventions only to assert his own imperial will above the law. Lovelace's relation to the law replicates his relation to all authority: he addresses it only to vanquish and supercede it. That is, Lovelace's performances at his trials, in a sense, are themselves criminal, for they replicate the subversion of the law (religious, legal, social) that summons him there in the first place. This is contempt of court with a vengeance.

Although Clarissa refuses to prosecute him, Lovelace twice appears on trial for her rape. The first "trial" occurs in a fantasy related in Letter 208 before the actual rape of Clarissa, and the second occurs afterward in Letters 323–25, where Lovelace narrates to Belford his confrontation by his family. Richardson omitted Letter 208 from the first edition of *Clarissa* but then restored it in order to confirm Lovelace's criminal character to inappropriately sympathetic readers.[81] Relating a fantasy in which he, along with a crew of fellow rakes, kidnaps and rapes Anna Howe, Mrs. Howe, and their servant and then appears in "triumph" at court, this letter expresses the ways in which Lovelace's criminality adheres, beyond the actual, largely unnarrated rape of Clarissa, in the very stuff of his moral being. Some critics, such as Carol Houlihan Flynn, may be persuaded that the relegation of Lovelace's worst crimes to his imaginative world actually mitigates their extremity: "His fantasies of seduction, both ridiculous and grandiose, undercut the seriousness of his villainy," that is, they are only frolics.[82] However, I think that Richardson substantiates rather than equivocates, with such fantasies, the indelibly delinquent, even sadistic hue of Lovelace's character. That Lovelace approaches the imagining of such deeds as pack rape in such a playful, even comic spirit is meant to reveal not the preeminence of his imaginative powers but their grotesque depravity. From Richardson's severely anti-theatrical perspective, the sheer staginess of Lovelace's customary imaginative modes is itself an indictment of his character.[83] If Gay's Mohocks are excused because what is merely theatrical cannot be truly criminal, Richardson's Lovelace is indicted on the obverse principle: the theatrical *is* criminal.

The trial fantasy in Letter 208 is imagined much like a dramatic farce. Lovelace in his "pea-jacket and great watch-coat" is director and star in the rape scenes on board a pirated ship and then in the "*mob-attracting* occasion" of his trial (186, 189). As we shall see in the next chapter's discussion of celebrity highwaymen such as Claude Duval, James Maclane, and Dick Turpin, the scene Lovelace draws of glamorous criminals winning the support of the crowd, especially of women, is well established by the conventions of criminal biography:

> How bravely shall we enter a court, I at the head of you [fellow rakes and rapists] dressed out each man, as if to his wedding appearance!—You are sure of all the women, old and young, of your side.—What brave fellows!—what fine gentlemen!— There goes a charming handsome man!—meaning me, to be sure!—who could find in their hearts to hang such a gentleman as that? whispers one lady. (187)

Lovelace depends on his performative style, here played as erotic appeal, to redeem him with the ladies. With the men in the audience, including judge and jurors, he is further supplied with sympathy and prestige by virtue of the sexual double standard. Engineer of the rape of three women, two of them elite gentle-women, he anticipates an accrual of prestige: "Would not a brave fellow choose to appear in court to such an arraignment, confronting women who would do credit to his attempt? The country is more merciful in *these* cases than in *any others*: I should therefore like to put myself upon my country" (187).[84]

Lovelace has two additional lines of defense, both of them more than plausible. First, it would be unlikely for women such as the Howes to put their reputations at risk through such a public ordeal; and second, even if they did, and Lovelace were convicted, his family's status would secure him a pardon. Much later in the novel, we see Clarissa confirm Lovelace's assumptions when she writes to Dr. Lewen outlining her rationale for not prosecuting. First, she refuses to put her reputation in danger through a public trial where her name would be "bandied about, and jested profligately with" (1253). Second, even if Lovelace were sentenced to death for this capital crime, "can it be thought," Clarissa poses, "that his family would not have had interest enough to obtain his pardon?" (1253).

The grandiosity, perversity, and sheer narcissism of this fantasy is registered in Lovelace's account when he summons the redemptive vision of "a dozen or two of young maidens, all dressed in white" who go to court to plead for his life: "And what a pretty show they will make, with their white hoods, white gowns, white petticoats, white scarves, white gloves, kneeling for me, with their white handkerchiefs at their eyes, in two pretty rows, as his Majesty walks through them and nods my pardon for their sakes!" (190–91). Prosecuted for rape, Lovelace imagines a couple of dozen virgins pleading his pardon, quite literally whitening over the blackness of his crimes with their performance.

The scene Lovelace choreographs here soars with celestial and angelic figures and so implies the granting of a more-than-earthly pardon for his sins. Yet even this grotesquely fantastic travesty of justice is grounded in juridical actuality by the offhand remark with which Lovelace closes his scene: "And, if once pardoned, all is over: for, Jack, in a crime of this nature there lies no appeal [that could revoke the pardon thus obtained], as in murder." Thus Lovelace acknowledges the heinousness of his crime even as he operatically stages his immunity from its consequence. By consistently connecting Lovelace's monstrous fantasies to actual juridical process and realistic social expectation, Richardson links his rake's criminality to the very system responsible for legal reprisal. That this system works together with sociocultural sexual double standards and elite exceptionalism actually to service the criminal self-authorization of antisocial rakes like

Lovelace is one of the ways in which, as Goldberg puts it, the whole "male world in *Clarissa* is seen as potentially criminal."[85]

Lovelace's immunity from legal prosecution is secured by his status. But his more general social and cultural defenses engage as well the aesthetic and performative alibis conventionally summoned to preserve the prestige of rakish criminality. He pictures himself, not as a rapist and kidnapper, but as a fashionable gentleman, much too fine a figure of a man to condemn to death.[86] Lovelace's fantasy trial renders him a kind of celebrity, publicizing his sexual performance and enhancing its cachet.[87] Performed in the theatre of a public court and located most fully in his personal prestige, Lovelace's sovereign will triumphs over the law, even that of capital crime, exactly as Charles I had failed to do in 1649. This, anyway, is the fantasy—a cruel, farcical fantasy supported by much reasonable assumption. Finally, the fantasy realized at this trial is one that imagines the limitless pursuit of individual will without consequence. In her examination of the role of conscience, intentionality, and contractual law in *Clarissa*, Sandra Macpherson underlines Lovelace's commitment, as a rake, to such a denial of the consequentiality of action. Thus, in Macpherson's terms, Lovelace is "a master of the limited liability defense."[88] As we see in the next chapter's discussion of Ainsworth's Dick Turpin, this fantasy is translated by historical romance into a mythic timelessness, where masculine privilege, power, and transgression can be savored outside history and accountability.

Something like an actual test of Lovelace's forensic powers is posed when his family confronts him with damning evidence of his rape of Clarissa, of his forgery of Lord M.'s signature, and of the impersonation of his aunt, Lady Betty, and his cousin, Lady Sarah. Not surprisingly, Lovelace rises to the occasion and stages a heroic performance designed to render his audience "lost in admiration" (1029). In Letter 323, Lovelace begins his narrative, announcing to Belford: "Now, Jack, have I a subject with a vengeance. I am in the very height of my trial for all my sins to my beloved fugitive" (1026). As this first sentence intimates, the entire narrative of this trial twists and turns around Lovelace's stagy, comic perversity. Although this scene is presented as one that actually occurred, Lovelace's representation of it is just as reliant on the stylistic trappings of the stage as is his earlier, purely imagined fantasy trial. It is clear that here, as always, Lovelace seeks to control, through his theatrical metaphors, actions brought against him for his crimes. Yet finally, rather than attenuate Lovelace's criminality, such theatrics only compound it.

It is solely by virtue of Lovelace's metaphor that this family scene is played as a "trial" and he as a defendant. While certainly, as Douglas Hay and Peter Linebaugh have discussed, there is something theatrical about the eighteenth-century courtroom, Lovelace seems prone to fashion something judicial with his theatrics: "*And now I enter upon my* TRIAL," he inserts, center-spaced, italicized, and capitalized, in his letter to mark the beginning of his dramatic script (1026).[89] At one climactic point early on, he styles the scene as an opera: "For my part I hardly knew whether to sing or say" (1027). He reproves his aunt for her inappropriate response to the drama: "By my soul, Miss Patty, you weep in the wrong place: you shall never go with me to a tragedy" (1029). He styles his uncle, Lord M., as "my Lord Marplot."[90] As defendant, Lovelace writes his character as the underdog, the victim of aggression rather than its perpetrator, and accrues to himself the "right" of a fair trial: "But, pray now, ladies, if I am to be thus interrogated, let me know the contents of the rest of the letter, that I may be prepared for my defense, as you are all for my arraignment" (1030).[91]

As the narrative proceeds through three letters, the theatrical figures persist. At first Lovelace costumes and casts his aunt and cousin as "tabbies" and "grimalkins," and so in effect performs a degrading translation of their characters in a manner related to the personification, "the prostitution of character," for which he stands indicted (1033). For here Lovelace is made to confront not only his drugging, rape, and forcible detainment of Clarissa Harlowe but also his transgressions against his own family. This trial scene emphasizes Lovelace's criminal assault against his own family, the prestige of which he depends upon to shield him from judicial reprisal. This is part of the more generalized conflict in which the rake conventionally participates as he pits his own nonpareil sovereignty against the aristocratic status system in which such claims originate.

All three crimes—rape, impersonation, forgery—are related as violations of the person, whether as body, as character, or as identity. The phrase Lady Betty uses to reprove Lovelace points up the affiliation of his crime against Clarissa with the crimes against herself and Lady Sarah: "I don't think my character, and your cousin Charlotte's, ought to be prostituted in order to ruin an innocent lady" (1033). Lovelace's violation of Clarissa's body sexually assaults her honor and thus threatens her character just as the impersonation by prostitutes of Lady Sarah and Lady Betty degrades theirs. Both cases confound the distinction between reputable women and prostitutes. Thus, Lady Sarah opens her complaint against Lovelace: "Are all women alike with you?" (1027). Lovelace's forgery of his uncle's signature corrupts the legal integrity of the family name, just as both the impersonations of Lady Sarah and Lady Betty and the rape of Clarissa discredit their integrity. Impersonation and forgery are in a sense decidedly performative crimes; in each case, one self is acting as an other in ways that displace and diminish that other.

Judith Wilt's thesis notwithstanding, Lovelace actually has committed the capital crime of rape.[92] In his performance of his "trial" before his family, he meditates as well the capital crime of murder. Resenting this family interrogation and fantasizing the murder of Lord M., Lovelace recalls to Belford his recommendation that his friend murder his own ailing uncle: "I began to think of the laudanum and wet cloth I had told thee [Belford] of long ago; and to call myself in question for a tenderness of heart that will never do me good" (1027). Both capital crimes, murder and rape are identified explicitly at the end of *Clarissa,* as Richardson drives home the fact that with his rape, Lovelace has incurred the guilt of Clarissa's murder as well. In a scene narrated very late in the novel, Lovelace presents to Miss Montague and Lord M. a self-defense that he hopes will clear him of guilt for Clarissa's death.[93] Dismissing his nephew's specious analogies of his rape to mere "theft," Lord M. rules that "if by committing an unlawful act, a capital crime is the consequence, you [Lovelace] are answerable to both" (1438). Macpherson traces this principle to a body of case law "conventionally known in the eighteenth century as the law against dueling." This ruled that "if two persons fought and one was killed, the survivor was guilty of murder *regardless of who provoked the affray;* and, if in the process of committing another felony a death resulted, the perpetrator was guilty of murder *whether he intended to harm the victim or not.*"[94] So although Lovelace does not intend Clarissa's murder when he commits his rape, his uncle and his author nonetheless assign him full guilt for it, according to a body of law on dueling meant to manage the damage incurred by that most elite of crimes.

Thus while Lovelace is never prosecuted for his crimes in a court of law, he nonetheless frequently appears, by his own figurative device, as a defendant on trial. In his first fantasy trial in Letter 208, drawing on all the conventions of rakish performative mastery and elite exceptionalism, he emerges triumphant. Then, hauled before the tribunal of his own family in Letters 323–25, he manages to extricate himself from retribution for impersonation and forgery, and to undertake reparation for rape through marriage. But Clarissa not only refuses this compensation but also dies in a manner that places the blame fully at Lovelace's feet. Yet even then, Lovelace seems unconvinced and petulantly pleads at the end of Letter 515, "Was I the cause of her death? or could I help it?" (1439).

Is Lovelace, then, ever really brought to justice? He dies at the end, killed in a duel by Clarissa's cousin Morden. Lovelace's death in a duel draws on a doubled, not merely a "poetic," logic of justice.[95] It is the body of dueling law that convicts him of Clarissa's murder and the act of a duel that executes him for it. Lovelace's crimes are committed and resolved purely within the customary conventions of the aristocratic ethos. Morden's murder of Lovelace violates the law and so "returns to the pre-civil principle of blood feud," yet it realizes Jonathan Swift's proposal by which the Lovelaces of the world would conveniently cleanse society of their own contaminants.[96] Swift argues against any legal sanction against dueling since he "can discover no political evil in suffering bullies, sharpers, and rakes to rid the world of each other by a method of their own."[97]

From beginning to bitter end, Lovelace acts the consummate rake, following the part scripted for his character to self-annihilation. Yet although Lovelace must die, future rakes live on, each propelled by the narcissistic fantasy of existing as a "peerless peer" outside the very ideology that engenders him. The rake is dead. Long live the rake.

CHAPTER THREE

Romancing the Highwayman

A Few Good Highwaymen

The highwayman shares a number of features with the rake and the pirate. Like them, the modern highwayman emerges from the sociopolitical upheavals of the seventeenth century, and like them, he embodies the aesthetics and ideology of nostalgia that I articulate in the previous chapters. Like other criminals, the highwayman is chronicled at exhaustive and repetitive length in volume after volume of popular biography.[1] But from the seventeenth through the nineteenth centuries, the highwayman traverses a range of representational modes; he is nothing if not a mobile figure. The mythic figure of the highwayman, then, takes shape in relation to the conventions and ideologies of the various kinds of texts in which he appears. In the previous chapter, I use the rake to show how criminality and masculine prestige can operate in relation to notions of subjective authenticity and performativity. In the next chapter, contextualizing the pirate in the West Indian cultural matrix from which he emerges, I examine how distinctions between law and outlaw shift and falter in ways that are revelatory of colonial and postcolonial powers. Here, looking at the highwayman, I attend to some of the more specifically rhetorical and formal factors at work in his generation and establishment as a culturally mythic figure.

The romantic figure of the gentleman highwayman is exceptional; very few of the figures recorded in early eighteenth-century criminal biographies foreshadow the type. A handful of the seventeenth-century highwaymen of criminal biography might be glamorous, and John Gay's Macheath (1728) consolidates the most gallant features of those earlier highwaymen, but not until William Harrison Ainsworth's treatment of Dick Turpin in *Rookwood* (1834) is the highwayman properly romanticized.[2] Approached historically and contextually, the generic conventions of these different textual manifestations—in criminal biography, in mock-heroic dramatic satire, in historical romance—disclose the moral, socio-political, and cultural issues they are employed to address. Predictably, from the seventeenth through the nineteenth centuries, attention to prestigious criminal masculine figures such as the gallant highwayman foregrounds issues of authority and autonomy, legitimacy and corruption, liberty and license, self-preservation and social cohesion. However, the means by which the highwayman's self-authorization and thus his prestige is configured differs from text to text, from period to period. Thus, representations of the highwaymen provide one popular way that people thought through these issues, the prominence and urgency of which might be understood sensibly as a legacy from the seventeenth century. Like the rake and the pirate, the highwayman is a culturally mythic figure valuable for our reading of the passage into modernity of forms of masculinity closely reliant on criminality for their significance and prestige.

In three sections, this chapter examines three definitive incarnations of the highwayman: the seventeenth-century gallant highwayman of criminal biography; John Gay's gentleman highwayman, Macheath, as figured in James Boswell's journalist self-fashioning; and Ainsworth's romantic highwayman, Dick Turpin. In the first section, my subject is not criminal biography per se, or even highwaymen in general, but one precise figure from these volumes of biography: the gallant highwayman. There are really only a few figures before Macheath appears in 1728 whose biographies suggest those features of distinction, gallantry, principle, and prestige so prominent in the gentleman highwayman of cultural myth. Our notions informed by Gay's Macheath and Ainsworth's Dick Turpin, we might be tempted to look retrospectively in early criminal biography for the kind of reckless, glamorous lady's man at the center of Gay's sophisticated sociopolitical satire or for the rollicking boys' adventure hero that Ainsworth serves up. Faced with the substantially more ambivalent, often monotonous, usually less sophisticated criminal biographies of the highwayman's earlier incarnation, we might find ourselves disappointed and perplexed. A few, two of which I examine here, have a sharply focused sociopolitical point, but these are exceptions.

It seems significant that of the three figures treated in this section—James Hind, Phillip Stafford, and Claude Duval—most eligible for the title "gallant highwayman," two, Hind and Stafford, are also politically principled royalists who fought for the Stuarts.[3] A Frenchman, Duval is also connected with the political upheavals of the seventeenth century and with the Stuarts; he came to England at the Restoration as a servant to a royalist who had been residing with the exiled court at St. Germain. The gallant highwayman who might sensibly be viewed as a precursor to Macheath is an exception among his criminal compatriots, one distinguished by his close affiliation with the Stuart cause and the brand of cavalier, libertine masculinity associated with its supporters. As this type is cycled through the eighteenth and nineteenth centuries, he retains his nostalgic allure and continues to figure the convergence of the culturally prestigious (the gentleman) with the judicially and morally illegitimate (the criminal).

The second section of this chapter looks at how Macheath figures in James Boswell's engagement with the commonplace juxtaposition of the criminal and the gentleman that informs eighteenth-century notions of masculinity. Boswell's idealization of Macheath highlights the highwayman's erotic appeal. Macheath is emulated for his sexual prowess as much as for his personal courage and his enviable immunity from the disciplinary reprisal of the law. Looking at Macheath's place in Boswell's journalistic self-representation, we see how a historical individual handled, socially and emotionally, the particular cultural contradiction captured in the oxymoronic figure of the "gentleman highwayman." Boswell's journal provides a record of how the tension between authority and individual will that structures the criminal biography, and that between cultural prestige and criminal illegitimacy that structures the character of the gentleman highwayman, could be internalized. Moreover, Boswell's journal reveals how this internalization maintains the completely stereotypical nature of the figure even as it tailors the type to Boswell's own psychological makeup. This instance, then, provides a stunning illustration of the integration of the public and culturally conventional with the private and psychically specific.

In the third section, concerning Ainsworth's *Rookwood*, the accommodation of the commonplace juxtaposition—the criminal and the gentleman—occurs through the devices of the "modern romance" identified by literary scholar Ian Duncan.[4] The gentleman highwayman is a nostalgic figure; Ainsworth's *Rookwood* fixes nostalgia in a romantic rendering of historical anachronism as cultural archetype. Ainsworth locates his gentleman highwayman in the nationalistic Neverland of Merry Old England. He consigns all heinously *criminal* activity to the gothic romance that proceeds side by side in *Rookwood* with the historical romance of Dick Turpin. Translating the Turpin of popular eighteenth-century text and legend through the discourse of historical romance, Ainsworth's novel produces the modern myth of the romantic highwayman. Whereas the eighteenth-century Turpin appears in contemporary accounts as the "Famous Highwayman," Ainsworth's romantic Turpin is refigured as a *gentleman* highwayman. Bluff, athletic, utterly independent and self-reliant, a blameless emblem of the world we have lost, Ainsworth's Turpin becomes a boys' adventure hero; and this is what he remains for the rest of the nineteenth century.[5] Immune from the corruptions of patriarchal authority enacted through the gothic plot, the last of the noble clan of gentlemen highwaymen, Turpin is removed from historical continuity. Ainsworth's Turpin thus fixes the highwayman in romance, where his criminality is removed from consequence and so liability.

Early criminal biographies epitomize the tension characteristic of life-writing between individual self-assertion and authoritarian restraint, between the contingent ramblings of the individual and the providential determination of narrative. In *The Beggar's Opera* Gay's satire explodes the division between transgression and authority, fully exploiting the moral tension available from criminal biography. Yet the satirical implosion of the divide between crime and authority always presumes its availability. In Boswell's journal we see how the tension between transgressive individual will and legitimating authority is psychically and socially enacted. Moreover, there we see how performativity serves as an alibi and the aesthetic realm as an arena of authorization that provides an alternative to the harsher tribunals of paternal and judicial judgment. In *Rookwood,* this tension between patriarchal authority and individual will is completely dissolved, and with it any remaining shreds of contradiction within the term "gentleman highwayman." Fixing the character as mythic type, this romantic dissolution removes it from history—and thus from consequence—into the realm of escapist boys' stories and heritage-industry legend. As such, Dick Turpin as romantic highwayman furnishes a model of mythic criminal masculinity to generations of boys and tourists.

So effectively have Ainsworth, mass culture, and the heritage industry mythologized the figure of Turpin that historian James Sharpe perceives their shameless popularization as contributing to the assault on "the professional and technically skilled" approach to the past cultivated within his own academic discipline.[6] He devotes the final chapter of his recent book on "the myth of the highwayman" to deploring the damage inflicted on historical studies by the kind of appetite for infotainment fed so abundantly by the legends of Turpin and of other "celebrity" historical figures. Turpin, for Sharpe the historian, becomes emblematic of "the clear distinction between the type of attempts to reconstruct historical reality at which historians struggle, and the historical myth that so often achieves widespread public currency and triumphs over the historians and their labours."[7] What I attempt with my discussion of the mythical highwayman is neither, a la Sharpe, the imposition of positivist historical reality, nor, a la Lincoln Faller, an explanation of the highwayman's functions in narrowly personal, moral, and psychological terms, but an account of how this mythic figure emerges and the kinds of cultural purposes he has served.[8] Rather than counter popular mythologies with "real history," I want to understand, historically and rhetorically, their forms and functions.

Gallant Highwaymen, Criminal Biography, and Reversals of Authority

Criminal biographies emerge from the more general narrative matrix of life-writing that includes spiritual biography and autobiography and their early fictional twins, some of which we call novels. Reflecting the tension characteristic of all these modes of life-writing, criminal biographies comprise two major trajectories of energy and intent: one generated from the individual's deeds, and the other from the orderly containment of those deeds within an authoritative narrative.[9] All life-writing must come to terms with potential conflicts inscribed by these two imperatives—to detail the deeds and sometimes the words and thoughts of the individual, on the one hand, and, on the other, to render significant and authoritative the record of that detail in narrative. The criminal biography throws the tension between them into sharp relief. The contrast between the everyday deeds of the criminal and their containment by the narrative could not be stronger, for it is a contrast between absolute transgression and absolute suppression. Form and content here sharpen each other's contours. The criminal's activities must be stopped, not simply because any narrative must have some shapely and meaningful end, but also *because they are criminal.* At the same time, the narrative gains authority, not simply because it is in ultimate control of the text, but also because it is identified with the law. The ending of the criminal biography is overdetermined: we always know how things will turn out; there is no suspense, only reaffirmation of the operation of law.

These features, I believe, contribute to the saturation of fictional criminal biographies among those texts usually cited as among the first English novels. For this peculiar intersection of criminal content with narrative form highlights the very problems engaged by novelistic discourse as it emerges. These issues, epistemological and ethical in their essence, have been articulated at length especially by Michael McKeon. The privileged place of the criminal biography in early novelistic discourse has been examined by Lennard Davis, who contends that there is "something inherently novelistic about the [early eighteenth-century] criminal," just as Bryan Reynolds maintains that there is something intrinsically dramatic about the early modern criminal.[10] Furthermore, Davis argues that "the literary trade" itself "was considered illicit, disreputable, and even criminal."[11] However, what I suggest here is not that there is anything inherently novelistic, or dramatic for that matter, about the criminal and his underworld as such, or anything necessarily criminal about the literary trade, but that the synergy between the content of the criminal life and the conventions of seventeenth-century life-writing underline the formal issues of the narrated within the narrative and thus the ideological issues of individuality and authority that have been identified as novelistic preoccupations.

The tension between individual and narrative authority so marked in criminal biography is usually read as producing a doubled and ambiguous, even contradictory text. These biographies seem to offer two sorts of readings: one engaged with the criminal transgressions and the other with the assertion of authority that will put a stop to them. Criminal biography, like life-writing more generally, presents the possibility, sometimes even the desirability, of the self-authorization of the individual whose life it narrates. This is most typically accommodated by the narrative of repentance, which allows an integration of the agency of the individual with the authority of the law (divine and/or mundane). Within this narrative, the criminal and the spiritual biography proceed in parallel ways. In *Robinson Crusoe* we watch as the prodigal castaway learns to match his perspectives and desires with those of providential design; thus, in criminal biography the transgressor repents and accommodates his will to providential authority.

But the more fully—and, from a rhetorical perspective, the more successfully—the criminal's circumstances, motivations, and rationales are narrated, the more completely his life seems to authorize itself, independent of and in opposition to the law. McKeon has given the most succinct articulation to this potential for the reversal of authority in the criminal biography: "The delinquent folk hero, whether Spanish picaro or Tyburn highwayman, is compelling enough in his pursuit of freedom to suggest that the common way of 'error' may in fact be the road of individual truth."[12] What makes this reversal thinkable and not "merely blasphemous" is the questioning of authority, especially absolutist authority, so prevalent and so profoundly consequential in the seventeenth century. Criminal biographies, in their absolutist fusion of divine and worldly authority, recall the problem of that identification even as they assert it: "It would not be surprising if readers . . . were distracted at least momentarily by the complacency of an identification—between God and the magistrate, divine decree and its human accommodation—which recent history had rendered extremely problematic."[13]

Criminal biography, then, with its doubled quality and thus its potential for *reversals of authority*, might be seen to encapsulate and recapitulate a central issue of England's "recent history" itself. The decisive event and enduring emblem of this issue is the conviction for treason of Charles I. This event produced the ultimate identification of authority and criminality. From a radical Republican perspective, the criminality adheres to the sovereign who so traduced his authority; from a royalist perspective, to the regicides whose sham "authority" sentenced the king to death. From the time of Charles's execution until his son's restoration in 1660, active service to the Stuart cause was itself criminal, as it was again after 1689. The set of political and ethical upheavals that the execution of the king epitomized are witnessed in a number of highwaymen's lives. What is more, royalist political preoccupations feature almost exclusively in the biographies of those few highwaymen who are figured as "gentlemanly" or "gallant."

Looking for the origins of the romantic highwayman in the compendia of criminal lives assembled by Captain Alexander Smith (1714) and Captain Charles Johnson (1734), the reader finds them among the housebreakers, footpads, pickpockets, con artists, and murderers, but finds few of any distinction.[14] Sharpe, with good reason, thinks an examination of the lives of James Hind and Claude Duval can tell us pretty much all we need to know about the glamorous highwayman before Macheath and Turpin.[15] I add the life of Phillip Stafford. These three highwaymen, Stafford, Hind, and Duval, are royalists. Having fought in the royalist army, James Hind and Phillip Stafford can properly be called Cavalier highwaymen. In their lives we see how the reversals of authority implicit within the criminal biography as a genre are thematized around the sociopolitical reversals brought on with the civil wars and interregnum. Claude Duval is significant to the myth of the gentleman highwayman, especially as realized in Gay's Macheath, because of the weight his legend gives to the highwayman's gallantry and erotic appeal.

Captain Phillip Stafford was the son of a gentleman farmer. From an early age his character is marked by the kind of energy and personal charisma stifled by sedentary and conventional pursuits. Stafford, the biographer tells us, would have excelled at school "had his Application been equal to the Sprightliness of his Wit, and uncommon Vivacity of his Temper" (77). Although never the best scholar, Stafford is always the head boy. He joins the royalist army as soon as war breaks out, distinguishes himself in battle, and is made a captain. With defeat, Stafford, like all Cavaliers, is dispossessed, so he mends his fortunes by turning highwayman, con artist, and general thief:

> As soon as the King was dead, and the Rebels had got all into their Hands, the Royalists were obliged to shift from Place to Place all over the Nation; and to use all the cautionary Means they could invent, to secure themselves. The small Patrimony of Mr. Stafford was sequestered, among the many larger Estates of Gentlemen, who

had continued in their Duty to the last, and he soon found himself in no Capacity of getting a moderate Subsistence. (77)

Stafford vows his revenge; he will rob only those who have robbed him: "The Resolution he set out with, was, to raise Contributions among the Enemies of the Master [Charles II] only, whom he vow'd never to spare in any Thing" (77). Stafford, a highly principled criminal, is a social bandit of sorts.[16] His crimes are heroically shaded as vengeance; his depredations on Republicans as noble deeds executed to reclaim his honor.

Not only is Stafford a royalist, but so is his biographer. Throughout the life there is almost unstinting admiration for Stafford and his exploits. The narrator only expresses disapproval of Stafford's crimes when Stafford departs from his own principles and robs a woman of no particular ideological stamp whom he has just seduced. Before detailing this event, the author breaks the narrative and delivers an apology for his protagonist:

> And now I wish I could conceal the Sequel of this Story. When such a gallant Man as our Captain robs only for Necessity, and then makes Choice only of such Persons to collect from, as he [a Republican] of whom we have been last speaking, the Reader is not much displeased with him. There appears something so agreeable in the Manner and Circumstances of such a Story, as takes away a great Deal of the Resentment, which would otherwise arise against the Felony. (82)

Stafford's violation of his own principle is rendered by the narrator as evidence of his common humanity and thus refigured as a ground of sympathetic identification with the reader: "If therefore this, which we are going to relate, be acknowledged as the Captain's one great Foible, the universal Weakness of human Nature will be ready to excuse him in some Degree" (82).

The narrator and his protagonist share not only their political stance but also their status as authors. Stafford is both an aristocratic highwayman and Cavalier poet. His biography incorporates two of his literary texts: one a song celebrating the sexual freedoms of a libertine golden age, and the other a verse satire against Protestant religions (81–82; 84). These, his biographer reports, are but two pieces from a larger oeuvre: "As to his Poetry, it is confidently affirmed . . . that many of the best Satirical Pieces then published, which have since appear'd under other Names, were in reality of his Composing" (82). Stafford's verbal prowess is witnessed in the biography not only by his literary accomplishments but also in several scenes where he convincingly mimics the religious cant of his enemies and victims. Stafford is a master of language and of disguise; the two talents work together in a sustained subplot where, feigning the role of a Puritan preacher, he gains the pulpit and the trust of a community, the young women of which he proceeds to seduce. A libertine masquerading in pursuit of sexual conquests, Stafford reminds us of Restoration comedy rakes, such as Horner posing as an impotent man to gain full access to society ladies and Dorimant assuming the persona of Courtage to ingratiate himself with Mrs. Woodvill.[17]

As the biography of a criminal with whom we are encouraged to identify and sympathize, Stafford's life fully activates the reversal of authority latent in the criminal biography. As a royalist whose loyalty is criminal, the sociopolitical content of his life is shaped by the most complete upheaval of authority in English history. As a libertine cavalier who takes on the persona of a Puritan divine, Stafford performs yet another reversal. As the subject of a criminal biography, as a political subject, and as an inventive and accomplished rogue, Stafford is defined by reversals: "In short, his whole Life, with respect to his Religion and Gallantry, was as confused as the Account which we now give of it. He was one Day a Saint, the next a Lover, the next a Satirist, and the next a Highwayman, or Imposter, according as the Occasion offered" (82). Stafford, certainly, embodies the instabilities of his age; predictably, this embodiment takes the generic and discursive forms specific to that age: the criminal biography, the loyal traitor, the libertine saint.

Within the perspective of the narrative, however, there is no marked opposition between the gentleman and the highwayman. According to prevailing libertine notions, Stafford is an accomplished gallant; the ideal of the civil, politely restrained gentleman is not in play here. Stafford's cavalier masculine prestige is affirmed by his repeated seductions of women from Republican families. The contest is a conventional one between Cavalier and Puritan, played out in a criminal biography that uses its royalist subject to lambaste the self-serving hypocrisies of those who profited from the civil wars.

By championing Stafford, the narrator dislocates the more conventional identification between narrative and legal authority. Rather than a resolution, through repentance, of criminal will and lawful authority, this biography seems to resolve the narrative authority into concordance with the criminal agency of its protagonist. Thus the narrative, in a sense, incorporates as its own perspective the reversal of authority implicit in criminal biography as a genre. We are encouraged to side with Stafford as long as he sticks to his loyalist, royalist cause. The contest for moral authority lies within the protagonist's struggle with his own integrity, as defined by himself and sanctioned by the narrative. We have noted Stafford's first violation of his own principle when he robs a woman he has seduced. His second, when he robs, from simple greed, a mere farmer, results in his conviction and execution. This conciliates narrative and judicial authority, for Stafford is guilty on both counts: from the moral perspective of the narrative, he has broken his word; from a judicial perspective, he has broken the law.

Stafford's royalist sympathies, his martial service, his libertine gallantry, his verbal dexterity and literary accomplishments all contribute to his image as a dashing Cavalier and thus, by a widely held standard of the time, as a gallant gentleman. The testament he leaves behind him at his death attributes his criminal conduct to "the Iniquity of the Times" (85). His criminality, then, can be read as the product of the sociopolitical revolution that produced, as well, the criminality of the king and of all those supporting the royalist cause. As long as Stafford's crimes maintain their ideological connection with that cause, the narrator defends them as a species of anti-revolutionary resistance. The style of Stafford's masculinity and of his criminality are royalist and Stuart; they take part in many of the same imperatives and alibis examined in the previous chapter on libertine rakes.

This brand of masculinity and criminality is shared by Stafford's contemporary, the renowned James Hind, whose status and fame overshadows Stafford's own and whose biography follows Stafford's in Johnson's compendium:

> There is no other Life so proper to follow Capt. Stafford's as that of his Contemporary Capt. James Hind; a Man as much talk'd of to this Day as almost any one of his Profession that ever lived, and who was distinguished by his Pleasantry in all his Adventures; for he never in his Life robb'd a Man, but at the same Time he either said or did something that was diverting. The Reason why we think him so proper to follow Capt. Stafford immediately, is more especially his Principles, which were truly loyal, and which induced him, like the former, to commit all his Depredations upon the Republican Party. (86)

Hind's criminal career is barely begun when Charles I is executed. This revolutionary event inspires him to politicize his crimes: "It was much about the Time that the inhuman and unnatural murder of King Charles I was perpetrated at his own Palace Gate, by the Fanaticks of that Time"; so Hind, like Stafford, resolves "never to spare any of the Regicides" he meets (86).

Here, as in Stafford's biography, we have a royalist subject and a royalist biographer. As a criminal, Hind differs from Stafford in that his activity is more closely confined to highway robbery, and as a personality, in his reputation for wit, generosity, and personal address. This is apparent from his first robbery, which he accomplishes "with such a pleasant Air, that the Gentleman protested

he would never hurt a Hair of his Head, if it should at any Time be in his Power"
(86). More than Stafford, Hind's qualities as a gentleman find expression in a
highly stylized manner that renders his crimes not merely tolerable but positively
diverting. While Hind, more consistently than Stafford, confines his robberies
to his political opponents, the license the narrative grants him derives as much,
if not more, from the finesse and appeal of his personal manner as from the
virtue of his ideological stance. That is, like the offenses of the libertine rake,
Hind's crimes are redeemed by the stylistic mastery with which they are committed. This is the quality captured in his celebrity—"a Man as much talk'd of to
this Day as almost any one of his Profession that ever lived"—and the quality he
contributes to the makeup of the glamorous highwayman of legend. In Hind the
political alibi is matched perfectly to its corresponding aesthetic alibi, an alibi of
manners, and one that the highwayman, pursuing his "Pranks," shares with the
Restoration rakes in their performance of "handsome mischiefs."[18] Of course,
this biography lies open to a reversal of authority that could read Hind's criminal
frolics not as enjoying the same stylistic immunity but as being tarred with the
same brush as all rogues, rakes, and rascals, no matter what their sociocultural
status.

However, that is not a turn led by a narrative devoted to depicting Hind as
not only charismatic, amusing, courageous, and loyal but also generous and humane. In contrast to Stafford, who is reproved for his personal greed, Hind "has
been celebrated for his Generosity to all Sorts of People; more especially for his
Kindness to the Poor, which it is reported was so extraordinary, that he never
injured the Property of any Person who had not a compleat Share of Riches"
(88). In Hind's character, then, the charisma and polish of the Cavalier are joined
with the social conscience of that archetypal English social bandit, Robin Hood.
Moreover, he strives to limit his crimes to robbery: "Never was Highwayman
more careful than Hind to avoid Blood-Shed" (89). Only once does he kill a man,
and then only by necessity, "in order to preserve his own" life (89).

The authorization of Hind's moral authority is most emphatically expressed
in the judgment he delivers, first against the regicide Bradshaw, and then, at his
execution, against the entire regime. Meeting Bradshaw on the road, Hind not
only robs him but also denounces him as a criminal. In a speech that takes as its
trope the very reversals of authority that shape the entire biography, Hind exults
over his victim, who is allowed to live only in order that he might later suffer
the criminal execution he deserves: "I have now as much Power over you, as
lately you had over the King, and I should do God and my Country good Service,
if I made the same Use of it; but live, Villain, to suffer the Pangs of thine own

Conscience . . . who art unworthy to die by any Hands, but those of the common Hangman, and at any other Place than Tyburn" (87).

Hind arrogates to himself the authority more conventionally installed in the law; in this topsy-turvy moral universe, the highwayman is the voice of justice that condemns the magistrate for capital crimes. The heavily politicized tenor of Hind's career shapes his death as much as it does his life. Unlike Stafford, who is taken for the inglorious, unprincipled robbery of a farmer, Hind is convicted for treason after serving in the royalist army at Worcester. He dies unrepentant: "He declared that most of the Robberies which he had ever committed, were upon the republican Party, of whose Principles he professed he always had an utter Abhorrence" (89).

We have seen how Stafford's criminality can be read as a product of the same execrable rebellion that criminalized Charles I. Hind insists that his life be read like this and that he occupy a place right alongside the martyred Charles I and the exiled Charles II. That he sees his own fate coinciding with that of his sovereign is apparent in the overlapping referents in his speech. Before he is drawn and quartered, Hind only regrets that he will not live to see the restoration of Charles II to the throne "from which *he* [Charles II] was most unjustly and illegally excluded by a rebellious and disloyal Crew, who deserved Hanging more than *him* [Hind]" (89, my emphases). The execution of Charles I, the exile of Charles II, and the execution of James Hind are equally crimes committed by the "rebellious and disloyal" Republicans and regicides here styled as a criminal gang or "Crew." Narrative approval is never withdrawn from Hind. Appropriating to himself the sanction of sovereign will and sovereign immunity, the criminal individual is acquitted by his own judgment against an invalid judicial authority. It is their shared criminality that provides this common ground for king and highwayman on which Hind erects the apology for his life. It seems unlikely that criminality could attain a more absolute purchase on prestige.

Both Stafford and Hind, then, figure a kind of criminal prestige intimately engaged with the reversals of authority emblematized by the execution of Charles I. The final highwayman that I consider here, Claude Duval, is involved in the same set of upheavals but enters at a later stage. A French footman serving a royalist Englishman, he accompanies his master back to England at the Restoration. Unlike Hind and Stafford, Duval's political principles are never declared; his status and renown seem completely founded on his personal accomplishments and charms. Hind and Stafford are the king's men; Duval is a lady's man. His gallantry and popularity with women lie at the heart of his fame. In an iconic scene, he dances with a lady whose coach he stops: "Here it was that Du Vall performed marvels, the best masters in London, except those that are French, not being able to show such footing as he did in his great French riding boots" (146). Duval's claim to the status of a gentleman is based on those French forms of personal address and gallantry associated with Charles's Restoration court. A lowly footman, Duval nonetheless so perfects these social and erotic arts that he garners substantial prestige, especially among the ladies. Stafford and Hind, both soldiers in the royalist army, both devoted to aggressive resistance to the Republican regime, enact the martial and political imperatives of the Stuart cause. Duval, devoted to dancing, drinking, womanizing, and gambling, enacts the excesses of the Stuart court.

A Frenchman, a footman, a celebrity highwayman, Duval provides a ready subject for Walter Pope's satire against the Francophilia he sees spoiling English society and manners.[19] Pope seeks to reverse the authority of the Frenchified court from which Duval ultimately derives his prestige by showing how it cultivates such "Mushromes" as this footman cum highwayman.[20] So insidious and corrosive is this fashion for all things French that even a footman, even a highwayman, can insinuate his way into society merely by performing the "marvels" of a dancing master. Like one of Rochester's "knights of the elbow and the slur" in *A Ramble in St. James's Park*, Duval apes his betters and courts their women.[21] Like Gay's Macheath, he is surrounded by female admirers in prison. At his death, he is laid out in state with a full complement of teary-eyed women mourners.

These three figures, Stafford, Hind, and Duval, provide a kind of template for the rakish gentleman highwayman that takes his most influential eighteenth-century form as Macheath in Gay's mock-heroic *Beggar's Opera*. At Macheath's appearance in 1728, the gentleman highwayman, like the rake, participates in modes of masculine prestige associated with the pre-1689 world. As Isaac Kramnick and Michael Denning have argued, Macheath is affiliated with "the gentry and noblemen of quality" whose reliance on the "paternalism, customs, ancient rights, a discretionary system of law" is challenged by the Peachums of the emergent commercial society governed by counting, rationalized law, and bourgeois morality.[22] The gentleman highwayman Macheath, then, is a nostalgic figure prominent in popular eighteenth-century cultural negotiations of legitimacy, masculinity, and social status.

The reversal of authority so determining in the narratives of Stafford's and Hind's lives is steadied into the sustaining condition of Gay's satire where high and low, authority and transgression, are held in mock-heroic equilibrium. Duval provides an earlier instance of the kind of eroticized cult surrounding the figure of Macheath that we see instantiated in Boswell's relation to the highwayman.

As Pope deplores the corruption of manners and morals that support Duval's pretensions, he underlines what seems to be the all-too-conventional proximity of sociocultural prestige and criminality in accepted notions of the gentleman. In the next section, I examine this juxtaposition of the gentleman and the criminal as it manifests in Boswell's *London Journal*, where each figure seems to make equal claim on Boswell's aspirations and assays at self-definition.

The Perfect Gentleman: Boswell, Macheath, and Mr. Spectator

As a self-consciously literary personal journal, Boswell's *London Journal* has interested eighteenth-century scholars investigating the interplay between life-writing and fiction, between autobiography and the novel.[23] Recording the first encounters between Boswell and Samuel Johnson, this journal is significant in the genesis of Boswell's masterpiece of biography, *The Life of Johnson* (1791). As the diurnal record of a genteel young man in London from 1762 to 1763, the journal provides a detailed picture of one sort of well-connected life in the mid-eighteenth century. To historians of gender and ideology, Boswell's self-reporting lays tantalizingly open the uneven psyche of a young man struggling to find himself within and against familial expectations and sociocultural conventions. It is this aspect of Boswell's *London Journal* that primarily concerns me here.

In early adulthood, Boswell's first concern, as Patricia Meyer Spacks puts it, is "to be—quite simply—a great man; any attainable greatness will do."[24] Seeking to so distinguish himself, Boswell revolves through a series of available characters, trying them out to determine both how they fit and how they fit in with his ambitions. His journal constitutes a kind of source book for stock masculine characters current in mid-eighteenth-century Britain. Moreover, as Felicity Nussbaum has remarked, the journal supplies not simply a variety of different characters but also a range of different approaches to character and to subjectivity.[25] Focusing this observation more sharply around Boswell's engagement with gender, with his own masculinity, David Weed reads Boswell's quest for character "as a guide to the significant changes in the social construction of masculinity in the period" and finds the unsettled younger Boswell especially valuable because of his "position at the nexus of several kinds of masculine identity."[26] Likewise, Philip Carter has tried to categorize and define Boswell's relation to a range of widely divergent masculine ideals.[27]

Here, I examine Boswell's relation to two of the most divergent ideals he emulates: the rakish highwayman, Macheath, and the arbiter of taste and architect of the autonomous realm of the imagination, Mr. Spectator. Rather than seeing these figures simply as emblems marking polar points on some sort of moral spectrum across which Boswell swings or along which he advances, I examine how they both serve together to accommodate Boswell's notion of his own manliness. Rather than charting a progressive narrative through which, as Weed has it, Boswell undergoes "a steady conversion of the dissipated man of pleasure into the dignified *retenu*," I see the *London Journal* laying bare the ways in which the rakish man of pleasure and the dignified gentleman are mutually constitutive positions more or less simultaneously available in Boswell's psyche.[28]

Looking at Boswell's relation to these two figures reveals the dominance in his own psyche of that commonplace juxtaposition of criminal and gentleman. While this juxtaposition certainly participates in the wider cultural logic of *concordia discors,* the union of opposites, it is so heavily conventionalized both by the habitual misconduct of elite men and by popular cultural representation, as in *The Beggar's Opera,* that the status of its terms as oppositional starts to seem compromised.[29] The mock-heroic, the modal form that most perfectly encapsulates this juxtaposition of opposites, realizes this compromise in its doubled logic, which holds high and low in equilibrium, momentarily suspending value hierarchies and so allowing the criminal and the gentleman to occupy a single register of representation. As William Empson writes, "It makes Macheath seem like the heroes and swains no less than the heroes and swains like Macheath."[30] In relation to eighteenth-century notions of masculinity, this, I believe, is the ultimate fantasy presented by *The Beggar's Opera* and one in which James Boswell, along with much of polite British society, eagerly participated.

Investigations into the cultural myths of criminal masculinity as embodied both in the rake and in the gentleman highwayman bring to attention the durable place that Gay's Macheath, the genteel, rakish Scottish highwayman, took in the intimate imaginings of James Boswell, the genteel, rakish Scottish man of law and letters. Boswell's *London Journal*, recording the years when he was in his early twenties, witnesses the prominence of Macheath in his psyche. "In one way or another," remarks Frederick Pottle, Boswell's modern editor, "the figure of Macheath dominates this entire journal" (252).[31]

Yet alongside the gentleman highwayman, Boswell's impersonation and identification target another fictional figure, Mr. Spectator. This pair of emulative models—one the glamorous, flamboyant (indeed, operatic) libertine outlaw Macheath, the other the reserved (indeed, mostly mute) Stoic doyen of the polite imagination, Mr. Spectator—seems incongruous, even paradoxical. Yet contradiction and paradox abound in Boswell's *London Journal* as he lurches between noble resolution and sinful backsliding, devotion to pleasure and fidelity to economy, self-aggrandizement and self-loathing, pride in his heritage and abhorrence of Scottish acquaintance, disciplined self possession and loutish outbursts of "low jocularity." Yet while Boswell's self-contradiction is widely confirmed, contemporary scholarship attending to his emulative identification with Macheath and Mr. Spectator does not focus on the contradictions this paradoxical pair might describe in Boswell's psyche. Indeed, the full relation of Boswell/Macheath to Boswell / Mr. Spectator is left largely unexamined in accounts that look discretely at Boswell's relation to either one figure or the other. In his essay on Boswell and *The Beggar's Opera*, Michael Friedman asserts that Macheath provides Boswell with a "paragon of manly conduct."[32] Looking at the role of the *The Tatler* and *The Spectator* in Boswell's emotional and imaginative development, Donald Newman elaborates how Mr. Spectator provides Boswell a model for the cultured and polite man of letters. Friedman's examination of the Boswell/Macheath pairing never attends to the Boswell / Mr. Spectator pair; Newman's Boswell / Mr. Spectator pair is viewed independently of the Macheath identification.[33]

I bring this paradoxical pair into analytical proximity, because I believe that "in one way or another," Mr. Spectator no less than Macheath dominates Boswell's entire journal. Moreover, I find that the domination of each often occurs in tandem with the other. It is a critical commonplace that Boswell, especially the young Boswell of the *London Journal*, is preoccupied with his own manliness, his own masculinity, for which one prominent figure is Macheath.[34] It is the pervasive domination of this concern with manliness, rather than the few—though crucial—overt appearances of Macheath, that justifies Pottle's remark. During the year in London, this preoccupation takes shape in large part around Boswell's dogged attempts to secure a place in the Guards, a smart martial occupation that conforms nicely to his emulation of Captain Macheath. Because the pursuit of manliness dominates Boswell's journal, and because of the obstacles that attend this pursuit, the Macheath figure becomes an emblem of this undertaking. Concomitantly, more than in any literal references to Mr. Spectator, it is in attitudes toward masculinity and subjectivity associated with this persona and his publications that his dominance might be identified.[35] So in the case of both emulative models, one way that their dominance is manifest is through their relation to Boswell's preoccupation with his masculine self, his manliness.

But both figures are also associated with specific realms of representation: a dramatic character, Macheath happens on the stage; his genre is theater. A fictional character, Mr. Spectator is most fully realized in that realm of the imagination he himself formulates. This is yet another way in which both Macheath and Mr. Spectator can be seen to dominate the *London Journal*. Both the theater and the aesthetic realm of the imagination provide sites of mediation that shape Boswell's relation to his own character and actions and their representation in his journal. Additionally, as arbiter of the taste of the town, Mr. Spectator models that arena of critical judgment that grants Macheath his reprieve at the end of *The Beggar's Opera*. In comforting distinction to his own father, Lord Auchinleck, who sat on the Scots bar to condemn to death criminals such as Macheath, Mr. Spectator provides Boswell with a more hopeful way of mediating his life and character.

Mr. Spectator and Macheath are only two among a number of roles that Boswell continuously tries out; what they primarily share is their status as culturally iconic fictional characters. As such, they have specificity and a genealogy more exact than the generic types Boswell also impersonates: the man of pleasure, the man of economy, the *retenu*, the *etourdi*, the man of consequence, the man of genius. Fixed in text, though perhaps modified in performance, both Macheath and Mr. Spectator have a greater independence from accident and change, a perhaps more dependable stability than Boswell's real-life role models: the urbane libertine Lord Eglington; the debonair actor West Digges; the authoritarian and demoralizing father, Lord Auchenlick; and, most notably, the brilliant and, to the young Boswell, surprisingly supportive man of letters, Samuel Johnson.

In the case of West Digges there is an overlap of the historical person, Digges, and the fictional persona, Macheath, one of Digges's signature repertoire roles. In a note to the *London Journal*, Pottle glosses Boswell's mention of Digges as one who "had long been Boswell's ideal of manly bearing and social elegance. He was especially captivating in the part of Macheath in *The Beggar's Opera*" (43). Digges, with his "manly bearing," replicates Macheath as an exemplar of "manly conduct." In turn, Macheath's claim to a "social elegance" comparable to Digges's is sustained by the mock-heroic register of *The Beggar's Opera*, where the rogues and whores speak in a style "that would rival the most elevated conversation of the upper classes."[36] Thus we might read Digges/Macheath as a kind of composite ideal of manly elegance. Furthermore, the Digges/Macheath ideal foregrounds the feature of *performative* masculinity so prominent in Boswell's writing. Boswell's composition of his own persona as "the hero of a romance or a novel" in his *London Journal* takes place through a dynamic psychic interchange with a range of characters—fictive, generic, and actual. That Boswell's "self" is conceived in such heavily textualized and performative terms itself confers special status on the figures of Mr. Spectator and Macheath.[37]

Both figures, I think, represent concerns and negotiations fundamental to all these impersonations: Macheath standing as a kind of icon of manliness; Addison and Steele, as sources for how Boswell's own persona might navigate the transgressive features of such manliness in ways conciliatory to literary culture, conscience, and the taste of the town. It is not that Mr. Spectator would in any way condone the criminal behavior of a Macheath or a Mohock or a Boswell, but that in *The Tatler* and *The Spectator* such figures, as we have seen in the previous chapter, are sentimentalized, narrativized, and aestheticized in usefully apologetic and redemptive ways. Their pages offer lessons to Boswell about being a perfect rake and a perfect gentleman; *Tatler* 27, in fact, shows these characters ultimately to be the same. Furthermore, *The Spectator* promotes a concept of an autonomous aesthetic realm where Boswell can situate his journal outside the autobiographical conventions of strictly accurate empirical record and potentially damaging moral confession.

The specters of both Macheath and Mr. Spectator hover in silent proximity at the beginning of Boswell's journal. Gordon Turnbull remarks how the youthful Boswell "sought to deflect guilt and terror by modeling himself on Mr. Spectator."[38] Turnbull does not elaborate this observation, but its aptitude is apparent even in the first pages of Boswell's Introduction to his *London Journal*. There, as frequently, guilt and terror, as the moral and psychological consequences of misconduct, are figured through the highwayman.[39] They are evaded by summoning the dispassion, self-containment, and invulnerability of the Spectator's perspective. Furthermore, as Newman discusses and as we see in the Introduction, the Spectator provides a literary aesthetic model for Boswell's aspirations as a man of letters.

In his Introduction, Boswell reports his perplexity in the face of two sometimes conflicting demands of his journal writing. On the one hand, he is keen to write candidly and fully. On the other, he would avoid potentially incriminating self-disclosure. Boswell confesses these anxieties to his friend Erskine, who, making light both of Boswell's worries and his wrongs, facetiously replies, "I hope there is no danger at all; for I fancy you will not set down your robberies on the highway" (40). Boswell "laughed heartily at [his] friend's observation, which was so far true," and he assures the reader that in writing the journal he shall be upon his "guard to mention nothing that can do harm." Erskine's and Boswell's exchange here adopts a glib hyperbole that both glamorizes and dismisses actual transgressions in a mode that corresponds to the parodic representation of criminal masculinity in Gay's *Beggar's Opera*, his *Mohocks*, and in the at once mocking and mitigating tone of the *Spectator* Mohock papers.[40] The remark is offhand, but Boswell uses it as a springboard to define the aims of his journal and the character of its narrator protagonist. "Truth," proclaims this man of honor and discretion, "shall ever be observed, and these things (if there should be any such) that require the gloss of falsehood shall be passed by in silence." Boswell, ever anxious to avoid scandal, continues: "At the same time, I may relate things under borrowed names with safety that would do much mischief if particularly known" (40). Moreover, in the text of the journal we see Boswell taking this masking of identity one step further when he relates mischiefs done by himself under borrowed names, for "greater safety" perhaps, but also in conformity with the performative conventions of criminal masculinity.

In the next paragraph, Boswell outlines the rationale and methodology of his journal; these center on the pleasures of self-representation enjoyed in retrospection: "I shall lay up a store of entertainment for my after life. Very often we have more pleasure in reflecting on agreeable scenes that we have been in than we find from the scenes themselves" (40). Here Boswell echoes *Spectator* 411, where Addison describes the refined entertainment that "A Man of Polite Imagination" can find in the *representation* of a scene: "A Man of Polite Imagination, is let into a great many Pleasures that the Vulgar are not capable of receiving. He can converse with a Picture, and find an agreeable Companion in a Statue. He meets with secret Refreshment in a Description." In his *London Journal*, Boswell is self-consciously engaged in the work of imaginative description and claims for it all the wholesome pleasures and uses that Addison had outlined some fifty years before.[41]

Whereas greater candor is valuable to the integrity of the journal and to Boswell's own project of self-knowledge, the final end of journal writing lies not in its status as an empirical record but in its status as a representation, what we would call its literary status, and in the reflective, imaginative pleasures it can provide. Discrete omissions or even dangerous confessions of "robberies on the highway," then, would not compromise the journal as a work of imaginative literature. For, finding a place for his writing in the aesthetic realm, Boswell is able to think about his journal in ways that transcend both the empirically centered recording of event and the morally focused confession of sin that conventionally characterize diurnal autobiographical writing. It is in the provision of such a literary-cultural site, I believe, that Mr. Spectator supplies Boswell with the most profound relief from the guilty anxieties of either recording or omitting his "robberies on the highway."

Highs, Lows, and the Highwayman

The marked instability of Boswell's "self" in the journals takes two, probably related, forms. There is the effect of fragmentation of identity as he cursorily adopts and casts off role after role. Then there is the emotional instability that attends his struggle with what he calls melancholy and hypochondria, and what we know as depression. The swings and cycles between exuberance and dejection recorded in these journals have led some scholars to diagnose Boswell as a "manic depressive."[42] Certainly his mood and energy levels swing up and down in dramatic arcs. Boswell's psycho-physiological highs and lows, recorded so vividly in his journals, frequently describe a circuit of high-spirited misconduct and the guilty self-loathing that follows it. Boswell, like Steele's sentimental rake, habitually "goes on in Pursuit he himself disapproves, and has no Enjoyment but what is follow'd by Remorse; no relief from Remorse, but the Repetition of his Crime" (*Tatler* 27).

As this passage intimates, psychological highs and lows follow closely on moral highs and lows, and these, in turn, as is so evident in Boswell's journals, can be articulated through the highs and lows of social class. Thus one common occasion of Boswell's guilty self-reproach comes with his sexual indulgences with prostitutes. On May 10, 1763, recovering from a bout of depression, his spirits lifted by a night at the theater, he picks up a prostitute and takes her to Westminster Bridge. "And then," Boswell reports, "in armour complete did I engage her upon this noble edifice. The whim of doing it there with the Thames rolling below us amused me much. Yet after the brutish appetite was sated, I could not but despise myself for being so closely united with such a low wretch" (255–56). Not exactly highway robbery, but an illicit act nonetheless, and one that Boswell converts into valiant exploit through glib mock-heroics—"in armour complete," "did I engage," "noble edifice." Language here follows the highs and lows of sexual feelings. It soars into the heroic and then falls into the quotidian, describing an arc of confident excitement and guilty dejection. The juxtaposition of high and low also informs the dramatic construction of this scene: the low act of sex with a whore conducted high up on the "noble edifice" of Westminster Bridge. As was completely commonplace, the expression of Boswell's sexuality frequently involved this kind of intimate link between "high" and "low," the gentleman and the whore.

These personal highs and lows that Boswell records, manifest as they are in the registers of emotion, morality, and class, constitute experiential analogues to the modal form of the mock-heroic that controls the aesthetics and ideology of

Gay's representation of criminal masculinity in *The Mohocks* and *The Beggar's Opera*. As we can see in the Westminster Bridge episode, the mock-heroic mode, in turn, shapes Boswell's own experience. This experience of rapid cycling between low and high, rising and falling, finds dramatic parallels in the action of both of Gay's dramas: in *The Mohocks,* where rakish rioter and citizen watchman switch places in a blink of an eye and an on-stage costume change; and in *The Beggar's Opera,* where the condemned Macheath is granted an eleventh-hour reprieve at the decree of the "taste of the town."

A figure often connected in Boswell's journals with guilt and terror, the condemned highwayman is also allied with the conquering spirit of confident assertion that overcomes all fears that might accompany misconduct. Ultimately, he represents both the fear of death and the successful and "manly" handling of that fear.[43] In the discussion that follows, I examine two appearances of Macheath: first in the person of the gentleman highwayman Paul Lewis, who Boswell sees in Newgate and whose execution he attends; then as impersonated by Boswell himself, when he takes two women off the street into a tavern and there stages a debauch. Both of these episodes are controlled through their theatrical contexts. The first plays out the drama of the condemned on the stage of Tyburn; the second produces Boswell's sexual escapade as scene 2.4 from *The Beggar's Opera*.[44] So we see how the Macheath figure takes center stage in Boswell's production both of his gloom and of his exuberance. Boswell's relation to Macheath thus articulates not simply either low or high spirits—Boswell the guilty, rebellious son or Boswell the exuberant, fearless, cavalier ladies' man—but the coexistence of both within a single persona, the condemned highwayman who plays out in the *London Journal* both as high tragedy and as mock-heroic comedy. Macheath, then, is not simply Boswell's model for manly elegance but also for the very instabilities, the highs and lows, of his own psyche.

In a sequence describing a major depressive episode that culminates with Lewis's execution at Tyburn, Boswell's alternating identifications with Mr. Spectator and Macheath are paired as they are in the Introduction, but here both figures are named. Whereas in the Introduction, Boswell moves from anxiety and allusions to "robberies on the highway" to comfortable anticipation of Addisonian imaginative pleasures, in this sequence, Boswell swings the other way, from Spectatoresque equilibrium into mortal despair. Fixated on the condemned highwayman Lewis, "a perfect Macheath," his melancholy hits its nadir at Tyburn.

Setting off for Oxford early on the morning of April 23, 1763, a Saturday, Boswell puts on his Mr. Spectator hat in anticipation of fresh imaginative adventures: "Between five and six we set out. I imagined myself the Spectator taking one of his rural excursions" (244). Yet the very next morning Boswell awakes "in miserable spirits." He spends the rest of his time at Oxford plunged in depression, vainly struggling to "work [him]self up to a little enthusiasm" (246). No Mr. Spectator resurfaces on Boswell's return to London on Tuesday, April 26. Instead, Boswell's imagination is occupied with irrational fears and highwaymen: "We had a very good journey. I was a little afraid of highwaymen, but we met none." He suffers cognitive disorientation: "My ideas were all changed and turned topsy-turvy" (248).

Back in London, Boswell remains captive in his own gloom. Finding there architectural and embodied emblems of his own mental state, Boswell visits Newgate on May 3: "I thought I should see prisoners of one kind or another," he explains (251). There he sees Lewis, a real live (for the next twenty-four hours) gentleman highwayman, awaiting execution: "He was a perfect Macheath. He was dressed in a white coat and blue silk vest and silver, with his hair neatly queued and a silver-laced hat, smartly cocked" (251). Drawn to Tyburn by a morbid attraction, "a sort of horrid eagerness," Boswell attends Lewis's execution the next day and, predictably, is "most terribly shocked" and reports himself "thrown into a very deep melancholy" (252).

Yet since the entries for every day since that gloomy Sunday in Oxford record Boswell's persistent and utter misery, it is apparent that Lewis's execution on May 4 does not initiate Boswell's depression but rather stages the mortal despair he had been suffering for several weeks. Viewed by a very depressed young Boswell, the execution of Lewis, "the genteel, spirited young fellow," serves as a projection for Boswell's own terrors. On the scaffold, Lewis, unlike Macheath on stage, receives no reprieve and becomes a figure of the tragic waste of youthful manhood.

By May 10, three days after Lewis's execution, Boswell has recovered his spirits enough to jocularly cast himself in the mock-heroic scene with the prostitute discussed above. The next morning finds him merrily singing popular tunes with Lord Eglington. On May 12, after a night at the theater, Boswell pronounces himself fully recuperated: "It gave me great consolation after my late fit of melancholy to find that I was again capable of receiving such high enjoyment" (257). The emotional inversions of the "topsy-turvy" time are set right: he cries at the tragedy *King Lear* and laughs at the farce *Polly Honeycomb*. The next day Boswell spends in a perfect riot of polite conversation, deporting himself as the perfect gentleman: "I have not passed so much rational time I don't know when. The degree of distance due to a stranger [Norton Nicholls] restrained me from my effusions of ludicrous nonsense and intemperate mirth. I was rational and composed, yet lively and entertaining" (257–58). Mr. Spectator would be proud.

Boswell's fine spirits, his self-possession and equilibrium, are reestablished fully when he enters onto the scene where, as Turnbull puts it, he watches himself play Macheath and thus is able to "turn transgression into comic theater."[45] The theatrical mediation provides Boswell with an arena of representation within which he can position himself as both actor and spectator, and so, as the latter, both distance himself from and pass judgment upon the former. But as with the invocation of Mr. Spectator's aesthetic realm of the imagination in the Introduction, here the theatrical metaphor imports a context of arbitration outside the journalistic conventions either of empirical record or moral confession. By sustaining this dramatic context, Boswell the spectator can judge Boswell acting like Macheath on the basis of his successful execution of the role and the overall value of the episode as entertainment. So Boswell, as arbiter of the taste of the town, can decree his own reprieve, just as happens in *The Beggar's Opera*.

This occurs on the evening of May 19. Having had some success toward the seduction of a Miss Watts, Boswell's campaign there is interrupted when the lady is called away. Boswell departs, encouraged, and "sallied forth to the Piazzas in a rich flow of animal spirits and burning with fierce desire" (263). He picks up two girls off the street and takes them to the Shakespeare tavern, where he buys them drinks and has sex with each in turn. The whole evening passes in impersonation and theatrics. Boswell introduces himself to Miss Watts under a false name and identity: "I told her my name was Macdonald, and that I was a Scotch Highlander" (263). At the Shakespeare tavern with the two girls, he progresses from the impersonation of a more-or-less generic cultural identity adopted to conceal his own, to that of an established dramatic character, the performance of which glamorizes and absolves his own sexual misconduct. Acting out perhaps the most outrageous sexual exploit of his life thus far, Boswell does so in the mock-heroic guise of Macheath: "I surveyed my seraglio. . . . I toyed with them and drank about and sung *Youth's the Season* and thought myself Captain Macheath" (263).

Even as he acts, Boswell self-consciously reflects on the quality of his performance: "[I] thought I was in a London tavern, enjoying high debauchery after my sober winter. I parted with my ladies politely and came home in a glow of spirits" (263).[46] As Boswell here enters more completely into mock-heroic impersonation, so does he seem able to hold more steadily to his Spectatorial immunity. Pronouncing the evening a triumph of "high debauchery," Boswell the actor seems to fully entertain and satisfy Boswell the spectator. The next day his judgment is wholly confirmed when he recounts the scene to the accomplished libertine Lord Eglington, "who was highly entertained" (264).

The Tatler and *The Spectator* papers examined in the previous chapter, along with Gay's mock-heroic drama, provide ways of exonerating what is criminal about Boswell's masculinity so that it can be accommodated to the character of the gentleman. This accommodation occurs through specific regimes of representation associated with Mr. Spectator (the aesthetic realm of the imagination) and with Macheath (the theatrical arena). But in the *London Journal* the most spectacular juxtaposition between Boswell's criminal conduct and his status as a gentleman occurs, not in the explicitly dramatized tavern scene, but in an episode a few weeks later where Boswell disguises himself as an underclass thug, a "blackguard," and goes roistering on the town.

On June 3, Boswell indulges in a bout of self-improvement, resolving to "get into a proper well-behaved plan" and "to study propriety of conduct" in order to be confirmed into "proper habits" (272). The entry for the next day then begins: "It was the King's birthnight, and I resolved to be a blackguard and to see all that was to be seen" (272). In costume, he proceeds to ramble through the town, drinking and picking up three women, one of whom he attempts to rape. The startling shift from pledges of sobriety to resolutions to riot suggest that Boswell's rampage represents a reaction against the inhibitions imposed by his own pledge to reform, taken just the day before, and, concomitantly, a rebellion against all those impediments to self-assertion, self-indulgence, and autonomy represented by political, religious, and legal authority: "It was the King's birthnight."[47]

Dressed as an underclass ruffian in a "second-mourning suit" filthy with two-months of wig powder, "dirty buckskin breeches," a soiled "shirt of Lord Eglington's," and "a little round hat with tarnished lace belonging to a disbanded officer of the Royal Volunteers," Boswell first poses as a "barber" to a prostitute with whom he has easy success. He picks up another "little profligate wretch" for six-pence, but when she refuses to have sex with him, he pushes her up against the wall and "volens nolens" attempts to rape her. She screams out, attracting a crowd of "whores and soldiers" whom Boswell manages to win over: "I got them on my side, and I abused her in blackguard style, and then left them." He then proceeds out of the city toward Whitehall, where he picks up another girl. Significantly, the report here suggests that Boswell, whose pockets are now empty, thinks that by posing as a highwayman he will have better luck getting sex from this girl gratis: "I called myself a highwayman and told her I had no money and begged she would trust me." She does not. Boswell returns home "much fatigued" by two in the morning, apparently too tired to attempt another rape (273).

Easily the most transgressive, violent, and offensive event in the *London Journal*, this episode witnesses Boswell's investment in criminal masculinity, the forms it takes, and the place it occupies in his psyche. With Boswell more like Mohock than Macheath here, though cycling through a range of personae all assimilated within the category "blackguard," the theatrical methods of this episode as well as its dramatic outcome resonate with those of Gay's farce. Boswell's status as a blackguard is just as explicitly theatrical as Gay's gentlemen Mohocks; it is taken on and put off with a costume change in full view of the audience. Perhaps paradoxically, the outcome of all this disguise, violence, and riot is not guilty self-reproach but Boswell's full and proud self-assurance of his own status as gentleman: "My vanity was somewhat gratified tonight," the penultimate sentence of the entry reads, "that, notwithstanding of my dress, I was always taken for a gentleman in disguise" (273). This episode, as summed up in Boswell's assessment, articulates the complicity between criminal masculinity and gentlemanly status, and the conventions that govern this complicity.

The number of ways in which a man disguised as a blackguard would be taken for a gentleman is multiple. First, the pleasures of slumming are reserved for the social elite, and Boswell is clearly slumming here. Second, although the supposition that he was always taken for the gentleman he is might be read as Boswell's own self-congratulatory construction, it can also be seen as evidence of the sheer conventionality of such inverted juxtapositions in masquerade.[48] But more profoundly, I believe, it speaks to an equally conventional congruence of expectation regarding the conduct, if not the dress, of a blackguard and of a gentleman. Boswell does not say that he was always taken for a gentleman "notwithstanding of *my behavior*," but "notwithstanding of *my dress*" (emphasis added). Moreover, Boswell's wording is erroneous: strictly speaking, he means to say that he was taken for a gentleman despite his dress, for he would have been taken as a gentleman *in disguise* precisely *because of* his dress, rather than despite ("notwithstanding") it. It is as if this sentence wraps Boswell, the gentleman, twice in his disguise: "notwithstanding my dress . . . in disguise." This redundancy of masking might be read both as reinforcing the irrepressibility of Boswell's gentility as it surfaces through not one but two assertions of disguise and as the utter insignificance of those disguises that, even doubly draped, fail to conceal the gentleman as rapist. Even while, in the register of class, sartorial conventions might differentiate the blackguard from the gentleman, they seem to falter when read within a register of masculinity and its prerogatives: everything reported in this episode suggests that the conventional expression of criminal masculinity, on some level, is common to both identities and that ultimately it compromises neither. Surely, Boswell's actions on this night are anti-authoritarian and antisocial, but, his conclusion implies, they are not in any way corrosive to his manliness, even his socially elite gentlemanliness. Very much like Steele's rake in *Tatler* 27, Boswell's criminal misdeeds do not compromise his "true" identity as a gentleman. Very much like the Mohocks at the end of Gay's farce, Boswell's apology for his misconduct has been well scripted by a discourse of masculinity that uses theatrical conventions both to express and to acquit criminality: "We are gentleman, Sirs, 'Twas only an innocent Frolick."[49]

In the lives of Stafford, Hind, and Duval and in Boswell's journal, we see how the gallant highwayman figures in two forms of life-writing: criminal biography and the diurnal personal journal. Furthermore, we see how this highwayman exerts pressures on and responds to the generic conventions of these texts. The gallant pictures of Stafford and Hind in their biographies depend to a high degree on that reversal of authority latent in criminal biography per se; in both lives, as well, this ethical reversal becomes a thematic and tropological element of the text. Walter Pope's satire against the manners of the jumped-up French footman Claude Duval commits an assault against the perceived reversal of cultural authority engendered by Charles II's court. Macheath is a product of Gay's mock-heroic satire that exploits the ethical duality that informs criminal biography. The gallant highwayman, in turn, works in tandem with the polite gentleman of taste, Mr. Spectator, in the *London Journal* as a figure through which Boswell negotiates the juxtaposed duality "gentleman" and "criminal" so prominent in eighteenth-century notions of masculinity. This negotiation depends on the literary-aesthetic and performative conventions associated with each of those figures, and these, in turn, shape the nature and aims that Boswell claims for his journal. Turning next to *Rookwood*, we see how the conventions of historical romance effectively work to dissolve such ethical and sociocultural tensions in the final incarnation of the highwayman, Dick Turpin.

Dick Turpin, the Famous Highwayman

More than any other figure, Dick Turpin exemplifies the modern notion of the romantic highwayman. In Turpin, claims made for the "innocence," the inconsequentially playful nature, of the gentleman criminal receive their fullest confirmation. In taking up the eighteenth-century legend of Turpin (d. 1739) and setting it alongside a gothic romance in his *Rookwood* (1834), William Harrison Ainsworth solidifies the myth of the romantic highwayman that subsequently appears in the weighty output of mass-cult nineteenth-century texts, especially in the "penny dreadfuls" aimed at a youthful, often working-class audience.[50] "It was Ainsworth," confirms Keith Hollingsworth, "who set Turpin going on so long a career as a hero."[51]

Rookwood, then, is a definitive text for the examination of the highwayman and, most particularly, of how this figure is fixed in the romanticized form in which he persists through modernity. For while the gentleman highwayman appears in glamorized forms from the seventeenth century on, his criminality persists in ambivalent relation to his prestige even through his apotheosis as Macheath in *The Beggar's Opera*. Macheath signals a watershed moment in the rhetorical construction of the figure, for with him the tensions that produce the reversals of authority in criminal biography are fully exploited by the thorough-going satiric identification of the transgressions of the criminal and the license of the authorities. What we find in *Rookwood* is a further, even more radical rhetorical transformation, one that removes the highwayman figure from the nexus of moral ambivalence and locates him in a romantic Neverland where his exploits can be enjoyed forever outside history and responsibility.

In contemporary eighteenth-century accounts, Turpin is first and foremost "The *Famous* Highwayman." The "*Gentleman* Highwayman" is James Maclane (Maclaine/Macleane), famous for his beau-ish good looks, his forays into polite society, his correspondence with Horace Walpole, and his twentieth-century portrayal by Johnny Lee Miller, alongside Robert Carlyle, in the film *Plunkett and Macleane* (1998).[52] While there is evidence from contemporary newspapers and from the transcript of Turpin's trial at York in April 1739 that his exploits were considerably renowned during his own lifetime, attention in these texts focuses more on his equestrian prowess and manly derring-do than on the more "fashionable" pursuits of gallantry and hobnobbing with bigwigs. There is some suggestion that Turpin self-consciously performs, especially in his handling of his execution, the celebrity role scripted for him, but this role, again, differs markedly from that cultivated by Maclane, the "Gentleman Highwayman." What may be most interesting about these contemporary accounts is that the Famous Turpin's representation in the media sometimes seems to produce the very features it reports.

In their popular history *The Immortal Turpin*, Julius Day and Arty Ash offer to counterbalance the weight of the "mythical" Turpin who exists "primarily in the imagination of the novelist [Ainsworth]" with a narrated compilation of contemporary eighteenth-century journalism.[53] Yet their account reveals how, well before Ainsworth's imaginative reconstruction, a celebrity, even legendary Turpin was generated through news media and hearsay during his own lifetime.

Furthermore, Day and Ash repeatedly suggest that Turpin himself consciously manipulated what we would call his "media image" in conformity with received notions of the gallant highwayman. A feature in the *Whitehall Evening Post* (April 30, 1737) reports that "the Famous Turpin, who rides with an Open Lace Hat, and his Companion . . . in a plain Gold Lac'd Hat, were last week at Bedford." Day comments: "The gold-laced hats show that they were entirely conscious of the effect of their exploits and looked upon themselves as characters of considerable importance in the reported happenings of the times."[54] While it remains impossible to verify the kinds of motivations and rationales that Day, with such cheerful positivity, attributes to Turpin, the litany of contemporary press reports he and Ash have collected confirms that Turpin was a legend in his own time. He is repeatedly referred to as the "Famous Turpin" in a press that had itself contributed to that fame.

Contemporary reports, both in newspapers and in biographies appearing at his death, also include instances of Turpin's civility and thus put in some claim for a gallantry of manners to complement his dashing "Open Lace Hat." The *Kentish Post* (June 22–25, 1737) reports an exchange between Turpin and the MP for Lynn, Sir Charles Turner, on meeting in Epping Forest: "Last week the Famous Turpin met Sir Charles Turner . . . and saluted him after this manner: 'Sir Charles Turner, I am Turpin, and do not design to offer you any Incivility or rob you of anything. In a little time I shall come to the Gallows, and hope that when I have Occasion, you will do me your best Service.' "[55] The *Newgate Calendar* biography, largely extracted from a life of Turpin published on the day of his execution, repeatedly notes Turpin's decency and forbearance while acting with the housebreakers known variously as the Essex Gang and Gregory's Gang. Having robbed a family called Saunders, Turpin and his associates got the lady of the house, who had fainted from terror, a glass of water, "put some drops in it and were very careful to recover her."[56] Similarly, taking their leave after robbing a Mr. Sheldon, they gave him back two guineas of his money, "asked for pardon for what they had done, and bade him good-night."[57]

But the historical Turpin's status as a gentleman is not named as such until the end of his short life, when in Yorkshire he passes as "John Palmer" and socializes with the gentry of the neighborhood: "While he lived at Brough, Cave and Welton he often took his diversion with the gentlemen of the country, in hunting and shooting."[58] Until he offends by drunkenly shooting one of his neighbor's fowls and then threatening to shoot the man who reprimands him for it, Turpin seems to have passed quite effectively as the sporting gentleman "John Palmer." However, after the man he menaced takes out a warrant against him and Turpin is unable to produce any sureties for good behavior, the authorities begin to look into his origins and identity. Finally, he is taken and charged with two counts of horse stealing. Although his identity as Dick Turpin, horse thief, is revealed, no witnesses appear against him in his more renowned role as highwayman. Jailed in York Castle, Turpin's celebrity brings scores of people to visit, and he entertains them graciously. At his trial, testimony given by a witness confirms his gentleman-like appearance:

> COUNSEL. What manner of visible living had he?
> GRASBY. He had no settled Way of Living, that I know of at all, tho' a
>   Dealer, yet he was a Stranger, and lived like a Gentleman.
>
> . . .
>
> COUNSEL. In what manner of Way used he [to] Support himself, or, how
>   did he live?
> GRASBY. He lived like a Gentleman.[59]

As the horse dealer John Palmer, Turpin creditably passes for a gentleman, but an element of impersonation is suggested by the witness's locution, *"like* a Gentleman."* Moreover, while a few instances of Turpin's sartorial style and of his civility are reported, he is never called a "gentleman" or even "gentleman-like" in his capacity as *highwayman.*

Found guilty on both counts of horse stealing and sentenced to death by hanging, Turpin impresses his public: "After his conviction he was as jovial, as merry and as frolicsome as if he had been perfectly at liberty and assured of a hundred years of prosperity to come."[60] His performance at his execution seals his reputation for manly aplomb. He is carted to the gibbet as a hero on parade: "All the way," reports an eye-witness, "he bowed repeatedly and with the most astonishing indifference and intrepidity."[61] He stages a proper exit for himself, hiring and outfitting five mourners to follow along the cart and valiantly surrendering himself to the noose. Turpin wins over his audience completely. A group of sympathetic well-wishers pay their respects by rescuing Turpin's body from the surgeons' anatomy knife, as reported in the *Ipswich Journal* (April 21, 1739): "They write from York that an attempt was made by the Surgeons of that Place to have got the Body of Turpin, but the Mob hearing that it was dug up, and being informed where it was, went and rescued it and re-interred it, having strewn it over with Lime to prevent it being anatomized."[62]

All this illustrates the contemporary celebrity and broad appeal of the highwayman Turpin, much of which was manufactured by, not merely reported in, the news media. Even that most renowned feature of Turpin's prowess—his preternatural speed on horseback and apparent ability to be two places at once—was in part the creation of media publicity. This is not to question the insistent fact of Turpin's exceptional horsemanship and his canniness in evading capture, but only to point to the ways in which these abilities were heightened to legendary, one could say mythical, status through the accidents of the press. Once Turpin's reputation, in part through newsprint, became solidified as celebrity prestige and his status as "King" of the highway confirmed, other robbers began to adopt his identity. So accounts citing "Turpin's" exploits at impossibly long distances within impossibly short periods of time started to appear in the newspapers.[63] These even produced miraculous reports of "Turpin's" capture and incarceration in three different jails: Chelmsford, Watford, and Hertford.[64] His emulation by these "lesser rogues" not only served to substantiate Turpin's celebrity prestige but also to produce diversions convenient to his own evasion of the law.[65]

Turpin's status as *the* Famous Highwayman was thus amply recorded and preserved for Ainsworth's nineteenth-century appropriation. Ainsworth underwrites Turpin's notoriety as a highwayman with amplitude of gallant, red-blooded manliness; the famous highwayman becomes the romantic gentleman highwayman, a role Turpin himself defines in the novel. In conversation with some local gentry gathered for the funeral of Sir Piers Rookwood, Turpin, as "Jack Palmer," delivers an extensive eulogy on the gentility of the highwayman:

> It is as necessary for a man to be a gentleman before he can turn highwayman, as it is for a doctor to have his diploma, or an attorney his certificate. . . . A real highwayman would consider himself disgraced, if he did not conduct himself in every way like a gentleman. . . . What are the distinguishing characteristics of a fine gentleman?— perfect knowledge of the world—perfect independence of character—notoriety— command of cash—and inordinate success with the women. (52)

As John Barrell has shown, much of the eighteenth-century discussion about gentlemanly status emphasizes the mutually supporting qualities of "independence of character" and comprehensive knowledge of society. Not confined to any specific sphere of knowledge or occupation, the gentleman might comprehend all and thus cultivate what Turpin calls here a "perfect knowledge of the world."[66] The other qualities listed—notoriety, "command of cash," and "inordinate success with the women"—while less abstract and lofty, reflect commonplace assumptions about the financial, social, and sexual prowess of the elite male. These qualities, while they might not be named as such in more polite, elevated discussions such as those Barrell examines, certainly mark his status in the widely popular imagination of his ideal. Specified by the Turpin character himself, these qualities are matched with his sportsmanship, equestrian prowess, and derring-do to form the image of the gentleman highwayman around which Ainsworth builds his nationalist, nostalgic, romantic myth of merry old England.

The Modern Romance of the Gentleman Highwayman

As I have suggested, it is not that the eighteenth-century Turpin, especially as "John [or "Jack"] Palmer," lacks all gentleman-like qualities but that, first, these are not paramount to his fame and, second, they are not tied tightly to his occupation as a highwayman. How, then, does Ainsworth romance the famous highwayman into the gentleman highwayman Dick Turpin?

First, Ainsworth produces a romantic genealogy of the "real" highwayman that positions Turpin as the end of the line, last scion of a noble clan. Thereby he eliminates any competing claims on prestige that might be made for successors, such as Maclane, and erects a bar between the ordinary, real-life criminals that his audience might fear and revile and his own gallant historical highwayman. In the "Memoir" of Ainsworth from the *Mirror* (1842), Laman Blanchard contrasts the easy popularity of *Rookwood* with the moral panic surrounding Ainsworth's *Jack Sheppard* (1839):

> Critics, who had always a passion for heroes in fetters before, now [with the *Jack Sheppard* phenomenon] found that housebreakers are disreputable characters. They were in raptures with the old-fashioned brigand still, and the freebooter of foreign extraction; they could hug *Robin Hood* as fondly as ever, and dwelt with unhurt morals on the little peccadilloes of *Rob Roy*; nay, they had no objection to ride behind *Turpin* to York any day, and would never feel ashamed of their company; but they shook their heads at Sheppard, because low people began to run after him at the theatres; he was a housebreaker! (xvi)[67]

These comments reflect a hierarchy of criminal prestige in which housebreaking is ranked far below highway robbery and culturally institutionalized cattle rustling. More emphatically, they call attention to how, for their nineteenth-century audience, Robin Hood, Rob Roy, and Dick Turpin are all successfully quarantined within a romantic, nostalgic past, safely removed from the realities of the present and its grubby everyday criminals.

Such romancing seems to have been less uniformly successful in the case of *Jack Sheppard*. As a cultural phenomenon, indeed a media event, "Jack Sheppard" breaks out of novelistic conventions to appear in eight popular stage plays running concurrently. These created among the largely working-class audiences a kind of Sheppard mania that critics feared reactivated the hero's transgressive energies in dangerous, sociopolitical ways.[68] Such a reception of Sheppard, it seems, broke through the romantic quarantine, transferring the hero from the pages of historical romance to the London stages, to the London streets, and, most dire of all, to the houses of the London elite. In an early and heavily publicized instance of "copy-cat" crime, on May 5, 1840, one B. F. Courvoisier, a valet, slashed the throat of his employer, Lord William Russell, citing Ainsworth's novel as inspiration.[69] The role of popular culture in class-based crime and delinquency only increases as a social concern as the nineteenth century progresses, predictably focusing on the mass market of literature produced for the working classes and for boys. So Jack Sheppard's mass celebrity in popular theater brought to the fore class issues apparently less agitated by the narratives of Dick Turpin, Rob Roy, and Robin Hood.

Yet the reader who reflects on the commonalities between the historical Turpin and Sheppard—both eighteenth-century figures, both notorious criminals from tradesman backgrounds, both wholly English, and both from the south of England, largely based in and around London—might well be startled by a grouping that sets Turpin alongside Rob Roy and Robin Hood and apart from Sheppard. Certainly, on the face of things, it would seem more sensible to pair Turpin with Sheppard in distinction to the medieval noble robber Robin Hood and the Highland cattle rustler Rob Roy. But the features that associate Ainsworth's Turpin with Robin Hood and Rob Roy—temporal distance and cultural exoticism—are foregrounded by Ainsworth's exploitation of the conventions of historical romance, best known from the novels of Sir Walter Scott.[70] In *Rookwood*, Turpin is figured as an "old-fashioned" brigand and given a gloss of exoticism by his association with and adoption into a gypsy community.

In a narrative eulogy for the vanished tribe of "real" highwayman, Ainsworth effuses:

> Turpin was the *ultimus Romanorum*, the last of a race, which (we were almost about to say we regret) is now altogether extinct. Several successors he had, it is true, but no name worthy to be recorded after his own. With him expired the chivalrous spirit which animated successively the bosoms of so many knights of the road; with him died away that passionate love of enterprise, that high spirit of devotion to the fair sex, which was first breathed upon the highway by the gay, gallant Claude Du-Val, the Bayard of the road—*le filou sans puer et sans reproche*—. (163–64)

Ainsworth, then, nostalgically records the world and its highwaymen heroes that we have lost. In ways that are notable in relation to Ainsworth's own romantic Jacobitism and, more significantly, to the tradition of Cavalier highwaymen from the seventeenth century, the representative of this world is the Frenchman Claude Duval, who came over to England at the Restoration in the employ of a English adherent to the exiled Stuart court at St. Germain. The line from Claude Duval to Dick Turpin lightly traces a hint of the Stuart line to which, in 1739, some were still loyal, but which in 1834 is only the heavily romanced (by Scott among others) token of a lost cause, the impossible might-have-been rendered null by the irresistible forces of modernity. As in Scott, in *Rookwood,* Jacobitism and the entire nexus of crises to which it responds is presented, not simply as part of a different time and a different political climate, but as part of a different culture, a different world. The line between "then" and "now" in Ainsworth's *Rookwood* is a heavy one that so surely sequesters the past from the present that political and personal crimes can be safely reclaimed into a national mythology.

As one critic notes, by presenting Turpin as the last of his line, Ainsworth employs a figure familiar from Walter Scott's historical romances such as *Waverly,* with its rebel Highland chief Vich Ian Vohr, representative of a culture doomed to extinction.[71] Yet as I have been suggesting, I see in Ainsworth's treatment of Turpin a much more comprehensive use of the romance strategies that Duncan has so eloquently claimed for Scott. Consequently, I think *Rookwood* achieves, in its different cultural register, some of the same nationalist ends that Scott realized. Certainly *Rookwood,* complete with its Blackadderesque "sizzling gypsies," is an unabashedly populist novel, with little of the lofty tone and serious imaginings of a romance such as *Waverley.*[72] By many critical accounts, *Rookwood* is a failed novel, compromised by the perceived disjunction between the gory gothic romance of the Rookwood family and the rambunctious, rollicking historical romance of Dick Turpin.[73] Nonetheless, in this novel Ainsworth participates in "the construction of the archetype as a rhetorical figure" that Duncan sees as central to "modern romance" and as Scott's transformative legacy to literary culture. Positing naïve romance "as modern culture's construction of a symbolic form prior to itself," Duncan attends to the role of the modern romance in the promulgation of cultural nationalism, the "invention of tradition."[74] In *Rookwood* Ainsworth romances the figure of Turpin, nostalgically constructing him not only as the archetypal "knight of the road" but at the same time as an archetype of English masculinity construed according to that oxymoron "the gentleman highwayman" inherited from the eighteenth century.

Whereas I have suggested above that the eighteenth-century Turpin is to a great extent the product of print journalism, Ainsworth's Turpin manifests, not in the realm of print, with all its connotations of urbanity, modernity, and self-reflexivity, but in the immediacy of the aural and of nature—in tales told and heard that incorporate Turpin into rural England. Moreover, Ainsworth's Turpin is approached nostalgically through the lens of childhood imagination, itself troped as a site of romantic subjectivity, naturally open "to the influences of legend and fable":[75]

> Turpin was the hero of my boyhood. I had always a strange passion for highwaymen, and have listened by the hour to their exploits. . . . There was the Bollin, with its shelvy banks, which Turpin cleared at a bound; the broad meadows over which he wings his flight; the pleasant bowling-green of the pleasant old inn at Hough, where he produced his watch to the Cheshire squires, with whom he was on terms of intimacy; all brought something of the gallant robber to mind. No wonder, in after years, in selecting a highwayman for a character in a tale, I should choose my old favourite, Dick Turpin. (xxxvii)

A boyhood hero, Ainsworth's Turpin, along with his Newgate novel cohorts such as Paul Clifford and Jack Sheppard, becomes a boys' adventure hero.[76] In a novel that consigns all real criminality to its gothic plot, Turpin's masculinity is written as a kind of cheerful rural athleticism, very much in the tradition of the hearty squire and very much to the approval of the squire in *Rookwood,* Sir Piers Rookwood, who pronounces Jack Palmer a "deuced good fellow" who "rode well, and stood on no sort of ceremony" (47). The portrait Ainsworth sketches of Turpin evokes, only to displace, the New*gate* physiognomy of the criminal with the New*market* physiognomy of the plucky horse dealer: "His face was one of those inexplicable countenances . . . a regular Newmarket physiognomy— compounded chiefly of cunning and assurance; not low cunning, nor vulgar assurance, but crafty sporting subtlety, careless as to results" (47). Although "somewhat showily dressed," Ainsworth's Turpin has a hearty manliness that avoids the highly urban, almost effeminate personal extravagance of that gentleman highwayman, James Maclane, who is dropped from the line of "real" highwaymen by Ainsworth's romantic genealogy that ends in Turpin.

In fact, Ainsworth's gentleman highwayman seems drawn almost in opposition to the fashionable figure of the eighteenth-century James Maclane. Whereas Turpin is "a man's man," Maclane is the ladies man: "The speciousness of his behaviour, the gracefulness of his person and the elegance of his appearance combined to make him a welcome visitor, even at the houses of women of character."[77] Indeed, Maclane's habitual fondness for fancy dress ultimately proves his ruin; he is arrested while fencing a laced waistcoat. Horace Walpole, whom Maclane had robbed and with whom he conducts a published correspondence, calls Maclane a "fashionable highwayman."[78] This status seems to have been expressed in at least four related ways. First, by Maclane's personal self-fashioning; second, by his admittance into polite, even elite company; next, by his choice of and relationship to his victims; and finally, and as a summation of all these factors, by the way that a fashion *for* Maclane takes hold of the polite spheres of London society. The preface of a contemporary life of Maclane highlights the features of the highwayman's life and character that render him an object of public interest: his "genteel Treatment" of his victims; "his gallant Behaviour to the Ladies"; and the esteem he inspires in "Persons of Rank" who "have not only been induced to contribute to support him in Splendour while under Confinement, but to solicit and use their utmost Interest to save him."[79] Maclane's fate, this biographer suggests, may lie in the hands of those fashionable ladies among whom he is such a favorite: "By the Laws of his Country He is undoubtedly to be deemed an enemy to Society; but how far the prevailing Passion of Pity, and Female Tears, so natural to their Sex, when a Man of Parts is in Distress, may influence to procure Mercy, we will not presume to determine."[80] The tension that defines Maclane's life lies between the claims of the criminal law and those of the beau monde, where women, fashion, and sentiment govern through the laws of attraction. Maclane may be an "Enemy to Society," but he is a pet of society ladies. Notable for his sartorial finery, Maclane conforms to other fashionable habits: he keeps a "famous" mistress at a posh address in St. James's Street; he challenges men to duels. Walpole names with himself three other society figures robbed by Maclane: James Boswell's friend, Lord Eglington; Sir Thomas Robinson of Vienna; and a Mrs. Talbot. In prison, Maclane is visited by a group of London's elite so large that Walpole remarks that he is "almost single in not having been to see him." Walpole calls Maclane and his partner Plunkett his "friends," and neither he nor Lord Eglington appears against him in court.[81]

While the historical as well as the romantic Turpin is admitted to a sphere of gentility, this is of a very different arena, where access is gained through male social connections forged, not in the drawing rooms and clubs of St. James, but through the pursuit of rural sport in the English countryside. Whereas Maclane's prestige is urban, fashionable, and highly dependent on female-dominated institutions and spheres of sociability, Turpin's is rural, athletic, and oriented around masculine pursuits. Furthermore, as he moves among the local gentry, the gypsy band, and his own criminal compatriots, Turpin's independence from any single arena of sociability and identification is underlined.

Certainly, Ainsworth's Turpin can be read correctly as more rural, masculinist, and naïve in comparison with the highly sophisticated Maclane; this is simple enough. But more profoundly, these features do not simply differentiate Turpin from Maclane but also authenticate and naturalize him in ways that contribute to his mythical status. Whereas accounts of Maclane reveal his dependence on highly artificial external social networks and cultural codes, his mastery of which wins him access to polite society and the title of gentleman, Ainsworth's Turpin has no time for "artificial" social distinctions: "he stands on no ceremony." Though he consorts successfully with local gentry, his status in the community is not reliant on that association but rather on his easy good nature, physical prowess, and derring-do. Whereas Maclane's absorption in fashion ties him strongly both to a particular moment and milieu and to forces of temporal change and instability, Turpin's independence from this sphere of fashion, as from any other determining arena, his embeddedness in nature rather than in culture, in the country rather than the city, establishes the aura of timelessness and immortality that contributes so strongly to his mythical status.

Finally, Turpin's status as a gentleman not only is independent of any social connections but is also prior to any particular exploits as a highwayman. According to "Jack Palmer's" disquisition on the gentility of all real highwaymen, success as a highwayman does not win status as a gentleman, but rather only attests to the presence of this inherent status. His gentility is inborn and transcendent. On the one hand, this reflects notions of heritable nobility—status, properly speaking—yet, on the other hand, the terms in which Ainsworth laments the extinction of this breed of gentleman highwayman reflect ideas of racial nationality: "Turpin was the *ultimus Romanorum*, the last of a race" (163). As the final figure in a long and distinguished line of knights of the road immortalized for Ainsworth in the stories his father told him, Turpin is idealized in ways that approach and elevate the authenticity of "a popular culture of living speech and song and tale-telling" that Duncan cites as one of modern romance's major ways of imagining the vanishing origins of an authentic national culture.[82]

In the tradition of romantic antiquarianism with which Scott is identified, *Rookwood* is heavily garnished with ballads and popular songs. Itself inspired by traditions of tale-telling, the novel incorporates the "authentic" folkways of a national culture in such ditties as the cant song "Nix my doll palls—fake away!" ["It's nothing my good companions—let's get out of here!"] (177–79).[83] Ainsworth proudly fabricates these pieces of tradition. In the preface to his novel, he cites as a major achievement that he has been the first "to introduce and naturalize amongst us a measure which, though common enough in the Argotic minstrelsy of France, has been hitherto unknown to our *pedestrian* poetry" (xxxvi). The text of "Nix my doll palls" is annotated copiously so that Ainsworth's readers might comprehend its meaning. In *Rookwood* the criminal subculture inhabited by Turpin and the gypsies becomes the site of "an archaic native culture" that Ainsworth portrays as "vanishing into the past," retrieves, and makes available to his audience. Thus, Ainsworth's romance, like Scott's, is marked by the process of "revival" of passing traditions, of recovery of cultural forms and characters.[84]

Turpin moves easily among and between both the colorful "canting crew" in the gypsy encampment and the commonplace local gentry at Rookwood manor. He is bilingual, fluent in both Standard English and "cant." Confined to neither sphere, criminal or genteel, Turpin partakes of the authenticity and exoticism of the former and the familiarity of the latter. He is a man of both worlds; this underlines his independence from either and facilitates his function as a kind of mediating figure between Ainsworth's contemporary audience and the criminal and exotic subculture of the gypsy "canting crew." Turpin's participation in both worlds also underlines one of the ideological points of "modern romances": "More than anything else, this romance revival involved the confrontation with cultural origins that were at once native and alien."[85] Even taken independently of Turpin, the gypsies, or "Romany" people, speaking their own language and developing their own culture on English soil for hundreds of years, are ideally suited to this role of representing what is at once native and alien. But what Ainsworth's novel highlights and what Turpin's ritual "adoption" into their clan underscores, is the long history of exchange and interdependence between gypsy culture and those criminal subcultures usually understood as properly English. This history is revealed best of all, perhaps, in the language of cant.[86] The exchange between Turpin and the gypsies romances both into a nostalgic English historical landscape; it associates the highwayman with a larger milieu that serves as a site for the romantic revival of cultural origins, and it translates the gypsies and their cant into a romantic national heritage comprehensible to Ainsworth's audience.

Situated by Ainsworth in a rural English landscape, Turpin's presence is written there in ways that make him a permanent feature of the cultural topography. The very calling of the highwayman, in its "authentic" and noble form, is itself distinctly English. Uttering a cultural commonplace, Turpin, again as "Jack Palmer," proclaims: "England, sir, has reason to be proud of her highwaymen. They are peculiar to her clime, and are as much before the brigand of Italy, the contrabandist of Spain, or the cut-purse of France—as her sailors are before all the rest of the world" (53). Turpin, the eighteenth-century "Famous Highwayman," becomes Turpin the boys' hero and at the same time Turpin the nationalist hero.

Finally, the nationalization of Dick Turpin achieved by Ainsworth's *Rookwood*

seems to participate in extra-literary cultural effects similar to those that Walter Scott's romances had on the Scottish highlands: "Scott, from *The Lady of
the Lakes* onwards, instigated something like the industrial-scale expansion of
Scottish tourism."[87] To similar effect, though perhaps with less historical and
cultural scope and weight, Ainsworth's novel, with its romance of the Turpin
legend, especially its remarkable and completely fictional ride from London to
York, invents a tradition for England profitably maintained by innkeepers and
tourists. That Ainsworth's novels were used by tourists as maps to England's past
is attested by a letter of appreciation to him written by Baltimorean Benjamin H.
Latrobe: "I am an American . . . visiting England for the first time. . . . Your volumes . . . were my companions and vastly enhanced the pleasure of the visits."[88]
In their account of the historical Turpin, Ash and Day devote two chapters to the
recital of the English landmarks connected with Turpin.[89] A number of inns that
are still standing boast Turpin as a former guest, and many preserve parapherna-
lia associated with the highwayman. Turpin, like George Washington in America,
seems to have slept everywhere. Moreover, in Essex there is a "Turpin's Lane"
and in Hounslow a "Turpin's Walk." Well into the twentieth century on Finchley
Common there stood a "Turpin's Oak" in which the highwayman took cover.
Ainsworth's approach to his heroic highwayman is that of the heritage industry:
both write Turpin into the landscape, naturalizing him and romanticizing it.

Ghostly Independence

For Ainsworth, Turpin's presence is so strongly felt in the Yorkshire countryside that it amounts to a haunting: "When a boy, I have often lingered by the
side of the deep old road where this robbery [on Hough Green] was committed,
to cast wistful glances with its mysterious windings; and when night deepened
the shadows of the trees, have urged my horse on his journey, from a vague apprehension of a visit from the ghostly highwayman" (xxxvii). In a remark that
points up the shared ground of the gothic and the historical romance, Duncan
comments on how attention to precise localities as sites of vanishing native culture produces "local countrysides seen as haunted by their passing historical
difference" (14). Romantic historical passing smoothly slides into gothic supernatural "haunting." This is evident in *Rookwood*, where the English countryside
provides the quite literalized common ground shared by the two strands of the
narrative, the gothic romance of the Rookwood family and the historical romance
of Dick Turpin. In his preface to the novel, Ainsworth describes his plan of domesticating the gothic into the English landscape by "substituting an old English

squire, an old manorial residence, and an old English highwayman for the Italian marchese, the castle, and the brigand of that great mistress of romance" (xxxiii). What is most homely and familiar, these stereotypical figures of Englishness, is thus put in dialogic tension with the foreign and uncanny, an arrangement that Duncan identifies as the structure of the modern romantic archetype. Of course, the relationship works both ways: the gothic is domesticated even as Englishness is gothicized.

"The ghostly highwayman" in the rural landscape is the central romantic archetype of Ainsworth's childhood and of his novel; gothic conventions are readily available to signal historical changes, differences between then and now, and, most crucially, the haunting presences that occupy the space between. In this sense, Turpin himself is fundamentally a "gothic" character. The realization of the "ghostly highwayman" as the red-blooded Turpin in the narrative *Rookwood* involves no less a literalization of the supernatural than the manifestation of other ghosts and animation of other corpses in the gothic plot; it simply occurs at a prior stage of conceptualization.

That said, perhaps the major relation between Turpin and the gothic plot of the Rookwoods resides in his marked evasion of its criminality, horror, and constraint. Celebrated as a highwayman, Turpin is not named as a criminal in *Rookwood,* where the real crimes are committed by the Rookwood males, fated to betray one another and murder their wives. "A monster race," the Rookwoods continue their murderous ways unpunished until "men wondered when the vengeance of Heaven, so long delayed, would fall and consume [them]" (15, 30).

The inheritance crisis narrated in the novel originates in the days of Sir Reginald Rookwood, a libertine rake at the court of Charles II who indulged his lust for power, wealth, and women in defiance of "all human laws and obligations" (15, 31). This Reginald seduces his brother Alan's wife and goes on to marry three other women and leave three children, the eldest a girl, Eleanor, who despises him and runs away, and two sons, one of whom is killed fighting for William of Orange at Killiecrankie and the other, Sir Piers, who succeeds to the title and the estate and whose funeral opens the novel. Alan, betrayed and intent on revenge, disappears with his daughter, Susan, and then returns with her to the estate disguised as Peter Bradley the sexton. Susan becomes the mistress and then the secret wife of her cousin, Sir Piers. She is strangled with the consent of Sir Piers, leaving behind a son, Luke Bradley, who is sent into the care of gypsy matriarch Barbara Lovel. Luke is then engaged to marry his foster mother's granddaughter, Sybil. Sir Piers has another wife, openly recognized, and another son, Ranulph, by her. Ranulph, the heir apparent, has a disagreement with his father, who forbids his marriage to one Eleanor Mowbray, whom he meets fortuitously on his European travels and who turns out to be his cousin, the daughter of the runaway Eleanor, daughter of Sir Reginald.

As this brief sketch of the genealogical plot suggests, the course of the novel witnesses a train of confusion, impersonation, incest, betrayal, suicide, and revelation dizzying in its complication. Armed with a wedding band from his mother's corpse and lured into his grandfather Alan's plot for revenge, Luke challenges his half-brother Ranulph's claim on the inheritance and on Eleanor Mowbray. Yet it is revealed that neither son is the true heir; for Sir Reginald had willed the estate to his daughter Eleanor and her descendents, thus passing the estate to Eleanor Mowbray, Ranulph's fiancée. In the end all is resolved, but only at the cost of a number of lives, including that of the innocent, martyred gypsy girl Sybil.

The Rookwoods' history is a chronicle of horrific, ruthless cruelty, greed, and murder. Ainsworth locates the "moral" of his novel not in any connection with the highwayman Turpin but in the examples of "the Tempter, the Tempted, and the Better Influence," that is, "in the Sexton, in Luke, and in Sybil" (xxxvii). Turpin's offenses, even those he performs in the action of the novel, are celebrated as frolicsome exploits, not deplored as crimes; he is not guilty, he is not repentant, he is not brought to justice. He is totally removed from the providential moral world of outrage and revenge, of sin and retribution that drives the gothic *Rookwood* plot. Thus Ainsworth evades the conventions of eighteenth-century criminal biography that ambivalently fluctuate between an affirmation of the individual will as will to crime, and its containment by religious and judicial authority as repentance and punishment.

Most significantly for the ideal of masculinity promoted through the Turpin figure, this immunity from the complications and consequences of the Rookwood domestic horror show confirms his consummate independence from the crises of masculine authority that originate, as the Rookwood gothic family does, in the seventeenth century. Much of my discussion of criminality and masculine prestige thus far has posited the modern alignment of these qualities in those critical upheavals; much of Ainsworth's gothic plot elaborates how corruptions of authority originating in the seventeenth century continue to haunt the Rookwood patriarchy. A considerable critical tradition in the study of the gothic emphasizes its preoccupation with just such corruptions and crises of patriarchy. Shaped by conflicts about succession and inheritance and the nature of the power these maintain, the conventional gothic plot explicitly thematizes issues of masculine privilege, authority, and especially, transgression. The gothic commonly figures forth the "archetype of a damned masculine will-to-power" who shows that "to enact patriarchy is to rape and murder your children."[90]

The last of his line, independent of all domesticity and all of patriarchy's contaminants, conflicts, and crimes, Turpin is removed from historical continuity. His relation to patriarchal authority in general can be read in his relation to the house of Rookwood and its representatives. He partakes of patriarchy's masculinist priorities and prestige just as he partakes of the abundant hospitality served up by Sir Piers, yet he is never dependent on them. That, at least, is the fantasy offered by Turpin's particular brand of prestigious criminal masculinity. Here is masculine prestige and criminality removed from all consequence. At the end of *Rookwood,* Turpin simply disappears: "'I have done with Rookwood,'" he proclaims. "And springing through the panel, he was seen no more" (327). Turpin, the romantic highwayman, leaps out of history into mythic timelessness where masculine privilege, power, and transgression can be savored, unburdened by the accountability that so vexes patriarchy's gothic narrative.

Postscript: Highwaymen and Huckleberry Finn

Early on in Mark Twain's *Huckleberry Finn* (1884), Huck finds some relief from the strenuous domesticity of life with Miss Watson when Tom Sawyer calls him out one night.[91] They raft down river and gather in a cave with some other boys. Tom casts them all in one of his grandly orchestrated "adventures": "Now, we'll start this band of robbers and call it Tom Sawyer's Gang. Everybody that wants to join has got to take an oath, and write his name in blood" (9). Swearing secrecy and fidelity on pain of death, the boys sign up: "Everybody said it was a real beautiful oath, and asked Tom if he got it out of his own head. He said, some of it, but the rest was out of pirate-books and robber-books, and every gang that was high-toned had it" (10).

Questioned by Ben Rogers about the gang's intended "line of business," Tom Sawyer scoffs at the idea that they might rob "houses" or "cattle": "Stuff! stealing cattle and such things ain't robbery; it's burglary," says Tom Sawyer. "We ain't burglars. That ain't no sort of style. We are highwaymen. We stop stages and carriages on the road, with masks on, and kill the people and take their watches and money" (11). Skeptical and competitive, Ben continues his questioning. Tom explains, citing precedent for all his policies from "what's in the books." They do not have to murder everyone they rob, but can keep them in the cave and ransom them, just as it is outlined in the "pirate-books and robber-books." When Ben asks if they will "kill the women too," an exasperated Tom explains to him the proper decorum governing the relations between the gentleman highwayman and his ladies: "Well, Ben Rogers, if I was as ignorant as you I wouldn't let on. Kill the women? No; nobody ever saw anything in the books like that. You fetch them to the cave, and you're always as polite as pie to them; and by and by they fall in love with you, and never want to go home any more" (13).

Twain's *Huckleberry Finn* is set about "forty or fifty years" before its publication in 1884 and takes place in the small towns and country lining the Mississippi. In the 1830s and 1840s this region was on the edge of the frontier; Missouri had gained statehood in 1821, Arkansas not until 1836. Even in this American backwater, the myth of the "high-toned" gentleman highwayman thrived in all its hackneyed glory, immortalized in a body of cheap boys' adventure stories, the "pirate-books and robber-books" that inspire and authorize Tom Sawyer's own robber gang. The proper highwayman puts on a high style; he despises common "burglary," pursuing only the noble quarry of "stages and carriages"; he commonly hides out in a cave, as Dick Turpin was famed to do; and he is a gallant, "polite as pie" with the ladies who fall in love with him, as we know from the life of Claude Duval.

As Sawyer repeatedly emphasizes, these conventions are fixed by textual authority. Twain's joke here—or one of them—lies in the ironic juxtaposition between the august authority of the text constantly invoked by Tom Sawyer and the criminality, even brutality, of the deeds it is called upon to sanction. There is a right way and a wrong way to go about murder and highway robbery, as any enlightened boy knows. The tension between narrative authority and the misdeeds it catalogues that provides the ground for Twain's humor here is, as we have seen, one of the defining features of the criminal biography as it emerges in the seventeenth century. The mythic figure of the gentleman highwayman that so powerfully captures the imagination of the mid-nineteenth-century American small-town boy has its origins in seventeenth- and eighteenth-century England. In a sense, Twain's *Huckleberry Finn* invokes, only to displace, the imported, outdated myth of masculine self-authorization and radical independence embodied in the romantic highwayman. Tom Sawyer may play at being an outlaw in ways scripted by the dime novels he reads, but Huck Finn and the rest of the gang soon grow weary of the discrepancy between Sawyer's fantasies of glorious forays against Spanish merchants and "A-rabs" and the demeaning actuality of busting up Sunday school picnics. After a couple of weeks, they all resign from the gang (16–17).

Huck, however, goes on to live through real adventures; furthermore, he scripts his own life, authorizing his own independence. As Huck tells us in the last sentence of the book: "if I'd a knowed what a trouble it was to make a book I wouldn't a tackled it, and ain't a-going to no more. But I reckon I got to light out for the Territory ahead of the rest, because Aunt Sally she's going to adopt me and sivilize me, and I can't stand it. I been there before." Lighting out for the frontier, keen to keep his lead ahead of the march of "sivilization," Huck Finn, like Dick Turpin before him, jumps out of the frame of civilization and history into a romance of complete independence. But with Huck Finn, Twain gives us a boys' adventure hero who is actually a boy. Huck Finn leaves off playing highway robbers and goes on to star in his own narrative of male independence and self-authorization, a post-Romantic American fantasy of boyhood and the frontier. This, then, might be seen as an important moment in the highwayman's cultural obsolescence; for after Twain's novel, boys would be as likely to play at being Huck Finn as at Tom Sawyer's game of highway robbers.

Finally, the romance of the highwayman realized by Ainsworth's *Rookwood* and immortalized in the mass-acculturated imaginations of generations of boys like Tom Sawyer is one popularly shared out among his pirate brothers in those "pirate-books and robber-books" named by Tom in the same breath. Thus, turning to the examination of the pirate in the next chapter, I will trace another history, not of the romantic pirate of popular British and American culture, but of the radical pirate within his distinctly West Indian and countercultural context.

CHAPTER FOUR

Welcome the Outlaw

Pirates, Maroons, and Caribbean Countercultures

Introduction: There Is No Pirate Sex

Pirate biography forms a bulky portion of the body of criminal narratives that saturate early eighteenth-century literary history and that exist alongside the literature of conduct and civility in the period.[1] Like other criminal narratives, stories of the pirates take part in the genesis of the early novel, especially those by Daniel Defoe. The cultural myth of the pirate generated by these narratives reveals, more forcefully than those of the rake or the highwayman, how dominant culture exploits the powers and structures of authority that it officially renounces. So, while the early modern pirate brings with him various points of intersection with the other figures studied here, it is as exemplar of the complicities among law and outlaw that he is addressed in this chapter.

Nonetheless, it is useful first to orient the pirate within the topic of masculinity that serves as the conceptual and historical ground of this book as a whole and to place him more fully in relation to the other iconic figures examined in it. If, as I have suggested in chapter 2, the criminality of the rake has been defined largely by his sexual transgressions while his impressive repertoire of thuggish violence is overlooked, conversely, the pirate's criminality is most often depicted and understood as violent, always economic, often sociocultural, and utterly outside sexual representation. The possible association of the pirate's sociocultural deviance with sexual deviance (as "homoeroticism") has been forwarded only recently by literary critic Hans Turley.[2] Although there is a fairly ample record of the rake's nonsexual criminal violence that has been overlooked by literary and cultural historians, the literature of piracy reveals no analogous representations of his sexual performance. Lack of scholarly attention to piratical sexuality simply mirrors the emptiness of the record. There is no pirate sex.

Yet there is more than nothing to say about it. Here it is helpful to recall the developments within the sex/gender system outlined in chapter 1. For while actual pirate sexual practices are generally absent in contemporary early modern documents, the expression and interpretation of pirate masculinity, like that of all the figures examined here, takes shape in reference to the emergent paradigm of sexual difference and the heterosexual, domestic, and civil gentleman who stands as that ideology's iconic figurehead. Because this paradigm aligns gender with heteronormative sociosexual practice, the location within it of piratical *masculinity* reveals something about piratical *sexuality*. This something, however, has more to do with the negative refusals—of heterosociality, of privacy, of domesticity, of masculinity as an expression of sexuality—engaged by piratical masculinity than with its positive definition within the modern gender/sex paradigm as "heterosexual" or "homosexual" or "bisexual." If we admit the alternate category "queer" to encompass gender/sexuality positions that elude relegation to these classifications, and thus foil the paradigm's categorical claims, then perhaps piratical sexuality, like that of the fop, might belong in it. However, in this case, "queer" must remain just that; early modern "queerness" should remain distinct from, though not necessarily unrelated to, late modern gayness. This is not to suggest that historians of homosexuality should keep their hands off the pirates, or that contemporary modes of gayness might not find social and erotic resonance with piratical masculinity, but rather to insist on the integrity and persistence of modes of masculinity that disavow modern sex/gender definitions. I suggest, then, that piratical sexuality may be best understood as finally deviant from determination through the (increasingly domesticating and privatized) perspective of gender as defined by sexual performance. This insistence that gender is won and lost through sexual activity—homo-, hetero-, or bisexual—is one of the conditions of the modern sex/gender system and precisely one that the pirate evades. Thus, while the representations of the pirate do deviate from the norms established by the paradigm of sexual difference, this deviation cannot, as Turley's proposition of piratical "homoeroticism" would have it, itself be defined within those norms.

Unlike the highwayman, alongside whom he may be understood as an economic parasite, the early eighteenth-century pirate is rarely portrayed as "gallant" or gentleman-like in any way. Unlike the rake, whose devotion to transgressive homosocial communities may seem analogous to his own, the pirate is not perplexed in a contradictory relation to his own status and its privileges. Pirates, like sailors more generally, were from the lower rungs of the status/class hierarchy, and their formation of "pirate societies" operated more or less outside of conventional status distinctions. Typically, they situated themselves, not against one class or even one nation, but against the whole world as the "enemies of all mankind." Perhaps the most spacious and stable common ground shared by the pirate with other contemporary outlaw figures can be found in the ways that they all operate outside the field of heteronormative domestic privacy. The radical anti-civility of the pirate and, related to this, his refusal of modern institutions of complementary sex/gender relations, link him especially closely with the rake. Yet, as Thomas King has noted, the rake's refusal of civility and of domestic privacy connect him, in turn, to the fop.[3] The Restoration rake's sexuality, unlimited by notions of sexual difference, encompassed both male and female objects; his eighteenth-century heirs are straightened up in heterosexual conformity, though they pursue sex outside the pale of domesticity. The eros of the fop is typically narcissistic, directed toward the spectacular self and thus stands outside any affective, heterosexual relation. Like the pirate, the fop's actual sexual practices remain obscure, always subordinate to his social performances, just as the pirate's are always subordinate to his criminal exploits. Yet, from the perspective of sexual difference, the pirate's hyperbolic masculinity stands in stark distinction to the fop's gendered character, equivocated as it is by his investment in feminized arenas of fashion, spectacle, and performative display.

Just as the rake is widely understood to exist in competitive and endangering relation to the fop, both dependent, as they are, on publicity and performance, both deficient, as King notes, in privacy and its morally stabilizing affective capacities, similarly Turley has similarly suggested that the pirate might be understood in relation to the molly, or the "sodomitical subject." Molly societies exemplify the ways in which male subcultures might coalesce around same-sex desire through a mode of homosociality radically bifurcated from both heterosociality and heterosexuality.[4] Suggesting a parallel between pirate and molly societies and pairing the pirate with the sodomitical subject, Turley suggests that the pirate replaces the libertine rake "as a cultural icon, a figure of sexual and cultural anarchy" and that he challenges the sex/gender order in ways widely analogous to the sodomitical subject. Yet even as Turley notes that, unlike the rake, the pirate's expression of deviance *takes no sexual forms,* he nonetheless insists on this coupling of the pirate with the "sodomitical subject" whose outlaw status, conversely, is purchased *exclusively* by his sexual deviance.[5] Both pirate and sodomite, according to this argument, are defined by their cultural "otherness," which is an expression of their innate unnatural "desires." Both embody subjectivities at odds with the ideology of heteronormative domesticity.

While accepting this conclusion generally, I challenge the specificity of its pairing of the rake and the emergent sodomitical subject. *All* the iconic figures of criminal masculinity that I examine participate in such a refusal and/or evasion of modern heteronormativity. Furthermore, in relation to their definition through sexuality, the pirate and the molly seem contrasting figures—the one evading such identification, the other wholly dependent on it. In the terms guiding this study, the sodomitical subject is further distinguished from the pirate, as well as from the highwayman, the rake, and the gentleman, by his reviled, rather than prestigious, cultural status. Finally, Turley's argument does not stop with the observation that both the sodomitical subject and the pirate are understood as activated by unnatural desires, but he goes on to see these desires as analogously "homoerotic," albeit taking a repressed and displaced form in the pirate.[6] In distinction, I understand the pirate as a figure whose propensity for gender transgression is expressed by its operation outside sexuality. Again in distinction from Turley, I would insist that the libertine rake and the pirate are contemporaries well into the eighteenth century; therefore, the latter cannot be understood to supersede the former. The pirate does not take up where the rake leaves off but figures forms of independence and autonomy that the rake does not, especially after the rake has been updated through the heteronormative pressures of sexual difference. While the heteronormalized rake, like his Restoration progenitors, remains dependent on sexual performance for the expression of his masculine will-to-power, the pirate's masculinity, in this regard, might be seen as more fully absolute in its autonomy from this mode of confirmation.

Daniel Defoe's novel *Captain Singleton* provides in its protagonist a central exhibit of piratical subjectivity-and, for Turley, of its implicit "homoeroticism."[7] Turley arrives at his conclusions about pirate "homoeroticism" most generally by reading piratical and sodomitical homosociality alongside one another and by understanding piratical "excess" and "violence" as analogous to aristocratic libertine extravagance and thus transgressive not only of "the economic and cultural status quo" but also "implicitly" of the sexual status quo.[8] Pirate violence and brutality, then, are figurative "masks" that Turley strips away to reveal "the sexual connotations" latent in "piratical society."[9] Rather than granting the pirate a distinct form of gendered transgression, such analysis risks absorbing it into that of those other figures, the sodomitical subject (molly) and the rake.

In his reading of *Captain Singleton*, Turley presents a test case for these more global conclusions about piratical sexuality, focusing on the relationship between

Singleton and Quaker William. Singleton is the iconic pirate, without family or country, bred at sea from childhood, predisposed toward the lawless and roaming ways of pirate society. The first half of the novel chronicles young Singleton's adventures to Madagascar and then across the continent of Africa. In the second half of the narrative, Singleton's crew adopts the unlikely pirate Quaker William into its ranks. William proves a canny hand at piratical profiteering, and he and Singleton become fast friends. Forged in pirate society, the bond between Singleton and Quaker William becomes exclusive when they leave their crew and set off to establish a life together first in the Levant, then in Venice, and finally in England where Singleton marries William's sister and they live together passing "as Brothers."[10] These developments, argues Turley, remove their relationship both from "the anarchy of consistently unstable pirate desire" and from what any contemporary would understand as a "sodomitical" relationship. Ultimately, Turley insists, their relationship is recognizable to a twentieth-century reader as an affectionate, "but not necessarily nonsexual," bond "based on their desires for one another," one that "goes far beyond camaraderie," ripe as it is with "homoerotic desire."[11]

Defoe's characters, male and female, are notoriously reticent in their expression of affectivity of almost every sort, so it would not serve as a convincing refutation to Turley's speculations to simply note that any "homoerotic" desires between Singleton and William remain unexpressed. Moreover, there *is* one veritable gushing of heart-felt reflection from Singleton on his bond with his friend: "As I had a merciful Protector above me, so I had a most faithful Steward, Counsellor, Partner, or whatever I might call him [William], who was my Guide, my Pilot, my Governor, my every thing, and took care both of me, and of all we had."[12] Singleton's inventory of possible roles for William recalls Robinson Crusoe's similarly indeterminate attempts to define his relation to his man Friday: "a Servant, and perhaps a Companion, or Assistant," "my Slave," "my Savage," "a Child," "the aptest Scholar," "a grateful Friend."[13] So Crusoe personalizes, privatizes, and detoxifies what is at base a relationship between colonial conqueror and slave. Up to this moment on his island, Crusoe's faith in God and in himself has gone untested and unconfirmed by any social or personal relationship. With Friday as surrogate "son" and religious "pupil," Crusoe can express his mastery of the familial and spiritual institutions he had earlier defied and evaded in his propensity for adventuring. This, then, is Crusoe's first and most fully articulated attempt at the interpersonal integration necessary to his final deliverance from the social wasteland of his island and the spiritual desert of his error.

Just as Crusoe's narrative is propelled by a thoroughgoing evasion of personal

and social relationships and is resolved through his reintegration into these relationships in conveniently unthreatening and magically opportune ways, so Singleton's life, a pirate's life after all, has been defined through an equally thorough-
going defiance of all authority. Peter Hulme has discussed *Robinson Crusoe* as a
"colonial romance" in which fabulously generous benefactors and improbably
grateful slaves provide the occasions of Crusoe's success.[14] The pirate romance
of *Captain Singleton*, I believe, depends in a similar way on the unlikely figure of
the Quaker pirate William. The resolution to Singleton's life of antiauthoritarian
piracy comes through the provision in William of an ideal authority figure. Just
as Defoe's relationship to Friday—a willing slave—is founded on a contradiction
that would cleanse from it the taint of coercion, so is Singleton's relationship to
William—a superior, a "Governor," who is also an equal, a "Partner"—involved
in a contradiction that equivocates the relationship of subservience defined
within authority's hierarchy. A man without country, family, religion, Singleton,
as a pirate, is defined by his absolute refusal of any allegiance; so his new life
outside piracy is defined by his loyalty to his "Governor," whose protection of
him and his interests is as absolute as God's own with which it is identified:
"Just as I had a merciful Protector above me, so I had a most faithful Steward" in
William.

More recently and, to my mind, more convincingly than Turley, Stephen
Gregg has argued that Singleton's and William's relationship represents Defoe's
attempt to articulate a bond between men translated across mercenary "interest"
and personal "affection": "Captain Singleton . . . provides the clearest example
[in Defoe] of a male-male relationship in which mutual exchanges of gratitude
and obligation . . . form the central terms whereby affection and interest become
indistinguishable." Gregg's analysis allows that Singleton and William's relationship is rendered "problematic" and partially "illegible" by virtue of its extreme
privacy and thus of its failure to commit to the ends of civic virtue through which
male friendships were more generally validated.[15] Because Singleton fears being
recognized and tried for his crimes, he insists on living incognito. Thus Singleton and William's relationship remains private, secret even, unintegrated into
any larger cultural-social web of representation and determination. This secrecy,
then, creates palpable obscurity about the nature and ends of the relationship and
leads to the ambiguities apparent in its scholarly interpretation. Yet the overtly
articulated features of this relationship—its magical resolution of the problem
of authority with the "Governor Partner" William, its conversions of interest and
affection—are clear enough and resonant with the narrative's trajectory, Defoe's
preoccupations, and the social ethics of the early eighteenth century. Taking di-

rection from these concerns, a reading of the relationship between Singleton and William, then, honors the evasion of sexuality typical of Defoe's and most eighteenth-century pirates. Retained as silence, pirate sex is allowed to speak its deviance.

The pirate's flamboyant masculinity seems undeniable. His bluff derring-do and proclivity toward personal violence are allied with martial, heroic ideals of masculinity, while his despotic aggression, immoderate egoism, and antiauthoritarianism may recall those of the libertine rake. That recent scholars such as Turley, Gregg, and I are intrigued and sometimes perplexed by the juxtaposition of the pirate's hypermasculinity with the absence of piratical sexuality, I believe, speaks to our own modern assumption that masculinity depends heavily on the performance of sexuality. What we meet in the pirate is a form of pronounced masculinity affirmed outside of sexuality. It is easy to see how the appeal of the pirate might lie in exactly this evasion, which removes from the assertion of masculine power and privilege all those anxieties about sexual performance and association that plague the rake. As I discuss chapter 2, the central risk to libertine masculinity lies in how sexual relation submits the subject into a network of circulation that, as in Rochester's *St. James's Park*, threatens that subject (his "reputation," his "honor') by linking him to a socially damaging chain of associations. "Gods! that a thing admired by me / Should fall to so much infamy," exclaims Rochester's rambler, outraged that his mistress would sully *his* reputation through *her* associations with the reviled "knights o'the elbow and the slur" (ll.89–90, 43).[16] The peculiarly nonsexual mode of piratical masculinity also fashions a subject ready-made for his long career as a favorite character of boys' fiction and film. In the pirate, the preadolescent boy finds a model of autonomous masculinity outside not only the confines of the maternal domestic arena but also outside the as yet uncharted and anxious territory of sexuality itself. At the moment of his emergence, the culturally mythic pirate, then, offers all the sweets of absolutist masculinity without the risks and pressures of its sexualized validation.

Complicity and Continuity

In chapter 1 I suggested that much of the prestige of the criminal types examined here is produced by their maintenance of forms of absolutism discredited in both the political and social realms. In their association with powers understood as elsewhere lost and as evocative of a world superseded by modernity and its ignoble compromises, such figures, as we have seen in the discussions of both the rake and the highwayman, become nostalgic. The highwayman occupies modernity's romantic imagining of its own lost cultural past. The rake expresses nostalgic desire in erotic registers, as absolute will unlimited by the reciprocity of newer models of polite, complementary, and largely domestic gender relations. Declaring war against all humankind, forging purely male communities outside any domestic or social restraints, remaining politically autonomous and mobile even as the nation-state takes shape around him, the pirate has become perhaps the best-known avatar of those principles of absolute individual will activated in the legends of all of these types. But as with all such claims, the famed autonomy and independence of the pirate remain complicated both by the necessary interdependence of piracy with the very colonial powers it opposed and by the tenacious investment those colonial powers maintained in these maritime freebooters whose powers they would exploit.

While I have argued that all these prestigious criminal figures accrue and retain cultural prestige to a great extent because they figure forms of masculine license elsewhere outlawed, it is the pirate whose stories write this paradox of celebration and disavowal into the global, world-historical landscape. With the figure of the pirate, the logic of complicit disavowal characteristic of the cultural position of all these figures is inscribed into the history of colonialism in the Caribbean. As agents in this West Indian history, pirates should be understood not only alongside their Old World compatriots, the rake and the highwayman, but even more immediately together with their New World cohorts, the early modern Maroons and the late modern rude boys and Rastafarians. For together with the pirates, those are the groups most dramatically implicated in the history of resistance and complicity through which colonial and postcolonial powers have been forged. It is in league with these West Indian groups that the cultural history of the pirate becomes continuous with the sociopolitical history of colonialism and its aftermath. Finally, casting the pirate back into the Caribbean and its history helps secure an understanding of the potentials and limits of the outlaw as an agent of dissent and resistance.

In chapter 2 we saw how rakish criminality has sometimes been read as liberatory aesthetic and ethical innovation. Likewise, there is a prominent strand of eighteenth-century scholarship on the history of labor that claims for the pirate significant agency as a figure of principled opposition and even radical reform. Here that tradition is brought into line with analogous claims for the political status of West Indian subcultures in contemporary society. Whereas discussions in this study of the rake and the gentleman engage issues at the fore in the history of masculinity and manners, this discussion of the pirate takes place within the history of radicalism and dissent. Both of these histories, of manners and of dissent, take modern shape around the same set of seventeenth-century developments in the status of aristocratic ideology and its accompanying ethos of absolutism.

In representations so ambivalent and repetitious as to signal a cultural fixation, volume after volume of criminal biography has fixed the pirates of the early modern Caribbean as objects of popular fascination, glamorization, and, I think, nostalgia since the late seventeenth century. Locating themselves in a tradition of frontier outlaws that starts with the early modern pirates and goes forward through the Wild West gunman and Depression-era mobster, Jamaican rude boys self-consciously accrue the outlaw glamour produced by three-hundred years of popular culture. The popular glamour of the frontier outlaw is colored by nostalgia for a kind of fully licensed machismo already becoming outdated by the turn of the eighteenth century and yet one that still, at the beginning of the twenty-first century, remains active in fantasies of masculinity. As I have worked on this book, two and now three Disney *Pirates of the Caribbean* movies have appeared, and *Guardian* articles continue to chronicle "Yardie-violence . . . across the UK."[17]

It makes perfect sense that such hyperbolic, desperado forms of machismo are promoted within two groups, the pirates and the rude boys, that emerge from dispossessed underclasses for whom social, economic, and political powers are most circumscribed. One thing worth noting is that for those who have never had power, the taking of criminal liberties needs to be seen as a utopian as well as a nostalgic gesture. The other two Caribbean subcultures examined here, the Maroons and the Rastafarians, though also promoting strong ideals of masculine power and notions of independence, engage in what looks like a more explicitly sociopolitical form of nostalgia. Both the Maroons and the Rastafarians enshrine an African political and spiritual past lost to slavery, but do so effectively only through a complicity with colonialism that might be understood to compromise the power and validity of this preservation. The "Africa" replicated in the New World Maroon communities survived only by means of the collusion of these communities with the colonial military machine. In ways that look very nostalgic indeed, the Rastafarians reconfigure an inevitably New World and mythical Africa as both the locus of lost origins and the site of redemption and return. Yet, to reframe a point made below, the discrepancy between the Africa of the historians and ethnographers on the one hand, and the mythical and redemptive Africa of the Rastafarians on the other, reveals not simply a nostalgia for what never was but also a utopian site of resistance from which demands for justice keep on coming.

In April 1978, before an audience of twenty thousand people gathered for the reggae Peace Concert headlined by superstar Bob Marley, former Wailer Peter Tosh made an extended and dissenting speech. The concert had been organized to celebrate the truce between rival Kingston gang leaders Claudie Massop and Bucky Marshall and their political sponsors, Michael Manley of the Jamaican National Party (JNP) and Edward Seaga of the Jamaican Labour party (JLP).[18] For years these national political leaders had capitalized on the rivalries, desperation, and tactical expertise of Kingston youth gangs by arming and employing them as security forces. The Peace Concert, as Tosh suspects, itself involved a questionable exploitation of the iconic powers of popular cultural demigods such as Marley and himself. For better and, as Tosh fears here, for worse, politics and popular culture are inseparable, and he resents the complicity extorted from him by corrupt politicians opportunistically huddling under the Rasta-reggae banner of One Love.

Distrusting the declaration of peace where economic and social justice have not yet been served, Tosh's speech turns to the inequities of Jamaican society; these lie at the roots of the violence ripping through the streets of West Kingston, and until they are eradicated there can be no peace. From his call for equal rights and justice ("No Justice, No Peace"), Tosh goes on to connect the motivations and means of the rude boys of West Kingston to models presented by the glorified marauders celebrated in Caribbean history as discoverers and adventurers:

> Right now, Mr. Manley, me wan talk to you personal cos me and you is friends, so you seh. . . . I no seh that my brother is a criminal. Cos when Columbus, Henry Morgan and Francis Drake come up, dey call dem pirate and put dem in a reading book and give us observation that we must look up and live the life of and the principle of pirates. So the youth dem know fe [to] fire dem guns like Henry Morgan same way.[19]

Columbus, Drake, and Morgan, Tosh insists, took the Caribbean by violence. Historically, this violence has both constituted and enforced the exploitation and depredation of these territories and, across the Atlantic, of the West African nations from which the bulk of the West Indian enslaved labor was wrested. The Kingston youths, descendants of those slaves, looking to get some of the goods back for themselves, follow the models of success handed down to them. Peace, Tosh insists, is broken as the youths are recruited, ideologically and strategically, by schools and political parties, to serve the outlaw forces that have held sway in the Caribbean since its European colonization.

The rude boys in twentieth-century Kingston act like pirates for the same reasons that young men in the seventeenth and eighteenth centuries did: because it offers an available and potentially lucrative, if potentially lethal, opportunity in a life with too few chances. They turn pirate because pirates eat better, are paid better, and pack more heat than legitimate workers.[20] The rude boys, like the pirates, acquire prestige in at least two ways. First, because there is, among many, a sympathetic realization that the frustration and oppression suffered by the underclasses provokes an equally violent vengeance. Second, less admirably, because the cultural value of hyperbolic machismo, self-aggrandizing aggression, and ruthless predation is in no way diminished with their ostensible condemnation by "decent society." Outlaws are welcomed not only by the sufferers seeking vengeance but also by the privileged, both relishing and disowning, with envious resentment, forms of power they revere, and often depend on, yet cannot openly condone.

Yet this machismo and the often brutal misogyny that characterizes both rudie and Rastafarian cultures becomes a sore point for progressive cultural critics otherwise sympathetic to West Indian underclasses. Sometimes these are explained as an unfortunate legacy of colonialism. Thus Carolyn Cooper traces the hyperbolic machismo of the rudies to a reaction against the "diminished masculinity" available to West Indian black men within the strictures of postcolonial society and reads the persistence of the sexual double standard in Rastafarian society as an aggravated form of "the duplicitous gender ideology that pervades Jamaican society," which is ultimately an inheritance from the "Judeo-Christian theology" of Victorian evangelical campaigns.[21] It is precisely against the conservative and repressive dictates of both Jamaican middle-class and Rastafarian societies that Cooper then reads the sexually liberatory potentials of the dancehall culture dominated by the rudie ethic of transgression and personal bravado: "Though the denigration of 'slackness' seems to determine the concomitant denigration of female sexuality, this feminisation of slackness in the dancehall can also be read in a radically different way as an innocently transgressive celebration of freedom from sin and law. Liberated from the repressive respectability of a conservative gender ideology of female property and propriety, these women lay proper claim to the control of their own bodies."[22] Yet although women may enjoy expanded forms of personal and sexual expression in dancehall culture, these forms, while innocent of criminal violence, cannot be innocent of the contradictions attendant on that culture's relation to mainstream society. As Cooper argues so sympathetically, though women have inhabited dancehall culture in defining ways, nonetheless feminine slackness is a counterpart to male machismo and shares both its potentials and limitations: both are forms of sexualized bravado; both depend heavily on stylized forms of self-definition and self-assertion that, as in Cooper's analysis of the phenomenon, are articulated largely in reaction against perceived limits of legitimacy. Most importantly, both are vulnerable to the kind of simultaneous exploitation and disavowal that characterize the reception of subcultural forms in dominant society. And because that society is sexist, when these forms are both feminine and overtly sexual, their vulnerability to both exploitation and denigration is more acute.

Whereas the rude boys have had, since the 1960s, scores of critics and apologists, most align the ethos of these gangs, often called "yardies," with more temporally and culturally immediate iconic outlaws: the gangsters of organized crime, and even more, the Wild West gunfighters of North American legend and film.[23] Like early modern pirates, the gunfighters are the glamorous denizens of the frontier: the Caribbean was the first American frontier, the North American West the next. Inhabited by ethnic and economic outcasts, abandoned by business and industry, neglected by social welfare, demonized by the media, ravaged by the wars among gangs and the police, certain late twentieth-century urban areas, such as Tivoli Gardens and Trenchtown in West Kingston, Brixton and Hackney in London, and South Central Los Angeles and the South Bronx in the United States, stand as present-day heirs to earlier frontier outlaw zones such as Port Royal and Dodge City.

Tosh's speech points to the ways in which contemporary West Indian communities are heir to pressures rooted in the early modern formation of the English-speaking Caribbean and, in their struggles for socioeconomic empowerment, prone to responses that echo, often quite explicitly, that history with its icons of outlaw resistance. These icons were constructed largely within late seventeenth- and eighteenth-century colonial conditions, and a return to their early modern history helps us gain an understanding of their nature and function in late modernity. Tosh's remarks, then, frame two points this essay forwards: that early modern piracy has an analogue in late modern West Indian youth gangs, and that those celebrated as heroic discoverers and founders were engaged on an ethical frontier where the boundary between the law and the outlaw was prone to slip and slide in step with the sorry parade of institutionalized predation and exploitation. The pirate operates as a cultural repository for resonant historical memories of New World origins. The conditions of violence and exploitation that created what we now call the Caribbean continue to this day, generating modes of legitimacy and assimilation on the one hand, and of transgression and resistance on the other, whose distinction from one another is, and has been since the days of pirates, confused by the complicity between the law and the outlaw. These conditions are embodied in the culturally mythic persona of the pirate, whose ethical and aesthetic ambiguity becomes an iconic model for such justice-confounding and opportunity-bedeviling complicity.

Like the pirates themselves, the trope of piracy has always been highly mobile, a marker of the very instabilities of those lines that define social and ethical standards. In the eighteenth century, piracy is a concept useful for the definition of the line between legitimate and illegitimate commercial practices. The period's preoccupation with piracy and pirate stories seems largely linked to the ways these are used discursively to rationalize and mobilize commercial imperialism. In his *Review* for October 16, 1707, Defoe ironically ticks off the types of piracy central to English commercial institutions:

> It would make a sad Chasm on the Exchange of London, if all the Pyrates should be taken away from the Merchants there, whether we be understood to speak of your Litteral or Allegorical Pyrates; whether I should mean the Clandestine Trade Pyrates, who pyrate upon fair trade at home; the Custom-stealing Pyrates, who pyrate upon the Government; the Owling Pyrates, who rob the Manufactures; the privateering Pyrates, who rob by Law.[24]

Here, operating like the trope of highway robbery in *The Beggar's Opera*, the trope of piracy turns to indict the iniquities domesticated by licensed commerce. Conversely, in *Captain Singleton* Defoe turns the trope of fruitful commerce to equivocate piratical accumulation.

The ethical instabilities of the commercial realm, then, generate the same kind of reversals of authority already noted in their operation in criminal biography. In *Captain Singleton*, William, the Quaker turned pirate, proves that best practices for pirates are about the same as those for all prudent businessmen. He repeatedly convinces the crew to forgo the indulgence of revenge and the pleasures of violence in the interests of pure profit: "I only ask," he says to Bob Singleton, "what is thy Business, and the Business of all the People thou hast with thee? Is it not to get Money?"[25] William's rationalization places piracy next door to legitimate commerce just as the shady dealings on the Exchange place that institution within the frontiers of piracy. Defoe's speculations, narrative and expository, ironically and tellingly register the contiguities between piracy and honest commerce that prove so compelling to those concerned with the rationalization of capitalism in the early eighteenth century and to its critique in the late twentieth.

In both the early and the late modern periods, the complicity between law and outlaw has been generated by a political and socioeconomic milieu where dominant power, in its desperate attempts to secure its grip, exploits outlaw forces such as the pirates (as privateers) and the West Kingston gangs (as security forces) in ways often at odds with overt ideologies of law and order and with the result that these forces, enlisted initially to protect and enhance "legitimate" power, often come to pose grave threats to it.[26] But when the threat against dominant power is felt, those outlaw forces are ruthlessly quelled, and with impunity, for they are usually composed of underclasses whose claims to justice are weakened or obliterated by their lack of social and economic status. With his direct address to "Mr. Manley" and "Mr. Seaga" in the speech quoted above, Tosh smoothly reminds his audience of the real players who support and arm the youth gangs in the territories they both defend and ravish.

Dreadlocked, his speech peppered with Rastatalk and his thought informed with roots consciousness, Peter Tosh (aka Bush Doctor) embodies the Rastafarian Afrocentric tradition of sometimes heavily criminalized dissent and resistance that is distinct from, though socially and culturally mingled with, that of the gunfighters whose tactics he refuses but whose kinship he acknowledges. Coming from the same underclass ranks in the shanty towns of West Kingston, the social and cultural contiguity of rude boy and Rastafarian is close. Both the rudies and the Rastas express the consciousness of the "sufferers" battling poverty, political exploitation, and social ostracism in the shantytowns of West Kingston. And they do so in ways that carry on two traditions of outlaw cultures: rudies perpetuate the ethos of the armed desperado, with his glamorized violence, personal stature, territorialism, and bravado; and Rastas, that of the separatist Maroon communities with their focus on spiritual righteousness, consciousness of African tradition, and resistance to cultural and political colonialism. In the early modern Caribbean, the armed desperado took amphibious form as the buccaneer and the pirate. In ways reflected in the cultural positions of the rudies and Rastas in late modernity, the Maroons and the pirates were the two most prominent early modern Caribbean subcultures and together constituted the two most serious threats to colonialism in the West Indies.

Geographical and historical contiguity suggest that it makes sense to look at Maroons and pirates together. The cultural contiguity of the Maroon and pirate is casually assumed in late seventeenth- and early eighteenth-century literature. So in Aphra Behn's *Oroonoko* (1688), the Royal Slave plans a revolt against white rule that involves both marronage and piracy: "He said they would travel towards the Sea, plant a New Colony, and defend it by their Valour; and then they could find a Ship, either driven by stress of Weather, or guided by Providence that way, they wou'd seize it, and make it a Prize, till it had transported them to their own

Countries."[27] This passage also articulates two features associated with marronage for the next four hundred years: the Afrocentric trajectory of its ideals, and the notion of Maroons as the noble counterparts of the enslaved populace. Maroons are Royal Slaves whose heroic status is witnessed by their freedom.

In *Polly* (1729), John Gay's sequel to *The Beggar's Opera*, Macheath, antihero of the London underworld, runs off and passes for a pirate in the West Indies. He adopts the disguise of a black man and goes by the name "Morano." He becomes a white urban criminal passing as a pirate passing as a runaway slave, or Maroon.[28] Thus Gay's opera notes, in a tellingly offhand way, the link between pirates and Maroons in the eighteenth-century cultural imagination. It is as Morano, the pirate in black face, that the highwayman Macheath is executed; in the West Indian and colonial context, the threat of the pirate and the threat of the Maroon cannot be mercifully given the satiric/poetic reprieve that saves Macheath's skin in *The Beggar's Opera*. Taken together, these early modern examples of the proximity of piracy and marronage show as well how sociopolitical and criminal objectives intertwine in that area where freedom fighter exploits piracy and the highwayman's mask bears traces both of the sea marauder and the righteous African rebel.

Perhaps the strongest link in the chain that connects pirate and Maroon is that both constitute sustained and organized refusals of participation in the two central institutions of the colonial machine, plantation slavery and the vastly expanded merchant navy, both of which qualify as total institutions and as precursors to the industrial factory of the later eighteenth and nineteenth centuries.[29] And while there are strong traditions of resistance within the merchant shipping force on the one hand, and plantation slave society on the other, both the pirates and the Maroons are exemplary in the militancy of their refusal and in the iconic, even mythical status granted to them, both contemporaneously and retrospectively.

Pirates and Maroons are culturally mythic figures in the early modern Caribbean. By virtue of their status at once within and in opposition to the conditions of colonialism and its aftermath, they have become repositories for two, sometimes overlapping, ethics of resistance and survival whose currency in the contemporary African-diasporic world is apparent in youth gangs (the rude boys or yardies) and Rastafarians communities. Living, in a sense, on the frontiers of the frontier, both pirates and Maroons hyperbolically embody instabilities—ethical, economic, political, sociocultural, linguistic, demographic—that typify the early modern Caribbean and, as well, the late modern urban frontier. As repositories of historical and cultural alternatives, both pirate and Maroon cultures have attracted considerable attention, especially since the 1970s, from historians, critics, and activists interested in histories of resistance and subversion.

Focusing on the maritime origins of globalization, Peter Linebaugh and Marcus Rediker's *The Many-Headed Hydra: Sailors, Slaves, Commoners, and the Hidden History of the Revolutionary Atlantic* sets out the circum-Atlantic context of those strategies, alliances, and ethics that informed the anticolonial, anticapitalist, and antislave revolts that have shaped modernity. Concerned with recovering the origins and multiracial ideals of an early modern proletariat, their focus is on labor history. Highlighting the racial and ethnic complexities within the seafaring communities, *Many-Headed Hydra* casts the pirates in a positive, progressive light, emphasizing their inclusiveness, egalitarianism, and institutionalization of alternative social forms: "They had . . . self-consciously built an autonomous, democratic, egalitarian social order of their own, a subversive alternative to the prevailing ways of the merchant, naval, and privateering ship and a counterculture to the civilization of Atlantic capitalism with its expropriation and exploitation, terror and slavery."[30] But while their status as *subcultures* of modernity is evident, the status of these groups as *countercultures,* I contend, is more complex, though one often granted to both the pirates and the Maroons. Moreover, my interests here are precisely in those complexities that threaten to unfix such positive definitions of cultural status.

The significance of the distinction between subculture and counterculture lies in the greater sociopolitical autonomy and coherence associated with countercultures and thus in the application and, I think, in the confounding of standards of legitimacy, both sociological and legal-political. Because subcultures are often distinguished by a greater integration with the "parent culture" in which they exist and often lack an explicit articulation of lofty social and political aims, their significance may seem compromised. Their actions, even when viewed sympathetically, may seem pre-political and in need of rationalized organization and direction in order to qualify as meaningful in any fully political-historical sense.

These distinctions color the current sociocultural situation. Jamaican gang violence remains in the foreground alongside attempts within Jamaican communities to culturally disarm it by retaining the rude boys' militancy and raw power but using these to fuel more consciously cultural and socially responsible messages. Such attempts can be heard in the work of DJs such as Terry Ganzie (whose cut "Welcome the Outlaw" provides a kernel of inspiration and the title for this essay), who combine the rude boy gangster style with a commitment to sociocultural critique. In his recent study of dancehall culture, anthropologist Norman C. Stolzoff has dubbed as "Rude-boy Rastas" artists whose lyrics "are intensely political in that they decry the corruption of politicians, the senselessness of violence, the exploitation of the poor, the misrepresentation of the truth." Yet while Stolzoff grants the immediate political jab of such DJs, he hesitates to grant them real ideological coherence; the lyrics, while political, are not "explicitly ideological."[31] This is a quality he reserves for the "Cultural Rastas" such as Tony Rebel and the reformed Rastafarian Buju Banton, "known for their moral integrity, celebration of things African, and revolutionary politics."[32] So the intimacy—and the divide—between rudies and Rastas, between contingency and coherence, between reaction and revolution, remain in force, with an ongoing hesitancy to attribute ideological force to the former even where political relevance is undeniable.

Most pirate societies are more accurately compared to contemporary outlaw subcultures, such as the rudies or yardies, than to contemporary countercultures such as the Rastafarians. Yet, as the formation of outlaw subcultures shows, the distinction between criminal and sociopolitical actions, between transgressive reactive complicity and truly political subversion, can be difficult to define. So in an evaluation of Jamaican subcultures, urban anthropologist Faye V. Harrison emphasizes the need to read such cultures politically; for even though rarely organized as part of "a coherent and long-term political program," they nonetheless are "shaped by variant struggles against exploitation and oppression" and may "antedate, accompany, or catalyze more coherent patterns of mobilization."[33] Conversely, as alternatives to dominant societies and with their emphasis on separate institutions, countercultures such as those of the Maroons and the Rastafarians flirt with standards of separatist purity and authenticity that are hard to maintain. And while such claims to ethnic and ideological purity may bolster a certain brand of legitimacy, they may also bind these cultures in limiting contradictions.

While I share Linebaugh's and Rediker's concern with the contributions to progressive ideologies recoverable from histories of the underclasses, here by examining the analogues among two iconographic early Atlantic subcultures—the pirates and the Maroons—and two contemporary African-Caribbean subcultures—the rudies and the Rastafarians—I strive to emphasize how such contributions are complicated by the complicity between the law and the outlaw, between alternative and dominant societies, and between subversive and repressive orders that seems a characteristic feature of the genesis and development of these groups. For this complicity is what threatens the value of the sociocultural achievements of these groups, especially as estimated by progressive standards. Yet this complicity is a feature of their cultural-historical tenacity and significance; its elision obscures not only the "historical record" but also the discursive operations that produce colonial imperialism, slavery, and global capitalism. That is, piracy is disavowed by legitimate power only at the risk of a hypocrisy that denies that power's indebtedness to it, and it is embraced by radical intellectuals only at the risk of overlooking the ways in which piracy mirrors as much as it subverts the very economic and social institutions it opposes. Likewise, marronage operates as a name for resistance and alterity in the African diaspora but only by dint of a historical complicity with slavery and colonialism that complicates the claims of unity and purity that marronage sets against the disabling hybridity those institutions impose.

None of the groups examined here, then, achieves a pure and absolute autonomy from the dominant institution in opposition to which it constitutes its own identity. Yet this failure of "pure" oppositionality, ideological or practical-strategic, does not invalidate the sociocultural power of these groups; rather, if anything, it constitutes one feature central to their continuing currency in a postcolonial world where lines between law and outlaw, black and white, inside and outside disappear almost as quickly as they are, often opportunistically, calculated and imposed.

In what follows, I look at connections between the Maroons and, first, the seventeenth-century buccaneers and, next, the second wave of post-1714 pirates. I trace the material and historical contiguities, as actual contact and as analogous social formations, between the two groups in the early modern period. As it pertains to these connections, I present the relevance of these groups to historical and cultural-ideological work motivated by a set of critiques of modernity, especially in respect to its capitalist, colonialist, and postcolonialist features. These critiques are forwarded not only in textual form by academics but also within the traditions of popular African-diasporic culture. The modern pirate is a figure of cultural myth generated, in large part, in a New World Caribbean matrix he shares with the Maroon, and both figures serve as repositories of cultural memory and alternative historical possibility in a variety of traditions: popular, commercial, and academic; Euro-American and African-diasporic. Because of the global currency achieved by their highly institutionalized and articulated form of Afrocentric ideology, the countercultural status of the Rastafarians, those contemporary heirs of the Maroons, receives particular attention. By attending to the contemporary West Indian heirs of the early modern pirates and the Maroons, I hope to facilitate a better understanding of how culture works in the historical relations between early and late modernity. One principle guiding this examination is that the histories of African-diasporic and Euro-American subversion need to be read together even as they are experienced together historically and culturally.

Desperados: Buccaneers and Maroons on the Caribbean Frontier

In his entry for May 19, 1750, Thomas Thistlewood, recently arrived from England in Jamaica to become an overseer, remarks on a meeting he had with the famous Maroon leader Colonel Cudjoe:

> Between 8 and 9 miles from Dean's Valley, met Colonel Cudjoe, one of his wives, one of his sons, a Lieutenant and other attendants. He shook me by the hand, and begged a dram of us, which we gave him. He had on a feathered hat, sword by his side, gun upon his shoulder, &c. Barefoot and barelegged, somewhat a majestic look. He brought to my memory the picture of Robinson Crusoe.[34]

Cudjoe and Crusoe link through a variety of associations: the mirroring echo of the names Crusoe/Cudjoe, and the visual resemblance that Thistlewood's sketch emphasizes. Going "barefoot and barelegged," perhaps by preference, but sustaining his "majestic look," Cudjoe possesses, as does Crusoe, a distinctly "hybrid" Caribbean identity, fractured from origins in signs and circumstance that speak of both the Old and New Worlds. Both stranded in the Caribbean bush, Crusoe in his goatskins, Cudjoe in his scanty tattered finery, both present an appearance that speaks of life on the frontier productive of an identity outside of the limits of conventional civilization yet irreducible to simple savagery, noble or barbaric. With infinite labor, Crusoe stitches together his suits of skins and maintains, in a fashion peculiar to his Caribbean island, standards of European decency. With great dignity, Cudjoe plucks the plumes of European martial prestige and uses them in the crown he wears as the leader of free Africans.

Perhaps most fundamentally, Cudjoe and Crusoe are associated as the black Maroon leader and the white marooned man; the link is etymological. The practice of leaving people stranded on uninhabited islands, a favorite discipline of pirates, was named after those African people, the Maroons, stranded by the European slave trade on the Caribbean frontiers.[35] Defoe's Robinson Crusoe, though stranded by Providence rather than pirates, serves as the archetypal image of the marooned man in Anglo-American culture.[36] Crusoe is marooned when he is shipwrecked on a voyage from Bahia to Africa undertaken to obtain a black-market cargo of slaves; Cudjoe evades his fate as a slave by becoming a Maroon. Both the marooned Crusoe and the Maroon Cudjoe are products of the slave trade, which stranded black and white together on New World frontiers in conditions of mutual hostility and dependency, violent subjugation and militant revolt, opportunistic alliance and exploitative legitimization.

From the first, European attempts to supply a Caribbean labor force from peoples taken from West Africa met with resistance, from the passive to the militant. Great numbers perished in the passage; others expired under the deathly labor discipline on the plantations. Still others ran off into the bush and formed communities whose size varied from small bands of several dozen to fortified towns of thousands, such as Palmares, in northeastern Brazil, a conglomeration of villages with a combined population estimated at some 30,000. This African "nation" was finally reduced by Portuguese colonial forces after six expeditions in the 1680s and a siege of more than two years in the 1690s.[37]

When not obliterated, Maroon communities persisted through successful military resistance, as was the case with the Haitian Maroons instrumental in the revolution; or through formal negotiations of treaties with the colonial government, as was the case, for example, with the Jamaican Maroons.[38] Maroon communities, then, developed in the New World, especially in the Caribbean and the coastal areas of South and Central America, from the beginning of the slave trade, and they continue to exist, most notably in Surinam but also in Jamaica. Predictably, Maroons came into contact with the early buccaneers and privateers/ pirates with whom they sometimes formed alliances and shared similar means of livelihood.

Maroons lived in settled communities and so were familiar with the territory and its Amerindian inhabitants (where there were any left). They were often hostile to the Spanish and thus open to alliance with English sea rovers, most famously with Francis Drake, whose international highway robbery in Panama was engineered in the early 1570s with the sustained assistance of a Maroon named Diego and his men.[39] Although officially commissioned by the English crown to conduct his depredations against the Spanish, Drake's was, as one recent historian puts it, a sensibility passionately "ambitious and piratical." His raid on the mule train carrying Spanish silver and gold across Panama brought him fifteen tons of silver ingots and about £100,000 in gold coin.[40] The Maroons, in turn, received the moral satisfaction of having foiled the Spanish, the opportunity to join Drake's company, and "gifts and favors of the sorts most pleasing to them, such as knives, iron, coloured ribbons and cloth."[41]

Drake's sacking of St. Domingo on the island of Hispaniola in 1586 weakened the Spanish hold there and left it open for successive raids of privateers, who then settled on the west and northwest coasts of the island, forming the first bands of what develops, in the next century, into a loose confederation of hunt-ers and raiders called buccaneers. These buccaneers were mostly French and English men who gained a livelihood from hunting the wild pigs and cattle left by the Spanish. When, after 1655, the Spanish attacked their holdings in Tortuga, the buccaneers took to the seas seeking vengeance and a livelihood, forming the core of the first of two major waves of pirates. The second wave came after the War of the Spanish Succession in 1714 and was based in Providence Island, Ba-hamas (now Nassau).[42]

The buccaneers are named after their process of curing meat; both the process and the name for it—*boucan*—were taken from the Amerindians. This way of curing meat, and the practice of selling it to ships put in for supplies, is some-thing the buccaneers shared with early Maroon communities and proto-Maroon communities in Jamaica, where the process and its product are known by the Quechua-derived term "jerk."[43] According to standard twentieth-century etymol-ogy, the word *maroon* comes from the Spanish word *cimaroon,* which first referred to the cattle gone wild in the hills of Hispaniola (the very cattle the buccaneers hunted). It then came to refer to the Amerindians who, resisting Spanish en-slavement, themselves took to the hills, and, as early as 1530, to runaway African slaves.[44] However, eighteenth-century etymologies assume a closer link between the Maroons and the wild boar they hunted and cured. "*Maroon,*" explains Bryan Edwards, following Edward Long, "signifies among the Spanish Americans . . . *Hog-hunters.* . . . *Marrano* is the Spanish word for a young pig."[45] This inflec-tion of the etymology—*Maroon* from *marrano,* the pigs they hunt, rather than from *cimaroon,* the cattle who are wild like them—stresses a contiguity between the Maroons and the buccaneers in the eponymous association of both with the hunting and curing of wild game.

The seventeenth-century buccaneers, settled in Tortuga off the northwest coast of Hispaniola, attracted to their ranks a typically Caribbean mélange of des-perate characters—"runaway slaves, deserters, escaped criminals, and religious refugees," especially Protestant seamen fleeing Richelieu's and then Louis XIV's France.[46] In 1654 they joined ranks with the English fleet sent out by Cromwell under Penn and Venables against St. Domingo. After failing miserably in that expedition, still determined to wrest an English foothold in the Caribbean away from the Spanish, Penn and Venables turned to Jamaica, which they took in 1655 and where some of these Tortuga buccaneers then settled. Henry Morgan, most famous of the British West Indian buccaneers, attended Penn and Venables on their expedition and soon after the taking of Jamaica became the captain of the "brethren of the coast," as the loose federation of buccaneers came to be called.

Under Morgan, the buccaneers found a new land base in the infamous Port Royal.

The culture and exploits of this society of buccaneers in Morgan's time is sensationally told in Alexander Esquemelin's *Bucaniers of America*. A Dutchman, shipped to Tortuga in 1666 under indenture with the French West Indian Company, Esquemelin is typical of many desperados who joined with pirate gangs as a means of escaping the inhuman forms of labor endemic to the Caribbean.[47] When the company recalled its men from Tortuga, all the servants, including Esquemelin, were sold. His new master, a "most cruel Tyrant," was the lieutenant general of the buccaneers. Brutalized, Esquemelin became ill and useless and was sold again, this time to a more humane man, a surgeon who, after a year's service, allowed Esquemelin to buy his freedom for 100 pieces of eight.[48]

Esquemelin lived during a period in Caribbean history when, as Sidney Mintz puts it, "slavery and other forms of labor coercion were hardly distinguishable."[49] Esquemelin deplores the condition of the many men kidnapped in Europe as "servants" and sold as slaves. These bonded men, he asserts, are used worse than African slaves; for their masters, with only three years to get their money's worth, often extracted that value at the price of the worker's life. Pressed beyond the limits of human endurance, they literally take leave of their senses: "These miserable kidnap'd people, are frequently subject unto a certain disease, which in those parts, is called *Coma*; being a total privation of all their senses. And this distemper is judged to proceed from their hard usage."[50] Experienced as a coma in the days when Haiti was called Hispaniola, this state of death-in-life induced by the "reduction of human into thing for the ends of capital" is now called zombification.[51] The zombie, like the comatose indentured servant, is a being whose identity and will are slaughtered in service to the exactions of unfree labor.

In order to escape this fate, Esquemelin buys his freedom and joins the buccaneers. He would have had few options; it was difficult, often nearly impossible, for free workers to compete in a market built on slave and bonded labor. His story is typical. Just as Africans ran off to found or join Maroon communities to escape the horrors of plantation slavery, so thousands of men responded to the constraints of an economy fuelled by unfree labor by joining the outlaw ranks of the buccaneers.[52] Although not confined by such absolute limits on their freedom and autonomy as were enslaved Africans, white indentured servants and even many nominally free men in the early modern Caribbean suffered severe restraints imposed by one or more factors: their bonded status; their class and educational background; their religious, national, and/or political affiliations;

their criminal identity; and the very nature of the economies being established in the Caribbean.

Though often deplored for their unruliness, the buccaneers were more often than not welcomed, if sometimes surreptitiously, by the governors of Jamaica, because they confined themselves to Spanish prey, they provided Caribbean-based military protection, and they spent a lot of money.[53] Indeed, in an action that reflects, if antithetically, the military connection between the Panamanian Maroons and Drake's forces, the buccaneers were used early on by the English military in Jamaica to hunt down hostile Maroon bands.[54] Certainly, however, the kind of "security" provided by such autonomous, violent, roving, and predatory groups was precarious. While the buccaneers may have provided Jamaica with some protection against hostile Maroons, the Spanish, and then the French, their presence on the island contributed to the general climate of social instability of the period.[55]

But while the buccaneers stand out vividly as emblems of that chaotic, licentious anti-society that many, from Edward Ward in the 1690s to Orlando Patterson in the 1960s, have seen as typical of Jamaica, the threat to law and order they presented paled next to the threat to white colonial rule posed by the Maroons from 1655 to 1738.[56] Not until a new generation of post-1714 pirates declared its war of predation, not against the Spanish or French but against the whole world, would England be moved to any sort of broad-based, policy-backed, action against maritime outlaws. As they attempted to turn a profit in Jamaica, the colonists were concerned not so much with the buccaneers profiting off Spanish spoils, but with the bands of Maroons whose very presence was an outrage to colonial domination and who provided motivation and strategic support for the "one long series of revolts" that took place during the first eighty years of English occupation.[57]

Grossly outnumbered by, and completely dependent on, a population of hostile, often recalcitrant African labor, the colonials held a grip on Jamaica that was white-knuckled and savage. Rather than provide living conditions, planters replaced their ever-perishing stock of slaves with continual new imports. Life was cheap: death from overwork, disease, malnutrition, and physical torture was epidemic; births were rare; continual revolt and continual reprisals caused endless violence. The history of slave resistance in Jamaica has been impressively documented; the central role of the Maroons in this resistance is set out by Patterson.[58] The story of the Jamaican Maroons presents a rich and curious mix of defiance and accommodation. Various bands of Maroons responded differently to the English occupation. One band allied with the English and in 1663 was granted full civil rights; but as its leader, Lubola, began to hunt down recalcitrant blacks for the colonial military, other Maroons grew resentful and assassinated him. A group under Juan de Serras orchestrated continual resistance to the occupation and, when prices were put on their heads, retreated into the uninhabited northeast. Newly imported slaves began to rebel and to form their own or join preexisting maroon bands.

The colonial establishment struggled with this problem of revolt during its entire tenure. Before the treaty negotiated with the Maroon leader Cudjoe in 1738, the situation looked especially dire. The English occupation faced the threat of death to white settlers and the depletion of its labor force but also a threat to its very hold on the island. For runaway slaves stayed, joining what eventually became two autonomous and armed Maroon communities. These should be seen as internal, yet independent African (Caribbean) nations; it is as independent nations within Jamaica that the military government had to treat the Maroons in order to manage their threat to its sovereignty.

The treaties made with Cudjoe's Leeward and then with Quao's Windward Maroons ensured Maroon autonomy but only at the price of their complicity with the colonial government for whom, from thenceforth, they served as police and militia.[59] From this point, the Maroons occupy a more ambiguous relationship both to the white colonials and to the population of enslaved Africans, with whom they maintained close contact. Sometimes, the Maroons acted in concert with the colonists to quell revolt, as in Tacky's rebellion of 1760; at other times they were suspected as instigators of revolt. At least two things seem clear: the Maroons were never completely trusted by the colonials, and they formulated and followed their own policies in the interests of their own nations. In doing so, they straddled the divide between law and outlaw, at least as it was defined from a colonialist perspective.

In their relation to the slave population, there is a record of resentment but also of inspiration and emulation.[60] Even as the Maroons were gaining a livelihood as bounty hunters and engaging with the colonial militia in the crushing of Tacky's revolt, they continue to provide the rebel slaves with models and motives of rebellion. Thistlewood notes in his entry for August 1, 1760: "The rebels give out they will kill all the Negroes they can, and as soon as dry weather comes fire all the plantations they can, till they force the whites to give them free like Cudjoe's Negroes."[61] As Patterson suggests, "All sustained slave revolts must acquire a Maroon dimension since the only way in which a slave population can compensate for the inevitably superior military might of their masters is to resort to guerrilla warfare with all its implications of flight, strategic retreat to secret hideouts, and ambush."[62] In relation to the power hierarchy structuring the master/slave duality, the Maroons occupy a role, as bounty hunters and as symbols of African freedom, that simultaneously reinforces and threatens colonial tenure. As long as the Maroons present visible, socially viable evidence of freedoms denied to other Africans, this threat cannot be completely controlled by the colonial treaties that recognize the two Maroon nations in an effort not to condone African liberty but to appropriate it in ways that inhibit its extension. Conversely, Maroon complicity with colonial rule threatens the equilibrium of their status as exemplars of African freedom.

The Maroon capitulation to terms that protected colonial interests might itself be viewed as a kind of strategic retreat, one that in turn guaranteed their autonomy and thus their heroic status as exceptions to a history of slavery. What has counted for every generation of freedom fighters from the eighteenth century to the present is the Maroons' independence from plantation slavery and colonial assimilation; their complicity with the colonial establishment is not overlooked so much as understood as a price extorted from them. Nanny, leader of the Leeward Maroons, and Cudjoe, of the Windward, head a pantheon of Jamaican national heroes that includes Sam Sharpe, Marcus Garvey, and Bob Marley as well. To this day, Maroon ancestry confers a prestigious, "noble" status; for example, the Maroon ancestry of contemporary reggae star Buju Banton is often noted as a factor in his phenomenal success and recent conversion to Rastafarianism.[63]

In contemporary Caribbean discourse, marronage has become a name for all sorts of preservative "retreats to secret hideouts" undertaken by African-diasporic people as they try to sustain lives apart from the pressures of exploitation and domination. The progressive memory of an Africa where past meets future in a time looped outside of bondage creates retreats and sites of resistance that may be cultural, spiritual, and symbolic. Developing an Akan-dominated culture alongside, but fairly distinct from, that of the slaves, the whites, and the free people of color, the Maroons are respected by contemporary progressive thinkers for their preservation not only of freedom but of traditional forms of language, dance and music, folklore, agriculture, social organization, and spirituality.

Marronage includes all those ways in which that which is seen as African survives the corrupting degradation of colonial and postcolonial domination by the Babylon of economic, ecological, and social exploitation.[64] No longer confined to the Maroon communities proper, marronage refers to the persistence of Afro-creole elements in society at large "in the Africanization of Christianity . . . in Garveyism . . . in the Rastafari movement . . . the Black Power movement of the 60s, and in the continuing African forms of marketing habits, family patterns, speech (dialect), magic-medicine (*obeah*) and religious practices: po/

kumina, vodun, shango, etc."[65] The Maroons become repositories for the notion that freedom is a black thing.

Worlds Apart: The Ship and the Plantation

Although not as directly central to political and cultural activism, piracy has become significant in academic discourses of resistance and liberation in ways somewhat analogous to those forms that the notion of marronage takes in African-diasporic thought. Like the intellectuals working with the idea of marronage, contemporary Anglo-American historians of pirates do their thinking in progressive traditions concerned with liberation politics. The case for radical piracy is usually made along three lines: piracy as a refusal of the labor discipline employed by the merchant navy; pirate societies as structurally democratic and egalitarian; and piracy as a haven for outlaw personal identities.[66] Most recently Peter Linebaugh and Marcus Rediker have included pirates in their archaeology of the "hidden history of the Revolutionary Atlantic," demonstrating the trans-Atlantic circulation among piratical rationales and strategies and those foundational to the establishment of organized labor resistance and political revolt.[67]

The notion of piracy as an outlaw version of the refusal of the forms of labor peculiar to England's merchant navy links piracy strongly to marronage and its own refusal of the labor on offer in that other total institution—the plantation.[68] Connections between these pirates and Maroons are constituted by the analogous cultural status of each, both in relation to their legitimate cousins, the merchant navy and the plantation, and by the contiguous relations of all four societies—legal ship and outlaw pirate, plantation slave and independent Maroon—to England and notions of civilized English society. Both the sailor and the slave occupy an outsider status that may fuse easily with the outlaw status of the pirate and Maroon. The alterity so ideologically useful in the cultural discursive constitution of piracy and marronage needs to be seen in connection with the position of difference, often understood as deficiency and deviancy, occupied by all ship and all slave societies in the eighteenth century. As outsiders, both ship and slave societies develop sociocultural features peculiar to themselves—ones that, in both cases, can be partially understood under the rubric of creolized cultural formation.

Not only the plantation factories, with first their indentured and then enslaved populations, but also the maritime forces that transported the products of the plantations and supplied and protected them, depended on labor recruitment and labor discipline notorious for brutality. Impressment, the legal kidnapping practiced by the Royal Navy, was common, and discipline on board was notoriously severe. In *The Adventures of Roderick Random*, Tobias Smollett, drawing on his own memories, paints a hellish picture of maritime service in the West Indies. From the press gang that imprisons him on board to the shipwreck that casts him ashore, Roderick's stint at sea is a chronicle of savagery. Like that of many young men, his service is coerced, and, as Linebaugh notes, "fully incarcerated": "After an obstinate engagement [with the press gang], in which I received a large wound on the head, and another on my left cheek, I was disarmed, taken prisoner and carried on board a pressing tender."[69] The harshness of the sailor's life, whether in the merchant or military navy, and its proximity to that of the criminal prisoner, is witnessed in Samuel Johnson's widely quoted opinion: "No man will be a sailor who has contrivance enough to get himself into a jail; for being in a ship is being in a jail, with the chance of being drowned."[70]

As Marcus Rediker argues, within the merchant navy, life for the sailor became increasingly brutal as the eighteenth century wore on. With the expansion and increased importance of colonial trade in the seventeenth and eighteenth centuries, the earlier shipboard practice of profit sharing was replaced by wage labor, and discipline grew more desperately severe.[71] Eighteenth-century ships were floating factories served by the (often resistant) wage labor of seamen whose "experience pointed in many ways toward the Industrial Revolution."[72] Pirates, on the other hand, reject their status as wage laborers in favor of a more egalitarian, "pre-capitalist" allocation of profit through the shares system and of a more democratic structure of ship government.[73] The articles documented in the account "Of Captain Bartholomew Roberts" assume the share system and stipulate the egalitarianism and collectivism on which Rediker bases his arguments:

> Every Man has a Vote in Affairs of Moment; Has equal Title to the fresh provisions, or strong Liquors, at any Time Seized. . . . Every Man to be called fairly in Turn, by List, on board of Prizes, because, (over and above their proper Share) they were on these Occasions allowed a Shift of Cloaths. . . . No Man to talk of breaking up their Way of Living, till each had shared a 1000 £. If in order to [do] this, any Man should lose a limb . . . he was to have 800 Dollars, out of the publick Stock, and for lesser Hurts, proportionably.[74]

Defying almost all the social institutions of their day, pirates formed the most radical sect of a group of seamen whose labor militancy, as Rediker demonstrates, was finely honed in these floating factories. Accordingly, pirate societies have been heralded by recent historians as bastions of earlier, more egalitarian forms of profit distribution and social relations that industrial capitalism was in the process of displacing.

But while pirates refused the economic and social conditions of the merchant navy, they were, in the main, trained in that institution, and their cultural situation is significantly similar to that of any ship society. Just as the Maroons share many features of the Afro-creole slave society, which they refused yet with which they were in constant, if sometimes oppositional, contact, so the pirates' demographic identity, language, way of life, and, to some degree, ethos, is contiguous with that of the general body of seamen. Both Maroons and pirates represent, in militant and extreme forms, features of resistance and alterity that mark early modern slave societies and ship societies more generally. In what follows, I point to a few large sociocultural features that plantation slave and ship societies, and Maroon and pirate societies as well, share in common.

Both the ship and the West Indian plantation were economically central but culturally alien to England. Pirate and Maroon societies were no less central, sometimes as armed threat, other times as armed allies, to English domination, even while they were even more completely outlandish. The world of the ship, like that of the West Indian plantation, was a "world apart," foreign and often incomprehensible to outsiders.[75] When challenged by a dinner companion with the observation, "We find people fond of being sailors," Dr. Johnson confesses his complete bewilderment: "I cannot account for that, any more than I can account for other strange perversions of imagination."[76] Describing the sailor communities of Wapping and Rotherhithe, John Fielding feels that he is "in another country," so "peculiar" are the sailors' "manner of living, speaking, acting, dressing, and behaving": "The seamen here are a generation differing from all the world."[77] Acclimation to life in this other country, like acclimation to life on the plantation (for blacks and whites alike), required a period of seasoning during which the initiate became accustomed to a new language; new and typically severe forms of labor discipline; a new, usually inadequate and distasteful diet; and new sets of social and labor relations—all peculiar to the floating world.

Plantation and ship societies altered all who entered them, white plantation dweller as well as black slave, ship's captain as well as common sailor, but the brutality of discipline and the violence of sociocultural alienation fell most heavily on the laboring masses, the slaves and the sailors. While the ship's mobility contrasts with stationary life on the plantation, once on board, the sailor, like the African slave, lived in a state of "virtual incarceration," isolated from all that had been familiar.[78] Both workers, sailor and slave, had to be "socialized anew." This process worked to strip the sailor "of previous attachments to local and regional cultures and ways of speaking," just as did slave seasoning.[79] The hard lessons of labor on board, as on the plantation, were taught with the whip. The violence of the slave driver is matched with that of the sea captain: both attempted to extract absolute discipline in a situation whose very isolation removed this discipline from conventional checks and limits. Authority was personal and absolute in both situations; the justice and severity of discipline wavered erratically with the temper of the captain or the overseer. Justifications for brutality in both cases came in assertions of the intractable nature of the sailor or slave, and often of their status as lesser humans whose natural insensibility rendered them immune to all but the grossest discipline: "Many seamen are of that lazy idle temper, that, let them alone and they never care for doing anything they should do, and when they do anything it is with a grumbling unwilling mind, so that they must be drove to it."[80]

With the logic of ethnocentrism, Henry Fielding makes difference hierarchical; the sailors, he marvels, "seem to glory in the language and behavior of savages" and to violate "the common bonds of humanity."[81] So in response to Boswell's assertion that "sailors are happy," Johnson asserts: "They are happy as brutes are happy, with a piece of fresh meat,—with the grossest sensuality."[82] Taken captive by the notorious Captain Low's pirate crew, Captain George Roberts describes their deportment: "In this Manner they pass'd the Time away, drinking and carousing merrily, both before and after Dinner, which they eat in a very disorderly Manner, more like a Kennel of Hounds, than like Men."[83] As members of a culturally distinct and despised underclass, sailors acquire an aura of bestial alterity that, again, parallels that often attributed to African slaves. Edward Long, influential lobbyist for the planters' interests, speaks at length of the African natural character—"brutish, ignorant, idle, crafty . . . lazy, thievish"—and the African natural body—insensate and only responsive to the "grossest" corporeal impressions, such as, one assumes, those bestowed on them by the whips of the overseer.[84] Degraded by their subjection to savage forms of life and labor, both the black slave and the white sailor are represented as different and worse than other humans. In both cases, notions of historically acquired cultural difference (understood as deficiency) serve to justify forms of labor discipline peculiar to the institutions of early modern colonialism, and they slide in and out of notions of innate ontological status: ethnic ideas coast into racist ones, and class identity verges on caste status.

Linebaugh speculates on the possibility that Henry Fielding's allusion to "savages" is specifically to the African peoples with whom sailors had extensive contact—contact of a variety including, but not limited to, that of the master to his slave.[85] Such association would be a factor not only for those sailors working in the Guinea trade, but more generally in a business where blacks comprised, by some estimates, as much as a quarter of the labor force by the end of the eighteenth century.[86] That language is a site of the sailors' "savagery" may in itself imply that Fielding alludes to a specific sort of difference, one at once African and maritime. As Paul Gilroy emphasizes, the modern Atlantic constitutes a distinct zone of contact and cultural formation. The ship, that "living, micro-cultural, micro-political system in motion," is the chief means of communication in this zone, and for Gilroy, the central trope of this cultural site.[87] As the linguist J. L. Dillard has shown, the British ship had its own language, one it shared with the coastal regions of England, Africa, the Caribbean, and North America.[88]

The extensive contact among sailors and the African peoples they transported, worked with, and were in casual contact with, brought with it specific "exotic" or "savage" forms of trans-Atlantic language. Cultural and linguistic contact took place in and between such cosmopolitan polyglot harbors as London, Bridgeton, Kingston, Charleston, New Orleans, Boston, and Philadelphia and coastal African factory settlements such as Bonny, Whydah, Cabinda, and Goree. A contemporary cultural historian describes the linguistic situation in early eighteenth-century Jamaica as one "not of diglossia, triglossia, or even heteroglossia but of panglossia, a state of 'generalized multilingualism,'" from which Creole emerges as the primary, if despised, language of the island.[89] Communication in the pan-Atlantic world did not take place in standard English (or any European language), but rather in pidgins and Creoles concocted out of European and African languages. J. L. Dillard has documented how "the Maritime Pidgin English, transmitted to West Africans in the slave trade and heavily influenced by West African languages, became the English Creole of the plantations from Nova Scotia to Surinam."[90] Sailors, naturally, were among the largest groups of speakers of this maritime English: sailors, slaves, and those populations of whites who owned and were raised by slaves from whom they learned this language which set them off, to no advantage, from the English.[91]

Pirate's language is distinguishable from that of the generality of sailors mostly by its blasphemy and its self-naming practices that, like the skeletons and hourglasses on the Jolly Rogers, stressed the irreverent, oppositional, radically autonomous, do-or-die ethic that controlled pirate identity. Such an ethic is apparent in the names pirates gave their ships: *Batchelor's Delight, Liberty, Night Rambler, Queen Anne's Revenge, Cour Valant, Scowerer, Flying Dragon, Most Holy Trinity, Happy Delivery, Bravo, Black Joke,* and *Blessing.*"[92] The linguistic relationship between the Jamaican Maroons and the plantation slaves is more complex. The first Maroons were probably bilingual speakers of Spanish and either a dominant African language (such as Twi-Asante) or a variety of African languages. Barbara Kopytoff suggests that "a common African language may have provided the first means of communication between Spanish and English Maroons."[93] Or perhaps they were trilingual. Layering the mix, Barbara Lalla and Jean D'Costa emphasize the contact between the Spanish African population and the Arawaks who originally occupied the island and thus the role the Maroons play as "a link both with their own African traditions and the language [Taino] and customs of the peoples [the Arawaks] with whom they had mixed."[94] By the eighteenth century, evidence from white commentators shows that the Maroons spoke the English Creole of the island, but they may have also retained strong Spanish and African elements in what could have been a distinct Creole of their own.[95] Additionally, into the twentieth century, alongside various forms of English (from Creole to standard) the Maroons maintained an Akan language, Twi-Asante (Coromantee), though finally only in the most ritualized contexts.[96] And while it seems proper to emphasize the distinct "cultural and linguistic heritage" of the Maroons, it is also clear from their ongoing contacts with whites and blacks that, alongside this distinct heritage, they shared the island's Creole.[97]

Jah Is in the Interstices

The linguistic position of the Maroons is indicative of their cultural position in relation to Jamaican society more generally, one that, like that of the twentieth-century Rastafarians, is "interstitial" rather than fully "marginal," to adopt the terms employed by Richard Burton in his recent analysis of Caribbean cultural politics and performance.[98] For Burton, the degree to which Rastafarian cultural forms are generated from within the dominant culture they oppose forecloses their hold on the locus of pure marginality whence, in his view, true resistance must originate. Following a dubiously derived and applied distinction between, on the one hand, resistance emanating from a place of pure alterity, and, on the other, opposition generated from within the culture it counters, Burton strait-jackets his reading of cultural formations with binary categories that prohibit the very movements between law and outlaw, inside and outside, complicity and resistance that the history of cultural formation in the Caribbean witnesses.[99] Contrary to Burton, I argue that this position complicates, but does not invalidate, the nature of the opposition and resistance both the Maroons and the Rastafarians present to that society. Indeed, rather than viewing this lack of pure marginality as an enervation of sociocultural force, as does Burton, it may be viewed as a feature of currency and power, if one purchased at the price of impurity and apparent contradiction. The contradiction is an easy one, a product of the way the Maroons, and now the Rastafarians, are valued and value themselves as inheritors and preservers of distinct—one is tempted to say "pure"—African cultural forms. In their rejection of the "Babylon" of western European sociocultural and political life, in their focus on African inheritance, and in their bid for cultural distinction—and one is correct to say for cultural "purity"—the Rastafarians self-consciously engage in the fostering of distinct, ideologically charged forms of language, cuisine, dress, and living habits styled in relation to notions of African roots and authenticity.

But Rastafarian societies, like those of the Maroons, are Afro-*creole* cultural formations, although certainly ones that distinguish themselves—as more purely African—from other Afro-creole societies. Accordingly, Rastatalk is a subdialect of the English Creole of Jamaica. It certainly does, as Burton claims, simultaneously invoke and subvert the language of Babylon, creating distinctions inseparable from the objects it disowns. But to call this relationship "parasitic," and to assert, as he does, that "because their diet, dress, hairstyles, language and ultimately their faith are in no way 'African' but are all oppositional products of the very 'shitstem' they hate, every protestation or would-be expression of Africanness is of necessity self-deconstructive and merely proves and reinforces their actual non-Africanness" abandons the very logic of creolization that the critic invokes in his dismissal.[100]

Any evaluation of the Rastafarians confronts the distinctly modern (both early and late) paradox that structures New World cultural formations, necessarily hybrid and creolized, centered on a notion of Africa as their site of unity and pure origin. The meaning of this paradox is not the self-negating logic of those cultures but, perhaps primarily, the assertion of a creolized consciousness that, painfully alive to the involuntary and exploitative context in which Caribbean cultural hybridity has taken place, seeks a different site for cultural regeneration, one defined in different terms, those of unity, purity, and autonomy. This place is called Africa. In cultural-symbolic terms, what modern "Africa" consists of is in part a product of what Afro-creole cultures have made it. On the one hand, it is simply counterfactual to deny the persistence of African-based cultural forms in the New World. On the other, it is mistaken to view the circuits of cultural formation as unidirectional: African cultures play a part in those of the New World; in return, cultures of the New World have formulated notions of the Old World in ways that are distinctly creole.[101] Since one of the most widespread and, in the context of slavery, most precious, of African-derived notions has always been the promise of a return to Guinea, to Africa, the very site and nature of this place "Africa" has been open, for four hundred years, to New World production. Africa is one foundational site of the transfigurative utopian conceptions that, as Gilroy puts it, construct "both an imaginary anti-modern past and a postmodern yet-to-come."[102]

To admit that, in their creolized production and invocations of Africa, the Rastafarians confront "an aporia inseparable from the fact of being Afro-creole, not African" should not, as it seems to with Burton, discount the value and efficiency of their culture.[103] Such an invocation of Africa is common to Afro-creole cultures; for an Afro-creolist to discount it as a violation of the purity of his paradigm of hybridity seems absurd indeed. Burton wants a hybridity as pure as the Africa he rejects. And here we are in the tiresomely predictable deconstructive vortex that so often surrounds issues of authenticity and essentialism, whether they have as their content ethnicity or gender or meaning itself.

Whereas a certain class of cultural critics devoted to the letter, if not the spirit, of hybridity could invalidate the Maroons as well as the Rastafarians for their impure, "interstitial" relation to the society they oppose, the cultural-political use of both groups in Jamaica has more often been a matter of inclusion, sometimes exploitative, than dismissive exclusion. The cultural symbols of the Maroons became fused with the middle-class and university-based Black Power movement led by Walter Rodney and given voice in a daily newspaper called *Abeng*, after the famous Maroon horn.[104] They were also co-opted, via their connection with the Rastafarians and reggae music, by the JNP in their campaigns of the 1970s and 80s.[105] While the clarity of eighteenth-century Maroon resistance may seem somewhat clouded by their complicity with slave labor discipline, the authenticity of these twentieth-century Afrocentric symbols of resistance may seem somewhat compromised by their exploitation by a dominantly bourgeois political party in its efforts to gain the allegiance of underclass sufferers. The difference between these two modes of "compromise" is that the first served the interests of survival and autonomy for a people whose existence was otherwise threatened with enslavement, while the latter served primarily the interests of those whose position of political power and social privilege is maintained through subordinate peoples.

Insofar as the rich and largely independently developed cultural forms of these peoples are exploited by dominant power groups who do not give back in return the kinds of economic and social justice sought by the underclass, this, in the Jamaican context, largely political appropriation of Afro-creole culture and Afrocentric symbols and slogans by the Jamaican ruling elite represents its own kind of theft, even piracy. With well-justified skepticism, Peter Tosh, as we have seen, signals his ambivalence about appearing on stage with, and in some sense for the benefit of, Seaga and Manley: "I man never love come in it."[106]

The culturally and ethically "compromised" position of both the pirates and the Maroons needs to be acknowledged, not in order to discredit the sociocultural efficacy of these groups, but in order to appreciate how their situation speaks to contradictions critical to processes of cultural formation in the English-speaking Caribbean. Parasitic on the very merchant navy they refused, pirates expose, even as they mimic, the aggressive self-assertion and ruthless greed of early modern global capitalism.[107] Acting as bounty hunters and police for the colonial military machine they had forced to recognize their own autonomy, the Maroons engender, even as they jeopardize, a notion of African freedom in the New World that cannot be fully contained within the limits of its enabling conditions.

Combating, in relatively peaceful and ideologically articulate ways, the effects of a cultural hybridity that threatens the remembrance of the very historical processes that define the matrix of its generation, the Rastafarians lay claim to an alternative site of roots purity where conceptions of time, knowledge, history, utopia, and salvation are developed as fundamental and resilient New World inheritances from African cultures. While ideologically centered in that utopian place called Africa, the significance, dissemination, and efficacy of these concepts is inseparable from their wider diasporic development. That such cultural riches are interstitial rather than fully marginal to society is a gift, not a liability.

Serving as security forces for a political machine they threaten to dismantle, contemporary West Indian gangs appropriate traditions of violent domination in ways that articulate the intimacy between African-diasporic and European cultural memory in the Caribbean and that seek to undo the inequities that are recalled in the very terms of their redress. The trade-off that these gangs negotiate with political parties—their armed "protection" in return for territorial control—recalls not only the tactics of the early modern pirates but also of the Maroons. Bound to political parties in death-sealed pacts that violate political process to such a degree that their actions seem drained of all but criminal motives and meanings, these subcultural criminal gangs challenge intellectuals trying to articulate the relations between politics and criminality, social protest and antisocial behavior, transgression and subversion, personal assertion and social amelioration. The articulation of these relations has proved extremely fruitful for both early modern and contemporary critical studies, for it has necessitated the examination of some of our more powerful ideological investments, whether they be in law and order or in radical politics. In the next and final chapter, we see how the radical political and social critic William Godwin uses the discourses of criminality to articulate these problems of complicity and resistance as he experienced them operating in the late eighteenth-century context of revolution and reaction.

CHAPTER FIVE

Privacy and Ideology

Elite Male Crime in Burney's *Evelina* and Godwin's *Caleb Williams*

In chapter 1 I looked at the intimacy of the discourses of criminality and of gentility in Daniel Defoe's *Colonel Jack,* and in chapter 3 at how these work in James Boswell's self-representation in his *London Journal.* In this last chapter, with Frances Burney's *Evelina* and William Godwin's *Caleb Williams,* I turn again to autobiographical writing and the issues of self-fashioning and subjectivity it foregrounds. Specifically, I examine how the masculine types that are the focus of this study embody competing ideologies of gender, authority, and subjectivity that both Burney and Godwin exploit as they forward their very different critiques of aristocratic privilege. By pairing these novels, this chapter returns to the two concerns whose synthesis shapes this study as a whole: the history of manners (*Evelina*) and the history of radicalism and dissent (*Caleb Williams*). Doing this highlights the mutually constitutive role that the conventional eighteenth-century discourses of masculine prestige and of criminality play in both texts.

Frances Burney's female novel of manners, *Evelina* (1778), is shot through with violence perpetrated by stereotypical characters—the rake, the gentleman highwayman, the brutal ship's captain—familiar in literature since the seventeenth century. Focusing on Burney's representation of elite male criminality and its counterpoint, ideal gentlemanly sensibility, this chapter revisits these guiding figures and concepts in ways that reveal some implications for *feminine* subjectivity and sociocultural power. I argue that this novel undertakes a reassessment of the nature and effects of such criminality from a point of view that assesses damage and reparation not through juridical or religious discourses but through the private discourse of sensibility. Lord Orville, the Grandisonian perfect gentleman, embodies the virtues enshrined in this discourse and thus provides the ideal ethical and emotional complement for Burney's heroine. As a model of masculine subjectivity, Orville represents the modern gentleman, not as feminized (like the fop), but as a privatized individual. Finally, the revisions of patriarchal power in *Evelina* depend on the absolute authority of the sentimental subject.

Using the conventional figure of the gentleman criminal, Godwin's *Caleb Williams* (1794) reorients the concepts and themes isolated by this study from the context of seventeenth-century revolutionary England to that of the French Revolution in the 1790s. Aligning his character of the ideal gentleman criminal, Falkland, with the Grandisonian model, Godwin insists on the incapacity of even the most perfect gentlemanly character to resist the lethal demands of the aristocratic ideology that is exposed as the matrix of both its virtues and its criminality. Godwin's indictment of aristocratic ideology extends to encompass non-elite subjects through an exploration of the ruinous effects on them of two of its central institutions: honor and patronage. Like Burney, who seeks reparation for elite male crime not in the judicial realm but rather in the private affective realm of sensibility, Godwin also dismisses the capacities of the law to correct injustice, but he locates any possible recognition of truthfulness and equity in a political awakening possible only outside the discourses of the novel itself, including the discourse of sensibility so privileged in Burney's text.

The discussions of *Evelina* and of *Caleb Williams* here are offered as case studies that reveal how the densely interwoven discourses of masculine prestige and criminality continue to operate throughout the eighteenth century in novelistic discourse. This reading of both of these well-known texts emphasizes, though more emphatically in *Caleb Williams*, their continuity with earlier novelistic "precursor" forms such as the criminal biography and thus shows the maintenance of this discursive strand well beyond its contribution to the early novelistic essays of Daniel Defoe. The pairing of these two texts, furthermore, shows how the juxtaposed figure of the criminal gentleman addresses a shared set of problems in both and how each offers a solution that throws the other into high relief: *Evelina* by excavating some newly privatized ground of reformative authority on the very site of the ideology whose corruptions she deplores; *Caleb Williams* by insisting on an evacuation of the site itself.

Mending Manners

Much as James Boswell's *London Journal* chronicles a constellation of current masculine types available as emulative models for a young, up-and-coming man in 1762–63, so Burney's first novel, *Evelina*, narrates how in the late 1770s a related set of masculine characters interact with the social and personal identity of a young woman emerging into the wider world.[1] Thus this much-studied text provides a highly recognizable instance of how these male stereotypes are imbricated not only, as with Boswell's journal, with masculine but also with feminine subjectivity as it is formulated and represented in the last half of the eighteenth century. Preoccupied with the abuses and reform of elite patriarchal privilege, Burney's novel participates in the critique of aristocracy underway since the seventeenth century.[2] In *Evelina* patriarchal dereliction and its redemption take narrative shape in the background story that generates the paternity plot of the novel.[3] Evelina's father, Sir John Belmont, had eloped with and secretly married her mother, Caroline Evelyn. Then, disappointed with his wife's fortune, Belmont denied the marriage and suppressed the fact of his paternity, leaving Caroline Evelyn to die in childbirth and the child, Evelina, to be raised by an old family friend, Arthur Villars. The fact of her public nonrelation to her father vexes Evelina's attempts to secure a social identity and tests to its limits the capacities of her private character.[4] Revolving its heroine through its set of masculine social stereotypes and their plots, the novel forwards nothing more insistently than the fact of female vulnerability to male power.

The cast of male characters we meet in *Evelina* are familiar from a literary history going back to the Restoration: the society fop, Mr. Lovel; the predatory rake, Sir Clement Willoughby; the gruff, indeed brutal sailor, Captain Mirvan; the excruciatingly gauche Cits, the Branghtons; the aspiring city "gentleman," Mr. Smith; the sleazy libertine, Lord Merton; the melodramatic, romantic poet, Macartney; and the perfect gentleman, Lord Orville. Among these we find versions of the criminal stereotypes that are the primary focus of this study: the rake Sir Clement, who threatens Evelina with rape on a number of occasions; Lord Merton, who, like Sir Clement, menaces her sexually; Captain Mirvan with Sir Clement, who, as "gentlemen highwaymen," act out a "frolick" against Evelina and her grandmother, Madame Duval; and finally, the young Macartney, who, in desperate straits, gets a set of pistols and makes a plan to go on the highway himself. While Captain Mirvan and Sir Clement pursue their "frolick" as a practical joke, Macartney, until Evelina rescues him from his doom, acts in deadly earnest. Indeed, Macartney has a number of narrow escapes, not only from highway robbery but also from the more primal, intimate, and familial crimes of incest, parricide, and suicide. The systematic violation of self and family that Macartney courts dramatizes the criminal effects of patriarchal corruption he and his half-sister Evelina are, quite literally, heir to.[5]

Evelina's own father, Sir Belmont, must take his place next to Lord Merton and

Sir Clement in the text's line-up of criminal rakes. His breach of his marriage vows and abdication of familial responsibility unwittingly generate Macartney's brushes with incest and parricide as well as Evelina's status as an apparent bastard, the foundational crisis of the novel. The narrative of *Evelina*, as of *Colonel Jack*, originates in elite sexual crime, here Sir Belmont's. But familial corrosion in Evelina's case is traced back two generations to her grandfather's ruinous marriage to the tavern maid we meet as Madame Duval, and it threatens to persist as the heroine must repeatedly ward off the advances of rakes such as Sir Clement who would destroy her as Sir Belmont did her mother.

The privileges and abuses of elite masculinity, expressed often in the conventional juxtaposition of the criminal and the gentleman, are central issues in Burney's novel, as they are in Boswell's journal and Defoe's fictional autobiography. However, here these are presented, not in the frame of a would-be gentleman's self-advancement, but in that of a young girl's attempt to preserve and assert her private virtues, her personal identity, within a field of characters and conventions that more frequently promise to compromise than to defend her integrity. Unlike Colonel Jack, although like him denied access to her paternity, Evelina does know who her father is. Again unlike Colonel Jack, who struggles with the concept of "the perfect gentleman," Evelina knows what genteel femininity—"being a lady"—is, and in perfect complementary fashion, she learns to recognize who is and who is not the perfect gentleman. So while the difficulties Evelina undergoes in securing her purchase on a socially legitimated identity form the content of the novel, her own private possession of virtuous, genteel femininity is never in question. Her character "develops" in that she acquires a mastery of manners that allows her both to represent and to protect her own virtue.

Critics have long noted in *Evelina* an apparent tonal and generic juxtaposition between, on the one hand, the "feminine," inwardly reflective, and emotionally attuned world of self and sensibility employed in Evelina's letters, and, on the other hand, the "masculine," often violently farcical episodes exploding in the social world these letters narrate.[6] This juxtaposition highlights an experiential dissonance between the heroine's interior life and the often emotionally disruptive public world peopled and actuated by the most stereotypical of characters and situations. It produces an ethical divide between a sometimes nightmarish world of seemingly senseless and, for women, often disempowering, sociocultural conventions, on the one hand, and, on the other, an interior world of sensibility and virtue that struggles through an evolving discourse of manners to find external social expression. This private world of finer feelings authenticates the manners through which the novel's sympathetic characters communicate their mutual recognition as members, alongside Evelina herself, of what Barbara Zonitch has termed a "neo-aristocracy of manners." As Zonitch emphasizes, "manners" in *Evelina,* as more generally, "are affiliated with forms of power; they are part of an elaborate code that upholds prevailing ideologies." In *Evelina,* good manners accomplish through the discourse of sensibility the goals of the modern ideology of complementary polarized sexual difference. It is through these manners, especially as they are enacted by the paragon male figure, Lord Orville, that *Evelina* forwards its reformulation of patriarchal authority in what Zonitch calls a "new bourgeois patriarchy."[7]

Chief representative of this new bourgeois patriarchy is the emphatically aristocratic Lord Orville. Zonitch reads Orville as a "*neo*-aristocrat," Burney's reformative solution to the corruptions of elite masculinity figured in Sir Belmont, Sir Clement Willoughby, and Lord Merton. Lord Orville might be called a perfect "bourgeois" gentleman because, unlike these other aristocrats, he does not presume on his elite status to secure the rights, powers, and distinctions that constitute prestige. Rather than assert his own preeminence, Lord Orville attends to others: "His manners are so elegant, so gentle, so unassuming, that they at once engage esteem, and diffuse complacence. Far from being indolently satisfied with his own accomplishments . . . he is most assiduously attentive to please and to serve all" (72). In a mode accessible to all gentleman and ladies regardless of inherited rank, Lord Orville integrates the operation of social power as manners with the expression of sensibility as benevolent sympathy with, rather than dominance over, others. The legitimating criteria for membership in this "neo-aristocracy" is the possession, not of inherited honors, or birth, but of authentic sensibility, cultivated and represented within refined, almost transparent social manners and recognizable to others with comparable sentimental endowments. Because of the grounding of these truly gracious manners in the subjective realm of sentiment, I would term the ideological revision accomplished in *Evelina* a "new aristocracy of sensibility" rather than, as Zonitch does, a "new aristocracy of manners."

In *Evelina,* the conventional aristocratic presumption that the fact of status confers worth and thus licenses will is expressed in the treacherous audacity, elaborate duplicity, criminal neglect, and callous imperiousness of its libertine characters. As discussed below, even where embellished by the most polished gallantry, such unfeeling manners perpetrate violence, often against women, and are allied with the brutal boorishness of a Captain Mirvan. Importantly, treacherously polite manners such as those of Sir Clement work, as publicly and ostentatiously as possible, to render motives opaque, to discount the agency and overwhelm the interests of their object: they are confusing and hard to read. In contrast, the authentically gracious address of a Lord Orville strives, with all possible delicacy and discretion, to clearly communicate desires, to enhance the agency and honor the interests of its object. Such manners are legible and reassuring. Thus, in Evelina's comparison:

> I could not but remark the striking difference of *his* [Sir Clement Willoughby's] attention, and that of Lord Orville: the latter has such gentleness of manners, such delicacy of conduct, and an air so respectful, that, when he flatters most, he never distresses, and when he most confers honour, appears to receive it! The former *obtrudes* his attention and *forces* mine; it is so pointed, that it always confuses me, and so public, that it attracts general notice. (330)

In this way, true benevolence and virtue may find social and textual representation in manners, and manners, where sensibly performed and understood, may supply the same kind of congruence between external and internal, appearance and truth, secured by traditional aristocratic ideology with its promise that "what could be seen on the outside and in public—rank, regalia, personal display, even refined complexion—was a dependable sign of internal and 'private' value."[8] Oriented toward a bourgeois pedagogy of self-improvement that it shares with conduct literature, *Evelina* represents not so much the female subject's cultivation of virtue as her mastery of the signs of its representation. It shows how Evelina learns to read manners so acutely that finally, as in this comparison of Sir Clement and Lord Orville, she can transparently recognize virtue and see how it inheres in sensibility rather than rank. That the ideal embodiment of this virtue is also a peer conforms to the status register of Burney's critique of elite male privilege that both exposes its abuses and imagines the nature of its reform: just as *Sir* Belmont, *Sir* Clement Willoughby, and *Lord* Merton personify abuse, so *Lord* Orville personifies the corresponding redemption.

Evelina, then, envisions a reformative restoration of (neo)aristocratic privilege by figuring the nature of patriarchal abuse as the violation, and its reform as the instantiation, of that inward arena of sensibility constitutive of authentic worth and selfhood. Drawing on a tradition of female ethical subjectivity generated in response to "outward injustice," *Evelina* realizes the absolute authority of this realm of sensibility by endowing it with powers of discipline and reform that supercede both judicial authority and the traditional laws of aristocratic honor.[9] The objects of admonition and reform take shape in a set of conventional male transgressions—the duel, the robbery on the highway, the sexual predation of the rake—that, as I have argued throughout, participate in a residual and devolved absolutism of individual sovereignty challenged by the critique of aristocratic ideology.[10]

Whereas the subjectivity represented in Boswell's *London Journal* remains, sometimes guiltily, invested in the masculine prestige accompanying outlaw figures even as it also affiliates with morally incongruent types, especially the Spectatoresque Man of Letters, things are more ethically straightforward in *Evelina*. The heroine's personal integrity may be under siege, but it is not internally overwrought by ethically polar allegiances; consequently, personal subjectivity enjoys greater reliability and authority here.[11] In relation to the notion of devolved absolutism, *Evelina* negotiates the displacement of hierarchically invested absolute individualism, expressed by figures such as the rake and the highwayman, by the absolute sentimental subject. In order to examine how the novel represents this confrontation between residual aristocratic absolutism on the one hand, and modern sentimental subjective absolutism on the other, we begin with an assault on the highway perpetrated by two gentlemen, Sir Clement Willoughby and Captain Mirvan, against Evelina and her grandmother, Madame Duval.

The Gallant and the Lout: Gentlemen Highwaymen at Howard Grove

At the beginning of the second volume of *Evelina*, the eponymous heroine returns to Howard Grove from London with the Mirvan family. Much to Evelina's mortification, they are accompanied by her vulgar grandmother, Madame Duval, whom they have met by chance in London. Although English by birth, Duval, having lived for decades in Paris, has adopted ostentatiously French manners, morals, language, and national chauvinism. Her showy Gallic and lower-class English traits meet in a kind of hybrid cultural identity that highlights the worst of both worlds. Throughout the novel she and Captain Mirvan, who has recently returned from a seven-year stint at sea, harass each other and everyone around them with their cultural combat—Duval fervently defending the greater refinement, gallantry, and politesse of the French character against Mirvan's advocacy of a hyperbolically masculine, staunch, blunt "Englishness." Having fought the French at sea for seven years, the captain brings the war home with him. Rude, bigoted, personally offensive, and verbally and emotionally violent, Duval and Mirvan are each as bad as the other; their presence on the country estate, Evelina remarks, has "ruined Howard Grove" (117).

Holding Evelina ransom to her inheritance, Madame Duval activates the additional humiliations of Evelina's financial dependence, of her dubious origins, and of her degrading connection to the Cit family, the Branghtons. "Surly, vulgar, and disagreeable," embodying the brutality, autocracy, and misogyny of ship society, Captain Mirvan exposes to a perplexed Evelina the stark fact of male domination, even over a wife infinitely his superior: "That kind and sweet-tempered woman, Mrs. Mirvan, deserved a better lot. I am amazed she would marry him" (38). Teasing Evelina and his own teenaged daughter, Maria, baiting Madame Duval, engineering practical "jokes" and intimidating his wife and mother-in-law into silent complicity, the captain entertains himself with his violence against others (38). His sole mode of relation to others is an uncontested domination secured through imperious command and violent practical "jokes." As Margaret Doody notes, Burney, in all her novels, is highly alive to the sadism and egotism of the practical joker: "A practical joker is a pain-bringer" who "for a moment seizes all the power present in the group."[12] In a novel preoccupied with modes of patriarchal powers and relations, Captain Mirvan embodies an absolutist mode of patriarchal autocracy, appalling in its primitive tyranny, unfettered and unclouded by any "affectations" of civility and politeness. Exploiting for all it is worth the naked sociocultural fact of male domination, Captain Mirvan lords it over Lady Howard's and Mrs. Mirvan's household.

Having married into this elite family, the captain disdains the frippery of its refined taste and manners even as he substantiates his own power by means of the connection. A sailor at heart, a "social buccaneer" and thus essentially a character all at sea domestically, Captain Mirvan supplies the portrait of what is most alien to that settlement most wished for by the heroine: a marriage and family secured by mutual and complementary interpersonal relations.[13] So " 'ultra-masculine' as to seem unmanly . . . [and] not quite human," Mirvan's gender status is compromised by the hyperbole of its assertion.[14] His masculinity is ship-bred, and rather than a constituent in a complementary coupling of male and female, it is autonomous and an anomaly in the polite domestic sphere. Where unable to exclude it, this kind of masculinity subjugates the feminine in all arenas of participation, sociocultural or domestic. Likewise, the very "Englishness" the captain chauvinistically promotes as unstintingly as his "manliness" is at least as equivocated by its pronounced maritime flavor. As a symptom of both his "unmanly" masculinity and his alien cultural identity, Captain Mirvan speaks a salty tongue foreign to Evelina, who has spent all her life in England, most of it under the tutelage of the pious Villars. "I can only give you," she apologizes in a letter to Villars, "a faint idea of his language; for almost every other word he utters, is accompanied by an oath. . . . And, besides, he makes use of a thousand sea-terms, which to me are quite unintelligible" (139).

But Evelina's misery at Howard Grove is only made complete when Captain Mirvan, the "social buccaneer," is joined by his partner in crime, the libertine rake Sir Clement Willoughby. Having all but abducted and raped Evelina in London, Sir Clement opportunistically cultivates a friendship with the captain in order to secure access to her in the country. While Sir Clement, in distinction to Captain Mirvan, cloaks his infamy in the conventions of libertine gallantry, Burney insists on the relation of both types as collaborators against marriage, the family, and the well-being of women. Both Sir Clement and Captain Mirvan abuse socioculturally protected aspects of patriarchal power in socioculturally conventional ways. So together, Sir Clement and Captain Mirvan execute their most egregious "frolick," an assault on Madame Duval and Evelina in the guise of gentlemen highwaymen. Pirate, rake, and highwayman come together here in an instance of male criminality redundant with stereotype and tradition.

This episode reiterates, from the point of view of its victims, the performative conventions of criminal masculinity examined in my earlier discussions of the rake, Mohock, and highwayman. Acting out their highwayman "frolick," Mirvan and Willoughby draw on the cultural template employed by Boswell when he casts himself as Macheath and stages his debauch in the London tavern as a scene from *Beggar's Opera.* In *Evelina,* the show has a dual lead; this isolates and defines two related sets of characteristics associated with the highwayman. On the one hand, armed and dangerous, the highwayman was feared for the very real physical violence he threatened; it is this aspect that Captain Mirvan embodies. That he restyles his atrocious violence against women as "sport" and "frolick" and enjoys it in elite male company, suggests that his is a species of sadistic pleasure also related to that of the Mohocks. On the other hand, traditions of the gentleman highwayman going back to the seventeenth century import to the character an erotic glamour and a reputation for polished gallantry; it is this aspect of the role that Willoughby plays to.[15] But, as Burney's narrative emphasizes, this duality defines a distinction without much difference: the discourse of gallantry employed by Sir Clement, no less than the brutal physical force preferred by Captain Mirvan, is designed to terrorize and violate women.

Having convinced Duval that her travel companion, Monsieur Du Bois, has been taken into custody on suspicion of "treasonable practices against the government" and is being held by a country magistrate, Mirvan and Willoughby mount their horses, mask their faces, and as "highway robbers" follow the carriage in which Madame Duval and Evelina are traveling to find Du Bois (141–48). They stop the carriage, Mirvan drags off Madame Duval, and Willoughby gets in beside Evelina. While Captain Mirvan is off in a ditch rattling Madame Duval's bones, Willoughby attempts once again, as he had done in his coach in London, to exploit Evelina's vulnerable isolation: "I could not refuse myself," he confesses to Evelina, "the so-long-wished-for happiness of speaking to you once more, without so many of—your *friends* to watch me" (146). "Tormented" by his sexual predation as much if not more than she would be by an actual robbery, Evelina begs Sir Clement to leave and is only released from his escalating importunities by the arrival of the other "highwayman," now finished with Madame Duval and eager to be off. "I've done for her!" Captain Mirvan exults to Sir Clement, "—the old buck is safe; but we must sheer off directly, or we shall be all aground" (146–47). A "social buccaneer indeed," Mirvan here speaks a ship's jargon—"sheer off," "be all aground"—that touches up his highwayman persona with piratical highlights. The "highwaymen" mount and depart. Evelina seeks her grandmother and finds her in a ditch tied to a tree, her dress in tatters, denuded of her hairpiece, bruised, shaken, enraged, and terrified.

Like Lovelace in *Clarissa,* like Sir Hargrave Pollexfen in *Sir Charles Grandison,* like himself earlier in *Evelina,* Sir Clement's criminal mode is primarily sexual and relies on the clichés of libertine erotic discourse. Captain Mirvan's mode of operation is not thus explicitly eroticized, but I believe is equally gendered and even sexualized. First and foremost, Mirvan wants to assert his brusquely English and bluntly masculine domination over the Frenchified and corrosively feminine Madame Duval. However, as the partnership of Mirvan and Willoughby suggests, and as I have noted in my earlier discussion of the rake and the Mohock, both forms of violence—sexual libertinism and loutish physical assault—are paired as a dual species of elite male criminality taking as its object the assertion of masculine prerogative through the violation of women. The differently pernicious characters of Captain Mirvan, with his thuggish brutality, and Sir Clement Willoughby, with his sinister gallantry, both find expression in the stereotypical guise of the highwayman.

Both modes of conduct are gendered, sexualized forms of sadism. Gina Campbell has noted how Willoughby perversely twists Evelina's language in a form of verbal sadism: "By insistently using the language of courtly love and responding to Evelina as though she too were using it, Willoughby seeks to pervert Evelina's own moral language." "No" can never mean no when constantly misread either as teasing coyness or as an expression of affected displeasure expressed only to petition even more assiduous erotic attentions. "The soft cover" of such language, as Doody says, "permits no lady to contradict or resent."[16] While Willoughby pursues his quarry with the weapons of gallantry, Mirvan's arsenal of insult and practical "jokes" comes out of an altogether more boorish bag of tricks. Nonetheless, the captain's magnetic repulsion from Madame Duval is, if anything, more passionately obsessive than Willoughby's attraction to Evelina. As the captain avers at the end of the novel, "She [Madame Duval] hit my fancy mightily; I never took so much to an old tabby before" (303). While Burney underscores the temperamental resemblance between Duval and Mirvan, she never suggests any affective correspondence between Evelina and Sir Clement. Outside of the libertine seduction plot that Sir Clement persistently intrudes, they have no relation. Unlike Marianne in Jane Austen's *Sense and Sensibility* (1811), Evelina never suffers and then overcomes an initial sympathetic attraction to her Willoughby; she finds his manners, address, and temperament unsettling and alien from the start.

Conversely, in their ferocity, coarseness, and absolute insensitivity, Captain Mirvan and Madame Duval are a perfect match, much more so than Captain Mirvan and his genteel, sweet-natured wife. Madame Duval demonstrates her identity with the captain nowhere better than in her invective against him: "She began, with great bitterness, to inveigh against the barbarous brutality of that fellow the Captain, and the horrible ill-breeding of the English in general. . . . (But nothing can be more strangely absurd, than to hear politeness recommended in language so repugnant as that of Madame Duval)" (67). Likewise, even as he mocks her, the Captain takes on Madame Duval's persona. At a public concert, Madame Duval loses herself in "extacies," and Captain Mirvan loses himself in a florid parody of her boisterous rapture, so, as in a feedback loop, one disturbance augments the other in a crescendo of commotion: "Madame Duval was in extacies; and the Captain flung himself into so many ridiculous distortions, by way of mimicking her, that he engaged the attention of all the company" (77).

The Captain's pleasure in Madame Duval is "insatiable. . . . He seems to have no delight but in terrifying or provoking her" (152). This insatiable appetite for sadistic pleasure takes on a sexual, if not conventionally erotic cast in a scene at Vauxhall that foreshadows the highway assault in the country. Enraged at the captain's mockery, Madame Duval, applying that celebrated Gallic gesture of contempt, spits in his face. In response, and just as he later does on the highway, Captain Mirvan shakes Duval violently and assures her "that if she had been one ounce less old, or less ugly, she should have had it all returned on her own face" (66). On the one hand, this suggests that the sheer sorriness of Madame Duval's condition as an old "French hag" limits the captain's aggression—she is too vulnerable, too pathetic even to "spit" on. On the other, in a covertly sexual register, it implies that she is too old and repulsive to qualify as a repository of even the most degrading of sexual impulses.

So both Sir Clement and Captain Mirvan use women for their "sport," which

Evelina aptly construes as their "love of tormenting" (150). Accounting for it from the point of view of its female victims, Burney then exposes such sport for the violent crime that it is. There is no glamorization of the gentleman highwayman here. Willoughby's seedy gallantry is condemned as a species of "torment" as vexing and as threatening to Evelina's integrity as Captain Mirvan's assault on Madame Duval. Posed as a practical joke, the highwayman episode has psychologically terrifying and physically injurious effects. Julie Epstein argues that Mirvan's assault on Duval demonstrates how "in *Evelina* . . . Burney concerns herself primarily with abuses of the façade rather than the edifice, the hair rather than the head" (87–88). However, given the sequence of psychological as well as physical violence that leads up to it and the emotional, deeply visceral terror it inspires both in Evelina and in Madame Duval, I believe that the damage inflicted by this assault on the highway is more than superficially cosmetic. Improving on an earlier disaster, where Du Bois, carrying Madame Duval away from the scene of a road accident, is shoved along with her into the mud on a rainy night at Vauxhall, Captain Mirvan ensures that Duval's discomposure here is complete (63–66, 73–76). Quite literally shaken up, bruised, enraged and terrified, deprived of the accoutrements of sartorial decency, Madame Duval is violated physically, emotionally, and socially. Evelina, while narrowly escaping physical violation at the hands of Sir Clement, has twice been subjected by his advances to mortal terror. The first time she is held captive by Sir Clement in a carriage, Evelina implores, "If you do not intend to murder me . . . for mercy's sake, for pity's sake, let me get out!" (99). More than a "euphemism" that avoids explicit sexual reference, "murder" here may be read as another way to name rape. Rape would itself entail the same sort of existential death for Evelina as it does for Clarissa. And, as Richardson makes emphatically clear in his novel, because he was her rapist, Lovelace is Clarissa's murderer as well.

While at Howard Grove, Duval remains the only person unaware that the "highwaymen" were actually Captain Mirvan and Sir Clement Willoughby. Although Duval's failure to identify and evade the plot is attributed to her "ignorance" and weak understanding, the failure of the other women at Howard Grove may be more significant: they fail to prevent the assault even though they know about it.[17] Evelina remarks Lady Howard's complicity: "There seems to be a sort of tacit agreement between her and the captain, that she should not appear to be acquainted with his schemes; by which means she at once avoids quarrels, and supports her dignity" (142). Motivated by the same fear of her husband's irascible temper, Mrs. Mirvan contributes to this complicity. So she tries to dissuade Madame Duval from seeking legal redress, "for she dreads a discovery of the captain, during Madame Duval's stay at Howard Grove, as it could not fail being more productive of infinite commotion" (154). Evelina herself sees through the story about Du Bois and is forewarned of the assault by Sir Clement; she as well fails to reveal the plot to Duval.

But afterwards, Evelina repents her collusion and resolves to resist complicity: "Should he make any new efforts to molest her [Madame Duval], I can by no means consent to be passive. Had I imagined he would have been so violent, I would have risked his anger in her defence much sooner" (152). The next day, in Mrs. Mirvan's and Sir Clement's company, Evelina summons the courage to petition the captain to abstain from further mischief. He responds by threatening to punish her for such "officiousness" (153). Sir Clement pounces on this opportunity to support Evelina's cause and so, he hopes, place her under obligation to him. Thus, in seeming solidarity with Evelina, Sir Clement leaves Howard Grove in order to deprive the captain of his collaboration. He begs Evelina to allow him "to place at [her] account the sacrifice" he makes by leaving her company (156). Even as Evelina, with her open solicitation to Captain Mirvan, makes a brave sally against the conspiracy of silence, she does indeed "pay" for her "officiousness" with the "debt" of gratitude claimed against her by Willoughby, one he would collect in erotic favors. And so, disciplining Evelina with the threat of sexual obligation, the "gentlemen highwaymen" continue to work in tandem to protect the invulnerability of elite criminality to either formal or informal check or redress.

Putting Crime Out of Countenance

Naming this "frolick" and "sport" for the sadistic torment it is, resisting the passive complicity imposed on the women at Howard Grove, and discounting Sir Clement's computation of personal obligation, Evelina's response to this assault exposes the dense web of cultural convention and sanctioned inequity that countenances it. The narrative accounts for the criminal damage of such actions across a wide spectrum of experience—physical, emotional, moral, financial, social, domestic; however, attempts to register it judicially are blocked. So while Evelina demurs from Lady Howard's and Mrs. Mirvan's complicity with the captain's plots, she nonetheless shares their aversion to legal redress. Back in London, when all finally becomes clear to Madame Duval, she again considers taking her grievance to the law. However, she is soon dissuaded from this course because of the lack of witnesses and the absence of positive identification and other evidentiary supports. Evelina is relieved: "I am extremely glad that this ridiculous adventure seems now likely to end without more serious consequences" (171).

A trial, Evelina and Mrs. Mirvan agree, would aggravate hostilities all around, solving nothing.

Madame Duval's resolution "that if ever she is so affronted again," she will be revenged in court *"even if she ruins herself"* unwittingly supports the judgment of those, like Evelina and Mrs. Mirvan, who oppose such action (171, my emphasis). The "ruin" a woman is likely to incur at court is both financial and, more significantly, social. The avoidance of legal redress speaks to the debilitating perils of female publicity even when risked to seek restitution for the most grievous harm. Thus Clarissa refuses to injure her "fame" by appearing in court against Lovelace for his rape, and Evelina similarly refuses to participate in a paternity suit against her father, Sir Belmont. The injuries to a woman's reputation are just as inevitable as the unlikelihood of an outcome favorable to her case. Lovelace, as he, Clarissa, and all subsequent scholarly accounts rightly claim, enjoys the unassailable protection of his corporate status. Belmont would enjoy the same immunity, and even the less stately Captain Mirvan has more than enough clout to silence charges brought against him by an expatriated ex-barmaid.

But there is more at stake in this resistance to the law here. In its association with a bourgeois culture devoted to the claims of property, judicial action is closely and damningly associated with the mercantile Branghtons.[18] In their initial eagerness for taking the captain to court, the Branghtons and Madame Duval would assent to the commodifying translation of personal injury into monetary reparation that a successful suit promises. This is part and parcel of their debased and mercenary sensibility. Rejecting this economy of harm, Evelina resituates the matter of redress back into the domestic and affective realm that she would protect from any additional "serious consequences" with which judicial involvement would compound the damages already inflicted by the captain and Sir Clement.

There is in this period a close imbrication of sin, as a violation of one's covenant with God, with crime, as a trespass against one's contract with society and its secular order of authority. In Richardson's *Clarissa*, the nature of Lovelace's trespasses and of Clarissa's injuries is always explored in both judicial and religious, as well as emotional and social, registers of significance. Clarissa refers her ultimate vindication and Lovelace's ultimate punishment to God, and claims her paternity only in a death that delivers her to that heavenly Father's house. However, in *Evelina* the religious realm recedes to a point of near invisibility.[19] Evelina's vindication and restoration are registered socially and accomplished sentimentally. The patriarchal crimes against herself, her mother, and, more generally, the sanctity of marriage and the family, are righted not through juridical or religious discourse but through the private discourse of sensibility, suited, as juridical discourse is not, to the realm of private familial relations that are the first object of repair, and accommodated, as religious discourse is not, to the secular and autonomous affective realm that serves as the matrix of all virtue and relation in the novel.

Importantly though predictably, Burney does not countenance the "gentleman's law" of the duel as an alternative to judicial law. Conventionally, this competitive opposition between the duel and the law articulates a sociocultural antagonism between aristocratic and bourgeois ideology: the duel, an instantiation of sovereign self-determination claimed individually in defiance of public judicial authority; the law, a participation in that authority as a subject whose sovereignty is both limited by it and protected by its limits on others. The novel recounts one actual duel between Macartney and Sir John Belmont; its awful criminality is compounded by its nearly parricidal result (227–28). As Lord Orville confronts Evelina's antagonists other duels loom, first with Mr. Lovel and then with Sir Clement Willoughby; yet in both cases he disarms the threat with diplomacy (83, 101–2; 345–47). True gentility, the novel suggests, avoids both the duel and the law, for both threaten ruin under the guise of reparation. The duel simply perpetuates the kind of elite violence admonished throughout the narrative. The court of law threatens a kind of public exposure especially damaging for women and particularly at odds with the text's investment in a realm of privacy protective of personal integrity.

The discourse of sensibility in the novel works both to protect and to correct. Because it is private, women may participate in it not only as objects but also as agents of amendment, as when Evelina saves the young Scots poet Macartney from a course of highway robbery and possible suicide. Macartney, a lodger at the Branghton's house in the City, had attracted Evelina's notice and compassion with his romantic, melancholy airs and the exquisite despair expressed in his verses (176–77). One day she notices a pistol fall from his pocket as he goes up the stairs; she then concludes, on the basis of his obvious "misery," that "he was, at that very moment, meditating suicide!" (181). (Macartney's later confession reveals that Evelina's assumption was slightly off the mark: robbery on the highway was his first object, and suicide only should he be apprehended [230].) Though at first paralyzed by fear, Evelina revives and follows her "impulse" into his room, where "almost involuntarily" she takes hold of his arms and exclaims, "O Sir! Have mercy on yourself!" (182). She takes the pistols away and goes downstairs, where he follows. Alternately overwhelmed into near insensibility and inspired into dramatic ecstasy, Evelina heroically declares that she is come to "awaken" Macartney "to worthier thoughts" and rescue him "from perdition"

(183). Called back to his senses, Macartney pronounces Evelina his "angel" of salvation: "'Wonderful!' cried he, with uplifted hands and eyes, 'most wonderful'" (183). The Branghtons return, Macartney rushes back up to his room, and Evelina faints dead away, the pistols beside her.

The scene plays out through the most exalted sentimentality, or melodrama. Beside herself with terror, Evelina acts out of pure feeling, pure sensation: "Strength and courage [was] lent me as by inspiration"; "wild with fright and scarce knowing what I did"; I "gave free vent to the feelings . . . in a violent burst of tears"; "I started from the chair, but trembled so excessively"; "I . . . sunk on the ground, without sense or motion" (182–84). Importantly, this scene links the virtue of courageous action to the almost involuntary impulses of the affections, to feminine sensibility, and thus reorients it from a more conventional realm of masculine, martial enterprise. The hero here is not the would-be highwayman, but the young woman who prevents him from becoming one. This fervent and redemptive encounter with the man whom she subsequently discovers to be her half-brother substantiates Evelina's and Macartney's kinship in sentiment far in advance of its conscious acknowledgment. As Evelina declares to Macartney when their blood relation finally is revealed: "I feel for you, already, all the affection of a sister,—I felt it, indeed, before I knew I was one" (363). As narrated here, sentiment authenticates genealogy and is prior to conscious knowledge. Feeling makes it real. The romance of the novel achieves the harmonization of affection and understanding in event. With its analogous celebration of the sentiments in which true relation inheres, this scene with Macartney foreshadows Evelina's later ardent meeting with their father, Sir Belmont.

In my examination of these two episodes, both involving variations on the "gentleman highwayman" theme, I have noted how their negotiation within the narrative seems to overtly discountenance or silently sidestep juridical, conventionally aristocratic, and religious ideologies and their attendant discourses. The scene with Macartney elaborates these evasions further by presenting a potentially sympathetic would-be gentleman highwayman and then upstaging him with a female agent, indeed angel, of salvation. In this way *Evelina* presents, in order to supersede, the popular discursive figure of the heroic highwayman, which reverses judicial authority as it sustains, in devolved and individualized form, the prestige of absolute sovereignty. Macartney's participation in these residual modes of individualized absolutism, dueling and highway robbery, is admonished and corrected by another kind of absolute authority, that of the sensible subject as embodied in Evelina. In a similar manner, Evelina's legal status as Sir Belmont's heir is restored, but only through the sentimental claims of affective relation claimed privately. The law does not restore private relationship, but relationship does repair public legal status.

As Evelina contends with Captain Mirvan's highway assault and its aftermath, the even graver plot of her paternity has taken a distressing turn. Having emphatically refused to prove her paternity in court, Evelina assents to Lady Howard's epistolary appeal to Sir Belmont. Just before she departs from London for Howard Grove, Evelina receives Sir Belmont's caustic response. The terms of his denial reveal that Sir Belmont believes the claim a fraudulent imposition. Evelina is crushed: "My doom is fixed. The various feelings which oppress me, I have not language to describe" (158). She does, however, describe her resentment: "I have, sometimes, sentiments upon this rejection, which my strongest sense of duty can scarcely correct. . . . Was it not enough to disclaim me for ever, without treating me with contempt, and wounding me with derision?" (159). Evelina feels her humiliation most sharply in Belmont's assumption that the claim made on her behalf is not merely mistaken but mercenary and fraudulent. Up to this point, her father's denial of his marriage and paternity identify her as illegitimate, a bastard. Adding insult to injury, now her father labels her a fortune-hunting imposter as well. Yet Evelina's resentment immediately turns to pity: "But while I am thus thinking of myself, I forget how much more *he* is the object of sorrow than I am! Alas, what amends can he make himself, for the anguish he is hoarding up for time to come! My heart bleeds for him, whenever this reflection occurs to me" (159).[20]

As she turns her feelings from her self to her father, from resentment to compassion, Evelina produces a sentimentalization of Sir Belmont that recalls Richard Steele's apology for the rake in *Tatler* 27. Here Steele argues, "A Rake is a Man always to be pitied; and if he lives is one Day certainly reclaim'd; for his Faults proceed not from Choice of Inclination but from strong Passions and Appetites." In Steele's apology, rakish criminality is a function of over-abundant feeling, sensibility, a physiological as well as emotional condition inevitably tempered by age. Sir John Belmont is still a young man with plenty of time to repent the error of his ways; the scenes with Evelina that activate this remorse demonstrate as well Sir Belmont's passionate sensibility. Unlike Sir Clement Willoughby and Lord Merton, Sir Belmont's character as a rake is not irremediable. Indeed, as events unfold, we learn that long before he meets Evelina, he has already begun to make amends, having years ago acknowledged and educated a girl he believed to be his daughter but who turns out to be a changeling imposed on him by her mother, Evelina's first nurse. So with Sir John Belmont, Burney draws on the conventional narrative of the reformed rake in order to initiate the sentimental

transformation of Sir Belmont that is vital to Evelina's reclamation of her paternity. This transformation is necessary in order that Evelina herself not be impossibly ambivalent about or compromised by her paternity. That Sir Belmont's
reform has high priority in the narrative is underscored by the changeling plot,
with its demonstration that Sir Belmont actually is not the monster of neglect he
has been taken for. The damaging misrecognition of Sir Belmont's character, the
counterpart of the misrecognition of Evelina's, qualifies him for some degree of
sympathetic indulgence.

However, as Richardson so emphatically demonstrates with Lovelace, the
rake's reform cannot by any means be assumed as "certainly" as Steele had earlier
suggested. Burney makes no such assumption.[21] Neither Sir Clement nor Lord
Merton evince any signs of reform, and Burney's single sentimental rake, Sir
Belmont, becomes fully aware of the consequences of his crime and thus most
fully penitent, only to drop out of the novel. So while she affirms Evelina's powers of sentimental renovation, Burney carefully sidesteps the most conventional,
and most dangerous, version of the reformed rake narrative, where moral and
affective probity is secured through marriage to a virtuous woman: the reformed
rake makes the best husband.[22] The failure of that narrative is bitterly recorded in
Sir Belmont's history with Caroline Evelyn. Marriage does not make a reformed
rake, and the reformed rake does *not* make the best husband; this is underscored by the courtship of Lord Merton and Lady Louisa Larpent, Lord Orville's
sister.

Having squandered half of his fortune and, as a "confirmed libertine," so sul-
lied his character that "he was rarely admitted" into polite company, Lord Merton
determines to bolster his credit through marriage to the respectable and wealthy,
if vaporish, Lady Louisa. As Lady Louisa's fiancé, Lord Merton may now "be admitted any where, for he is going to *reform*" (276). While Lady Louisa garbles
the discourse of sensibility with her affectation of nervous delicacy, Lord Merton
annuls affection in his parroting of sympathy. With a vapidity recalling the dia-
logues of the dead that Jonathan Swift records in his *Polite Conversation* (1738),
the couple engage:

> Just then entered Lord Merton . . . advancing to Lady Louise, [he] said, in a careless
> manner, "How is your Ladyship this morning?"
>
> "Not well at all," answered she; "I have been dying with the head-ach ever since
> I got up."
>
> "Indeed!" cried he, with a countenance wholly unmoved, "I am very unhappy to
> hear it. . . ."

"Your Ladyship's constitution," said Mr. Lovel, "is infinitely delicate."

"Indeed it is," cried she, in a low voice, "I am *nerve* all over!" (286).

Antitheses to Lord Orville and Evelina, Lord Merton and Lady Louisa perform the signs of sensibility as they have become conventionalized in social manners. Their inauthenticity is rendered transparent by Evelina's narrative, informed, as it is, by true sensibility and thus alive to Lord Merton's hypocrisy and Lady Louisa's comprehensive egoism. Lord Merton and Lady Louisa are all self and no subjectivity, all publicity and no authenticity. They have no personal relation; their empty social gestures signify only its absence.

Openly engaged to Lady Louisa, Lord Merton surreptitiously preys on Evelina. In public, Lord Merton presents himself, however indolently, as a "reformed rake." In private, he briskly wheedles Evelina behind closed doors: "Why now . . . if you was not the cruelest little angel in the world, you would have helped me to some expedient: for you see how I am watched here [at Mrs. Beaumont's house]; Lady Louisa's eyes are never off me. She gives me a charming foretaste of the pleasures of a wife! However, it won't last long" (311). Lord Merton's glaring incapacity for any proper conjugal and domestic role is a standing joke among his acquaintance. As Lord Orville exclaims to Lady Louisa, "What a metamorphosis . . . should you make a *patriarch of his Lordship!*" (111, my emphasis). Primarily, Lord Orville's remark exposes his skepticism about Lord Merton's character. However, read with different emphases—"What a metamorphosis . . . should *you* make a patriarch of his Lordship"—the statement also acknowledges that, all her feeling centered on self, Lady Louisa lacks sentimental authority; she will reform no rakes, make a patriarch out of no one.

In *Evelina,* patriarchy is remade and paternity reinstated in a set of concurrent melodramatic events: Evelina's engagement to Lord Orville and her meetings with Sir Belmont. Overlapping as they do, these two pivotal incidences at once reclaim Evelina's paternity and curtail its influence by transferring her in advance from the authority of her father to that of her husband. Even as Evelina appeals for the grant of her patronym, she has vowed to exchange it for another. So while Evelina's relation to Sir Belmont is affirmed, this recovery of paternity does not entail a redemption of his patriarchal authority; such authority, instead, is transferred to Lord Orville. Requiring no metamorphosis for either role, Lord Orville makes the best husband and the perfect representative of a reformed patriarchy.

The establishment of Evelina's relation with Sir Belmont takes place over three visits negotiated by Mrs. Selwyn. Returning confused and discouraged from an initial interview undertaken alone, Mrs. Selwyn reports to Evelina that although she "ceased not painting the enormity of his crime," Belmont insists that he has already acknowledged and provided for his daughter (366). The next day Mrs. Selwyn returns with Evelina. As with every scene in which Evelina encounters significant relationship, apprehension renders her almost paralytic: "I was almost senseless with terror! The meeting at last, was not so dreadful as that moment" (370). Brought before her father, Evelina lets out "an involuntary scream" and, as she had done in the scene with Macartney and his pistols, sinks to the floor. If anything, Sir Belmont is even more sensibly affected. Evelina, a dead ringer for her mother, appears to him as a reproachful specter: "My God!" he exclaims, "does Caroline Evelyn still live!" (372). He rushes away, unable to face the embodiment of his guilt.

However, he no longer questions his paternity. It is unequivocally confirmed by the "certificate of [her] birth" that Evelina carries in her "countenance," which "as it could not be effected by artifice . . . cannot admit of a doubt" (337). Evidence of Evelina's claim is given in terms set not by juridical but by sentimental discourse. Furthermore, since the text seeks resolutions outside of both judicial law and the "gentleman's law" of honor (dueling), so here sensibility provides an alternative both to juridical and to aristocratic ideology. Sensibility materializes truth in bodies, much as it may legibly code truth in manners, which, after all, are fully embodied social performances. Equipped with this means of authentication, the discourse of sensibility would "evade the ideology of aristocratic privilege" by providing its own terms of equivalence between internal and external, truth and appearance.[23] Thus, Evelina's paternity and so her elite status is confirmed through a system of legitimization outside the determination of the very order which invests that status. It is Sir John Belmont's presumption of aristocratic privilege that leads him to disown his wife and child in the first place; the reclamation of his paternity and affirmation of his error take place otherwise, in a discourse of sensibility that not only evades aristocratic ideology but even, to a degree, rectifies the abuses perpetrated under its cover. Sincerely remorseful, indeed, incapacitated by this confrontation with his crimes, Sir Belmont doubts that he can ever again bear Evelina's presence. Even if we do understand Sir Belmont as a reformed rake, Burney does not risk making him anyone's husband. His patriarchal authority is shaken to its foundations; it is withdrawn and superseded by the new order headed by the morally impeccable, irreproachably sensitive, "modern and feminized" masculine ideal: Lord Orville.[24]

Don't Hate Her Because He's Perfect

In many respects, Lord Orville realizes a tradition of the ideal gentleman of sense and virtue formulated in the early eighteenth century by Richard Steele in his *Christian Hero* (1701), his expositions of masculine virtue in the *Tatler* and *Spectator* papers (1709–1714), and in the character of Bevil Junior in the melodramatic comedy *The Conscious Lovers* (1722). The gentleman paragon, "a man of taste and imaginative refinement," embodies the integration of sociocultural refinement, "worldly graces," with moral virtue.[25]

This ideal is taken up and elaborated at heroic length by Richardson in *Sir Charles Grandison* (1753–54), probably the most influential articulation of the ideal gentleman in the eighteenth century.[26] Told largely from the perspective of female protagonist Harriet Byron, this last of Richardson's novels narrates the courtships and family crises so expertly managed by Sir Charles. Valued highly as a study of proper conduct, *Sir Charles Grandison* takes on most every topic of concern in eighteenth-century private life: family obligation, courtship and marriage, estate management, national loyalty, religious integrity, education, manners, and sentiment. As literary historian Sylvia Marks has observed, Richardson's novel lays open the wide range of moral and sociocultural issues central to conduct writing generally and, more particularly, to popular periodicals such as *The Tatler* and *The Spectator*.[27] As Samuel Johnson famously observed, one reads *Sir Charles Grandison* for the moral, not for the plot: "Why, Sir, if you were to read Richardson for the story, your impatience would be so much fretted that you would hang yourself. But you must read him for the sentiment, and consider the story as only giving occasion to the sentiment."[28] There is a major storyline—the torturous triangulated courtship of Harriet, Sir Charles, and the Italian Clementina—and any number of minor storylines involving Sir Charles's reformative management of problematic friends and relatives and his benevolent guardianship of the young Emily Jervois and of his younger sister Charlotte; but Johnson's judgment is sound. All of the events in the novel proceed to elaborate a comprehensive system of conduct as exemplified by that complete modern gentleman, Sir Charles Grandison.

In ways that dovetail with arguments I present here about the seventeenth-century matrix of the modern renegotiation of masculinity, Doody has traced a genealogy of Grandison's character, rooted in Clarendon's portrait of Lucius Carey, Viscount Falkland, and of Grandison's family in the royalist William Villiers, Viscount Grandison. Reaching beyond Steele's moral treatise of that name, Doody finds the seventeenth-century type of the Christian hero in Carey and emphasizes the moral and characterological resonances between Clarendon's dignified Royalist statesman and Richardson's genteel private gentleman. In his *History of the Rebellion and Civil Wars*, Clarendon eulogizes Carey at length, presenting him as an exemplar of those "great virtues" that it is "one of the principle ends and duties of history" to model for the emulation of subsequent generations. Falkland was "a person of such prodigious parts of learning and knowledge, of that inimitable sweetness and delight in conversation, of so flowing and obliging a humanity and goodness to mankind, and of that primitive simplicity and integrity of life, that if there were no other brand upon this odious and accursed civil war than that single loss, it must be most infamous and execrable to all posterity."[29] Furthermore, this link between the historical Viscount Falkland and Grandison supports the connection between Grandison and Godwin's fictional Falkland, written, as I discuss below, to refute the viability of elite authority even as embodied by its most promising representatives, such as Lucius Carey in the historical record and Sir Charles Grandison in the literary-cultural realm.

Sir Charles's associations with Carey and Villiers insist on his advantages of birth and fortune and on his relation to the upheavals of the seventeenth century. Doody thus surmises: "In using names of such Royalist associations, Richardson is suggesting a continuity between the old types of 'honour,' 'nobility,' and 'gentleness,' and the newer ideal which is non-military and non-political."[30] Resolutely private and magisterially benevolent in the exercise of his virtue, shunning any martial demonstrations of his honor, Sir Charles revises the traditional aristocratic ethos of honor in line with the domestic and sentimental orientation of the modern gentleman.

The moral and sociocultural failure of the elite is a topic to which Richardson returns in each of his novels and in each resolves differently. In *Pamela*, Mr. B. and Lady Davers are reclaimed through the heavily feminized virtue of the heroine; in *Clarissa*, the decay of aristocratic ideology takes pathological, murderous, and self-annihilating shape in Lovelace; but in his final novel, Richardson writes an elite hero who, unlike Mr. B., is in no need of reform, and, unlike Lovelace, eschews the predatory and self-aggrandizing prerogatives of elite masculinity. Instead, an always already perfect Sir Charles takes up the mantle of patriarchal responsibility to produce a fruitful amalgamation of masculinity, status, and virtue. In this, Sir Charles effects the consolidation of benevolent paternalism, sociocultural prestige, and moral value championed, for example, in *The Tatler* and *The Spectator*. Sir Charles's immediate and self-conscious rejection of the rakish and criminal character of elite masculinity is presented simultaneously with his cultivation of family honor in his relation to his father, the spendthrift, selfish, imperious, and sexually incontinent Sir Thomas Grandison. Even as his own character provides a damning foil for that of Sir Thomas, Sir Charles retains an almost fanatical adherence to the principle of filial piety. Maintaining his paternal connection intact, Sir Charles avoids unraveling the patriarchal mantle under which he would gather his community of dependents and restore the virtue and prestige of elite masculinity.

Predictably, as Sir Charles provides a vehicle for the resolution of each most pressing domestic, moral, and religious issue of his day, his character might seem improbably to encompass *every* virtue. Just so, Burney's Lord Orville has been faulted for his absolute perfection. Like Grandison, Lord Orville is a perfect "bourgeois" gentleman *and* an aristocrat; he possesses virtue *and* extravagant wealth and social power; he is supremely attractive to women *and* sexually continent; he has exquisite social polish *and* the most delicate personal sensibility. Orville supplies to Evelina the roles of father, best friend, brother, *and* husband. Grandison and Orville, then, embody what seems an almost impossible plenitude. With an ethical inversion, this may recall one of Lovelace's characteristics noted in chapter 2. While Lovelace's character seems inexhaustible in its diabolical, shape-shifting malevolence, so might Orville's and Grandison's seem in their Protean virtue.

Literary critic Mary Yates argues for a more extensive set of parallels between the paragon and the rake. She looks at how both Sir Charles Grandison's contemporary appeal and his subsequent critical obloquy, or at best, obscurity, lie in his resolution of a specifically eighteenth-century conundrum—how to square ethical virtue with sociocultural prestige—that is of little concern to the secular and irredeemably skeptical critics in the twentieth century. Thus Yates shows how a character such as Grandison or Orville that may seem to us woodenly prescriptive, insufferably officious, perhaps even hypocritical, was the product of a lively didactic and philosophic tradition. So while Grandison achieves very little purchase on the sensibilities of twentieth-century literary scholars, his contemporary currency in moral and aesthetic discourse was high. I have emphasized how such debates about masculine virtue and prestige took shape in the seventeenth-century critique of aristocratic ideology through the discourses of gentility and criminality examined here. We can trace the presence of this critique and those discourses in Yates's exposition of how Richardson tailors Sir Charles's character to a pressing contemporary cultural issue: the production, as an emulative figure, of a masculine type in which moral, aesthetic, and social merit support one another. That is, a male figure who is a gentleman and yet not a criminal.

According to Yates's reading, rather than a reformed rake, Sir Charles is a latent, unformed one, preserving all the rake's sexual charisma and self-authorized license but restraining himself from the rake's criminal courses.[31] Sir Charles, then, retains the charming exuberance of Steele's sentimental rake but resists the devolution into bad behavior. Just as its hero devotes a good deal of his time *not* becoming embroiled in duels, so *Sir Charles Grandison* dedicates much of its narrative to establishing (most significantly in the understanding of Harriet Byron) that this hero is not a libertine: for, "sooner or later, nearly everyone mistakes Grandison for a rake."[32] After all, while he never exploits his popularity in promiscuity, Sir Charles's major dilemma in the novel is how to cope with all the women who fancy him. Yates notes as well how Sir Charles, no less than Lovelace, single-mindedly pursues and always achieves his own self-authorized will—often, like Lovelace, manipulating and overwhelming others in the process. The difference is that Sir Charles uses his super powers for good rather than evil. Onto the character of his moral hero, then, Richardson transplants the attractive "vivacity" of the rake, and in his novel teaches his readers how to distinguish the charismatic rake from the captivating Grandison, Lucifer from the archangels.[33] Yates thus dubs Sir Charles Grandison a "Christian Rake."

However, these perhaps unsettling parallels between Lovelace, the villain, and Grandison, the paragon, do not extend fully to Burney's Lord Orville. Far from being mistaken for that of a rake, Lord Orville's character is only once cast under suspicion, when Sir Clement forges a compromising letter from "Lord Orville" to Evelina (256–57). In this instance, Lord Orville's virtue is so transparently communicated by his manner that Evelina knows the letter is not his and accepts his proposal even before its true authorship is confirmed by Sir Clement (355–58, 387–88). Standards of truth, as I have been arguing, are not juridical and conventionally evidentiary in this novel, but are sentimental. Evelina learns the truth of the letter, not from Sir Clement's confession, but by reading it in Lord Orville's character. While Grandison seems to share with Lovelace a "love of scrutiny, of prying into the female heart," Lord Orville, in contrast, waits patiently for Evelina's disclosures to be given in her own time.[34] Far from officiously running the whole show, as Sir Charles is apt to do, Lord Orville seems rather to achieve his stature by virtue of how he adapts to the necessities and desires attendant on its female protagonist. Without personal complications and abstaining from meddling, domination, and self-authorization, Lord Orville, then, is more purely perfect than even Sir Charles Grandison. If anything, this has earned him even more summary dismissal from contemporary critics.

Gerard A. Barker attributes the persistence of the Grandisonian paragon through later eighteenth-century fiction to its usefulness in accommodation to the needs of "the feminine novel." So it is as "young Fanny's [*sic*] wish-fulfillment of the ideal male lover" that Lord Orville flits through the pages of *Evelina*, "a shadowy, unrealized character."[35] With feminist skepticism, Judith Newton concurs: "Lord Orville is indeed too good to be true, and like all Prince Charmings, I suspect, his extraordinary virtues are not only compensation but justification for the way things are."[36] While attentive to the Cinderella narrative at play in *Evelina*, such appraisals discount the self-reflexive and critical manner in which Burney represents the figure of Lord Orville, the validity of the female desires it satisfies, and the larger sociocultural matrix in which these desires find expression not simply as individual female fantasies but also as part of a modern ideology of gender.

The possibility that Orville is indeed an idealized projection of female fantasy is self-consciously observed in the novel. Evelina reflects in a letter to her friend Miss Maria Mirvan:

> I think I rather recollect a dream, or some visionary fancy, than a reality.—That I should have ever been known to Lord Orville,—that I should have spoken to—Have danced with him,—seems now a romantic illusion: and that elegant politeness, that flattering attention, that high-bred delicacy, which so much distinguished him above all other men, and which struck us with such admiration, I now re-trace the remembrance of, rather as belonging to an object of ideal perfection, formed by my own imagination, than to a being of the same race and nature as those [the Branghtons and Madame Duval with occasional appearances by Sir Clement and the irrepressible Mr. Smith] with whom I at present converse. (172)

Refining a feature of Richardson's *Sir Charles Grandison*, where Harriet Byron's fraught negotiation of her relationship with Sir Charles constitutes much of the narrative, Burney focuses even more exclusively on the female response to and relationship with this perfect gentleman. In this passage, Evelina reflexively turns her attention to Lord Orville to question his existence independent of her own romantic fantasy. On the one hand, a critic such as Barker would read this as evidence that Orville lacks autonomy and substance as a character. Yet the shadowy "unreal" Lord Orville is so profoundly imbricated in the insistent realization of female desires in Burney's novel that to discount the one threatens to devalue the other. That is, rather than seeing Lord Orville as a diminished character because of his superabundant fulfillment of feminine needs and desires, it seems less perverse to read his character positively on these same grounds: his considerable value and substance derive precisely from the powerful feminine forces that find in them their complement and validation.

By questioning whether the figure in her imagination really corresponds to any actual Lord Orville, Evelina asserts a distinction between the fantastic and the actual character and acknowledges by this means the very value of Orville's independent autonomy that she, and Burney's critics, fear her idealization may obscure. Like the qualities of Orville's abundant perfection, those of his independence as a character "outside" Evelina's own imaginative realm are established characteristically, if somewhat paradoxically, through subjective self-reflection. In every way that is most telling and profound, Orville is indeed a product of Evelina's imagination, her private affective life. Especially as the narrative moves nearer to its conclusion, Lord Orville substantiates in action, and thus "independently" and "autonomously," his sympathetic responsiveness to Evelina's real, that is, her private and affective self. It is this quality of response that produces Evelina's frequent applause of his "delicacy"—indeed, his "almost feminine delicacy" of manners.

The Fop's Bad End

But the reading of Lord Orville as a "modern feminized gentleman," while apparently sensitive to his estimation within the text, suggests a kind of gendered identity between Lord Orville and Evelina that, I believe, violates the logic of complementary relations between polarized sexes to which the text ascribes. As has been widely explicated in recent scholarship, the modern revision of the sex/gender system from an analogical hierarchy into a field of polarized difference brings with it a notion of ideal relations between the sexes as the complementary juxtaposition of opposites.[37] Thus the neoclassical figure of *concordia discors* manifests in modern gender ideology: "Women in their Nature are much more gay and joyous than Men," asserts Joseph Addison in *Spectator* 128. "As Vivacity is the Gift of Women, Gravity is that of Men. . . . Men and Women were made as Counterparts to one another, that the Pains and Anxieties of the Husband might be relieved by the Sprightliness and good Humour of the Wife." In his recent study of seventeenth- and eighteenth-century masculinity, Thomas King emphasizes how such reciprocity, fostered in the domestic realm, models "an ethics of mutuality between same and other in the public sphere as well."[38] That this ethics of mutuality governs Lord Orville's public as well as his private interactions is recognized in the encomium on his manners quoted earlier.

Inattention to the prominence of this modern gender paradigm in the text may produce estimations of Lord Orville's character that reinforce its "vapidity" and status as product of empty feminine desire, unwittingly complicit with the status quo. Thus, locating Orville's desirability in the ways he "reverses the normal relation between male privilege and male control," Newton discounts this capacity as "not only compensation but justification for the way things are . . . the consistent courtliness of Lord Orville tends to justify ruling-class male control."[39] In contrast, I would emphasize the critical function of Lord Orville's manners that, rather than justify those of other elite men, most often contrast with them damningly. Lord Orville's principled refusal to exploit elite male privilege as domination, particularly domination over women, is consistent, not simply with Evelina's fantasy of an ideal husband, but also with the revision of patriarchal power as paternalistic benevolence that departs from a logic of hierarchal subordination in favor of one of complementary reciprocity. Granted, this modern notion of reciprocal relations between the sexes is ideological and obscures the fact of women's legal, financial, and social subordination to men; similarly, the recuperation of patriarchy undertaken through the figure of Lord Orville imports the fact of elite prestige and thus does not avoid an affirmation of "ruling-class male control." However, this modern gender ideology does revise the conception of relations between the sexes in ways that accord substantial power to the authority of the subject, and within such a revision neither ruling-class males nor the control they may operate legitimately remain the same.

Likewise, to label Lord Orville "feminine" distorts his role as an ideal patriarchal figure whose masculinity is not compromised but defined by his participation in modern complementary gender relations and their accompanying ethos of sensibility. In *Spectator* 128, where Addison eulogizes the perfect marriage, he also admonishes the temperamental obstacle standing in its way: female narcissism and its election of men characterized by their effeminate investment in superficial and social signs of identity and prestige. These are the men Addison and his contemporaries call fops, beaux, and pretty fellows, and who might in contemporary late modern parlance be labeled "queer." In defiance of the logic of complementary opposition, women, Addison laments in *Spectator* 128, are all too ready "to associate themselves with a person who resembles them in that light and volatile Humour which is natural to them [women]," rather than with "such as are qualified to moderate and counter-balance it." In choosing such "light and volatile" foppish men, women violate the ideology of gender difference: "To be short, the Passion of an ordinary Woman for a Man, is nothing else but Self-love diverted upon another Object." Such women can be brought out of their error into proper sexual relations; they are not gender misfits, simply vain and shallow narcissists. The object of such narcissistic affection, the "light and volatile" fop, however, manifests a gendered temperament at odds with his sexual assignment.

Like the feminine desire he attracts, the fop is an impediment to the establishment of natural, complementary sexual relations. It is not the Grandisonian or Orvillian man of sense, or even the man of feeling, but the fop who is (badly) feminine, who fails to achieve masculinity according to the terms of modern gender ideology.[40]

With its defining investment in this ideology, *Evelina* identifies threats to it not only in conventional figures of faulty masculinity such as Lord Merton, Sir Clement Willoughby, and Captain Mirvan, but ultimately in that ambiguous figure of the fop, whose femininity is as faulty as the masculinity that it compromises. As King emphasizes, the fop remains a kind of atavistic figure, invested in the specular social logic of court-based absolutism; he defies identification within the emergent regime of modern gendered sexuality with its "hetero-normative" strictures and its delegation of authority to the private, inward arena of subjectivity. Refusing participation in gendered complementary subjectivity, the fop, like the rake, refuses as well the new manners of reciprocity exemplified by modern men of sense such as Lord Orville.[41]

Whereas earlier theatrical representations of the fop exploit him as a comic character, Evelina's Mr. Lovel, the society fop, is an altogether darker, more threatening figure. He openly insults Evelina's "country breeding" and intimidates her with his rudeness: "But how malicious and impertinent in this creature to talk to me in such a manner! I am sure I hope I shall never see him again. I should have despised him heartily as a fop, had he never spoken to me at all; but now, that he thinks proper to resent his supposed ill-usage, *I am really quite afraid of him*" (82, my emphasis). So outrageous is Lovel's resentment that Mrs. Mirvan fears he might challenge Evelina's champion, Lord Orville, to a duel (83). The next day, however, Lord Orville disarms the threat in a private conversation with Lovel during which the fop engages "his honour never more" to humiliate or insult Evelina (102). The duel is a menace offered by the "weak and frivolous" fop and is avoided by the strong and serious man of sense. The fop and the duel are matched here as regressive manifestations of a court-based aristocratic culture successfully challenged by the new manners of a new, properly masculine man.

But the greatest threat the fop poses to the instantiation of modern gender ideology is registered only at the end of novel, where his indecorous humiliation and expulsion in effect clear the way for the marriage between Evelina and Lord Orville. In this ideology, the fop is a misfit and an impediment; in the narrative, he is punished and expelled. There is no happy ending for the fop.

Lovel takes a major role in Evelina's penultimate letter, the last to narrate any action, written just as she is off to marry Lord Orville and join Villars for a honeymoon at Berry Hill. Here the fop is exhibited as a degraded, repulsively effeminate, and finally subhuman creature. First, during a pleasure trip to Bath, Lovel's gentlemen companions contemplate ducking him for a wager. Addicted to gambling, this cohort, led by Lord Merton, earlier set up and placed bets on an appalling "race" between two old, infirm, and impoverished women (394–95). Just as that earlier "contest" dehumanizes and brutalizes the old women, so the ducking wager would demean Lovel as an object for the depraved "sport" of "gentlemen." Lovel's humiliating feminization provides amusement especially for Captain Mirvan, who baits and taunts him relentlessly. Lovel's status as the object of Captain Mirvan's persistent and gleeful harassment figures him in the role earlier occupied by Madame Duval. In their shared narcissistic self-absorption, obsession with fashion, and affectation, Madame Duval and Mr. Lovel each participate in a kind of bad femininity that compromises both. So Captain Mirvan comments on their sartorial identity: "Why his [Lovel's] coat . . . would be a most excellent match for old Madame Furbelow's best Lyons' silk" (403).

Lovel's torment at the hands of the captain takes final form in the practical joke with which the narrative closes. Here Captain Mirvan introduces into the drawing room a "little gentleman who desires to see Mr. Lovel" and then, as Evelina narrates to Villars, "to the utter astonishment of every body but himself, he hauled into the room a monkey! full dressed, and extravagantly *a-la-mode!*" (399–400). In his fury, Lovel canes the monkey, and the monkey, in his, bites Lovel's ear. Too cowardly to rebuke the human agent of his humiliation, Lovel reduces himself to the bestial level of his chosen opponent. While the captain enjoys the spectacle, Lord Orville catches the monkey and tosses him out. Though urged by the gentlemen to challenge the captain, Lovel declines and, following the monkey, departs (403). The company turns to peaceful pursuits and Evelina to the letter just arrived from Mr. Villars, giving his blessing to her marriage. The reformation of the patriarchal order represented in the novel requires at once the supercession of faulty forms of authority, such as that embodied by Sir Belmont, and also the dismissal of impediments, such as the simian fop, to the realization of the gender ideology in which it participates. The importance of the fop's exclusion to the resolution of the novel can be read both in its redundancy and in its climatic position in the narrative. Here the figure of the fop is doubled, as Lovel and as the monkey-as-Lovel, and thus expelled not once but twice, clearing the way for the happy ending: "You are now," whispers Lord Orville to Evelina, "all my own!" (404).

Lord Orville, I have argued, embodies a modern form of masculinity dependent on the authority of the gendered subject and one that supersedes the faulty masculinities figured by the libertine rake, the autocratic patriarch, and the fop. In this last episode, the narrative, in effect, pits these faulty types against one another in order to discountenance all of them in a farce that climaxes in the redoubled expulsion of the fop. Whereas the history of gender I have forwarded here as well as the trajectory of Burney's narrative insist on Lord Orville's progressive status in relation to these masculine figures that he supersedes, this relation is complicated by the ideology of reform that he instantiates. Noting how Lord Orville's gracious manners seem out of place in the company gathered at Bristol, Mrs. Selwyn remarks: "Certainly . . . there must have been some mistake in the birth of that young man; he was undoubtedly, designed for the last age; for, if you observed, he is really polite" (283). Paired with Mrs. Selwyn's later observation that "Lord Orville is almost as romantic as if he had been born and bred at Berry Hill," these comments emphasizing Orville's golden age paternalism and pastoral purity provide external confirmation of Evelina's own reveries in which the young Lord Orville mirrors the elderly Arthur Villars. So Evelina eulogizes Lord Orville to her guardian: "I sometimes imagine, that, when his youth is flown, his vivacity abated, and his life is devoted to retirement, he will, perhaps, resemble him whom I most love and honour. His present sweetness, politeness, and diffidence, seem to promise in future the same benevolence, dignity, and goodness" (72). So this modern reformation of aristocracy is pulled back again to the (mythic) past in a nostalgic turn that lends authority to transformation by positing it not as innovation but as restoration.[42]

This nostalgic modernity, with its mythologizing of the past, might be seen as at the core of all that is "conservative" in the resolution of Burney's text. Yet in relation to the nostalgia that, as I have argued in previous chapters, generates the absolutism of the modern outlaw figures, the rake, the highwayman, and the pirate, Burney's invocation of a golden age of paternalistic benevolence might also be read as substantially "progressive." Whereas the sovereign will claimed by the outlaw figures recalls, if in devolved and individualistic form, absolutism as hierarchical domination, the sovereign subject enshrined in Burney's novel remembers the past differently, as an epoch governed by benevolence and reciprocity. As the fissures in Grandison's character point up, both the paragon of masculine virtue and his outlaw brothers are species of the absolute individual. Characteristically, the outlaw resolves the contradiction inherent in this position through his domination over other competing sovereign individuals, whereas the paragon does so through the discourse of sensibility that refigures the contradiction within the individual himself, one whose authority as an absolute subject is only realized through his acquiescence to the authority of others.

Caleb Williams: The Criminal Character of Ideology

William Godwin's novel *Caleb Williams* (1794),[43] like his political treatise an *Enquiry Concerning Political Justice* (1793), addresses the nexus of sociopolitical issues prominent in the 1790s as England and all Europe clamored their responses to the French Revolution. The imprisonment and execution of Louis XVI and his family in 1793 and 1794 generated attention to a set of issues evocative of those raised by the 1649 execution of the English sovereign, Charles I.[44] Repercussions of the French Revolution in British intellectual and political life were immediate, as the government sought to limit Jacobin sympathies, stigmatizing and persecuting reformists more generally, and to fortify itself against an increasingly bellicose France. Edmund Burke's *Reflections on the Revolution in France* (1790) represents the dominant anti-Jacobin and conservative response to these issues of authority, transgression, right, and reform; Thomas Paine's *The Rights of Man* (1791–92), the radical, pro-revolutionary position. While Godwin's *Enquiry* provides an extended exposition of the evils of the social and political order, he proposes there not a revolutionary restructuring of the political realm but its gradual displacement through anarchic institutions. Thus Godwin would stand outside the illusion, corruption, and brutality of reactionary and revolutionary alike.

Just as Godwin's *Enquiry* looks beyond all existent settlements and reforms in its pursuit of political justice, his *Caleb Williams* posits only a negative resolution to its ethical and sociopolitical reversals and inversions that finally only double within one another, reproducing guilt and injustice in a kind of endless transfer of ideological illusion. Drawing on the characteristic eighteenth-century discourses of masculine prestige and criminality, Godwin's novel reveals the complications of both as they inhere in aristocratic ideology, its chivalric discourses, and its institutions of patronage and absolute honor; in the legal system and its penal institutions; in the sociopolitical hierarchies supported by government; and in that realm of emotional interiority realized here most vividly as an arena of terror and guilt, exultation and dominance, veneration and abjection (the Gothic). Exposing the ideological formation of the subject, which in this case is an ideological *de*formation, within these discourses, Godwin's novel discountenances the kind of salvation through the absolute sentimental subject forwarded by both Richardson and Burney. Armed with the fictions of this subject, in *Caleb Williams*, Godwin indicts the criminal character of ideology.

Because its procedure is so heavily weighted toward what we call ideological critique, and because this critique centers on the perfect gentleman criminal, Falkland, *Caleb Williams* self-consciously realizes many of the propositions about criminality and masculinity forwarded in this book: that the critique of aristocratic ideology initiated in seventeenth-century England and revisited in the 1790s produces a conventional, socioculturally intransigent juxtaposition between the criminal and the gentleman; that in the aristocratic code of honor persists conduct criminalized within the contexts of modern gentility and of judicial law; that modes of sociosexual relations associated with residual aristocratic ideology and its institutions, such as patronage, are discredited by bourgeois norms of complementary heterosexual difference; that while popular discourses of criminality might be understood as pronouncements of dissent against economic and social injustice, they remain dependent on the very institutions of discipline and reward against which they ostensibly arrange themselves. Indeed, *Caleb Williams* forwards an overt critique of eighteenth-century discourses of masculine prestige and criminality that, while oriented toward the sociopolitical world of the 1790s, might stand beside and, as here, complete their consideration more than two hundred years later. Finally, with his direct and weighty use in the novel of the popular stereotypes and motifs that are the object of this study, Godwin insists upon another important point: that cultural representation is an agent of sociopolitical ideology.

Briefly, Godwin's novel comprises two strands of narration: the first, a retelling of Falkland's early history by his devoted servant Collins; the second, Caleb Williams's own first-person narration of his involvement with Falkland's subsequent history. Returning to his English estate from a series of gallant exploits on the Continent, Falkland excites the competitive antagonism of his neighbor, Tyrrel. The first casualty of their quarrel is Tyrrel's orphaned and dependent cousin, Emily Melville, who falls in love with Falkland. Ever jealous of Falkland's influence, even where, as with Miss Melville, its effects are unintentional and the sentiments it produces unreciprocated, Tyrrel tries to ruin his cousin through marriage to a local lout, Grimes. By chance, Falkland rescues Emily from Grimes, but she is then dogged by her cousin for debt, is jailed, falls ill, and dies. Victim of a marriage plot that harks back to that of Richardson's *Clarissa,* Emily Melville likewise is a brutally realistic rewriting of *Sir Charles Grandison's* Emily Jervois, also a dependent with a schoolgirl infatuation.[45] Young, inexperienced, and with a heart "incapable of guile," Emily Melville, like her Richardsonian precursors, exhibits all the symptoms of an intense sensibility; but these, rather than finding their complement in the Grandisonian Falkland, only leave her vulnerable to delusion, indiscretion, and finally the fatal retribution of her cousin, Tyrrel (43). While Falkland does not participate in her passion, he does sympathize with her situation and saves her twice, once from fire, and again from abduction and rape.

Yet the homosocial hostility between Falkland and Tyrrel always overrides any routine courtesy between Falkland and Emily Melville; caught in their cross fire, she is destroyed, and with her any, even briefly sustained, romantic heterosexual element in the text.

The next casualties of this elite rivalry are two of Tyrrel's tenants, Hawkins and his son. When Hawkins refuses to allow his son to enter Tyrrel's service, Tyrrel has them convicted under the Black Act and imprisoned. They abscond, only to be falsely accused of Tyrrel's murder, actually committed by Falkland, and executed. Caleb Williams, then, is just one in a string of victims. In his narration, Williams tells us how he is recommended to Falkland's patronage as a secretary and how, having heard from Collins of Falkland's troubled history, he is goaded by curiosity to penetrate the secret of Falkland's melancholy. Through a series of calculating exchanges with his patron, Williams's curiosity solidifies into the conviction that Falkland himself, not Hawkins, is Tyrrel's murderer. Resenting his subjugation under Falkland's suspicious gaze, though having vowed never to reveal Falkland's secret, Williams flees the estate but is apprehended and jailed on a charge of theft that Falkland has trumped up against him. He escapes and re-volves through a series of adventures evocative of rogue and criminal biography. Apprehended again, Williams is released, only to be dogged through England and Wales by the thief-taker turned private agent Gines, and so remains incar-cerated within Falkland's net of surveillance. Finally, Williams appears against Falkland before a magistrate and presents his charge of murder. Falkland admits his guilt, confirming Williams's innocence of the theft with which he had been accused. Williams ends his narrative, defeated by guilt and remorse, emptied of significance, and abjectly apologizing for the confessed murderer whose end he sought and who sought his: "I began these memoirs with the idea of vindicating my character, I have now no character that I wish to vindicate" (337).

Caleb Williams builds its nightmarish tale of empty vengeance and retribu-tion, haunted doubling, terrorized pursuit and flight, and vain repentance from the conventional figures of eighteenth-century popular literature: the English masculine paragon with Continental tastes; the gentleman criminal; the boorish country squire; the romantic and sentimental ingénue; the band of robbers with their noble captain; the duplicitous thief-taker and informer; the rogue criminal. Likewise it fashions the narrative from tropes familiar from eighteenth-century fictional narratives: the pursuit of honor; the competition for masculine prestige; the forced marriage plot; imprisonment; uncanny prison break-outs; picaresque rambles; and, in its most profound relation with early criminal biography, the reversals of authority endemic to a topsy-turvy world of political and ethical inversions. We have here, then, material referencing popular criminal lives, such as those discussed in chapter 3, and popular novels, especially Richardson's *Clarissa* and *Sir Charles Grandison*. Thus, Godwin brings together the eighteenth-century source books for both the criminal and gentleman, weaving them together through a series of doubled reversals that articulate their proximity and indict their necessary collusion.[46]

As literary critic Eric Rothstein has noted, Godwin takes on not only the contours of plot and character found in Richardson's novels but, in his first volume, even the narrative framework of the flashback story.[47] As is everywhere acknowledged, Godwin's gentleman criminal, Falkland, is modeled on Richardson's male paragon, Sir Charles Grandison, as part of a strategy to discredit the powerful myth of the gentleman that sustains social inequities. Godwin, then, refuses the reforms Richardson sets forth in his Grandison, who, taking over from his decidedly Lovelacian father, Sir Thomas, repairs the abuses of libertine patriarchy and, long-windedly avoiding duel after duel, resists the criminal pursuit of personal honor. Falkland's early biography follows the Italian lines of Sir Charles's own; his refinement, gentility, liberality, and popularity match those of Richardson's paragon and recall those of his Royalist namesake, Lucius Carey, the second Viscount Falkland.[48] Falkland's honorable character is highlighted by its stark contrast with the vicious temperament of his churlish neighbor Tyrrel. The matched pair, Tyrrel and Falkland, embody the premise that Godwin revokes: that Falkland, as a modern polite gentleman, can subdue and supplant the violent enactment of elite masculine privilege so boorishly performed by Tyrrel. For Godwin's portrayal of his gentleman paragon insists on the persistence of Falkland's irresistible investment in the ethos of aristocratic honor, on the fatality of that "poison of chivalry" which Falkland "imbibed" in his "earliest youth" (336–37). Publicly insulted and beaten by a savage Tyrrel, his reputation mortally wounded, Falkland retaliates in fury and kills his opponent, not in a duel but covertly and disgracefully with a knife in the back. The perfect gentleman is the perfect criminal, stripped by Godwin of any trappings of gallantry and chivalry.

At the same time that Godwin's Falkland recalls, in order to revoke, the Grandisonian paragon, so does his life enact a psychologically and ideologically acute rebuttal to Edmund Burke's celebration of "chivalry" in his *Reflections on the Revolution in France*.[49] Instantiating Godwin's premise that the "characters of men originate in external circumstances," Falkland's internalization of the aristocratic ethos of honor makes and unmakes who he is: "To Mr. Falkland disgrace was worse than death" (100).[50] This principle both generates Falkland's murder of Tyrrel and predicts the consequences of that act; his secret disgrace wears him horribly away, making his a life in death. Williams describes the later Falkland, his vitality consumed by efforts to conceal his guilt and so maintain his honor: "His complexion . . . suggested the idea of its being burnt and parched by the eternal fire that burned within him. . . . His whole figure was thin, to a degree that suggested the idea rather of a skeleton than a person actually alive. Life seemed hardly to be the capable inhabitant of so woe-begone and ghost-like a figure" (328–29). Thus devolved into "the phantom of departed honour," Falkland fulfills his destiny, the gothic specter of Burke's definition of chivalry as "the spirit of a gentleman" (337).[51]

Godwin thus narrates the withering away of chivalry in the fulfillment of its own logic. Enthralled to the code of honor—"the slightest breath of dishonour would have stung him to the very soul"—the elite masculine subject sacrifices ethical and sentimental authority to its absolute decree. Such a subject, then, cannot be entrusted with social reform. That such a subject is *expected* to do so is driven home by Falkland's noble resistance to Tyrrel's malignant tyranny over the community, his own tenants, and his own cousin, Emily Melville. That he *cannot* do so spearheads the critique of aristocratic ideology elaborated through Falkland's imprisonment, pursuit, and final confrontation with his secretary, servant, accuser, and double, Caleb Williams.[52]

As Godwin's novel enlists the discourses of criminality and masculine prestige in its sustained exposition of sociopolitical inequity, it picks up the reversals of authority characteristic of criminal biography and follows them through both its narrative of pursuit and their internalization as moral inversions in the consciousness of its protagonists. The pursuer becomes the pursued and back again; innocence and guilt transfer across in an exchange that erodes distinctions, ethical and personal. These reversals produce identifications between Falkland and Caleb Williams; they first take shape through the bad kind of intimacy identified with the patronage system within which the relation of the two men is initiated. Robert J. Corber has argued that in *Caleb Williams* Godwin adopts the ready weapon of homophobia in his assault on elite privilege. Godwin, along with other radical thinkers, stigmatized the institution of patronage, and, associating it with sodomy, even criminalized it "as an especially pernicious form of male bonding" that "threatened to undermine the growing hegemony of the middle class." "Widely denounced as an aristocratic vice imported from the Continent," sodomy becomes part of the radical armory against the elite: "Contributing to the persecution of sodomites allowed the radicals to exacerbate the tensions between the aristocracy and the middle class."[53] By denouncing patronage, a persistent instance of what Thomas King calls "pederastic" gender relations, Godwin thus participates in the advocacy of heteronormative, complementary sexual relations even where he refuses their sentimental romanticization.[54] This bad bonding, then, shapes the relationship between Caleb Williams and his patron into the pattern of subjugation and rebellion, veneration and debasement, attachment and resentment, protection and persecution that drives the undoing of both.

In a novel so preoccupied with infatuated male-male antagonism, all powerfully charged relations—what Williams calls "the magnetic sympathy between me and my patron"—are between men (117). These are heavily eroticized and emotional, governed by a dynamic of identification and displacement, seduction and transgression. So Caleb Williams relates the illicit delights of prying into his patron's secret:

> The instant I had chosen this employment for myself, I found a strange sort of pleasure in it. To do what is forbidden always has its charms, because we have an indistinct apprehension of something arbitrary and tyrannical in the prohibition. I remembered the stern reprimand I had received, and his terrible looks; and the recollection gave a kind of tingling sensation not altogether unallied to enjoyment. . . . The more impenetrable Mr Falkland was determined to be, the more uncontrollable was my curiosity. (113)

Williams recognizes his danger, but is drawn on: "I had a confused apprehension of what I was doing but I could not stop myself" (118). Finally, Williams succeeds in wheedling something like a confession and some very passionate resentment from his patron: "Who gave you the right to be my confidant? Base, artful wretch that you are! . . . Are my passions to be wound and unwound by an insolent domestic? Do you think I will be an instrument to be played on at your pleasure?" (123).

The apparent advantage Williams gains through his knowledge of Falkland's crime quickly evaporates under Falkland's redoubled repression and Williams's own reactive guilt and abasement. Thus the narrative initiates its characteristic pattern of reversals between domination and submission, authority and transgression, innocence and guilt, pursuer and pursued. Williams exclaims against his "servile submission" to Falkland's surveillance: "I was his prisoner; and what a prisoner! All my actions observed; all my gestures marked, I could move neither to the right nor the left, but the eye of my keeper was on me" (149). Transgressive "curiosity" gives way to open defiance: "My patience," he records, "was at an end." He runs away. Anxious to retain control over Williams and his secret, Falkland fabricates a case of theft against his servant that provides the pretext for his apprehension.

Caleb's compulsion to rebel against the authority of his patron, and thus against "things as they are," is shown to be just as ineluctably embedded in the inequities of the patronage system as is the fatal devotion to personal vengeance in the code of honor. Under cover of favor, patronage barely conceals the inequities of tyranny and courts rebellious reaction. It is precisely this danger that the tenant-farmer Hawkins would avoid for his son, whom he refuses to submit to Tyrrel's patronage, which he regards as a "risk" to his "boy's welfare" (73). Independent, if poor, young Hawkins "is sober and industrious, and without being pert or surly, knows what is due to him" (73). Under Tyrrel's patronage, his father fears, these habits of sobriety, self-reliance, and self-respect would be corrupted by its compulsions of domination and revolt, favor and obligation. Just so, within the dynamic of patronage, Williams's independence is degraded to rebellion, his curiosity to guilty transgression, his relation with Falkland to one of obsessive "magnetic sympathy" in which intimate knowledge makes each the guilty party.

In *Caleb Williams*, then, private authority and personal relations are criminalized by elite ideology and its institutions. The public and ostensibly more impersonal tribunal of the law offers no alternative oasis of legitimacy. The novel foregrounds the conventional competitive discrepancy between judicial authority and traditional forms of status-linked power earlier remarked in discussions of *Colonel Jack, Clarissa,* and *Evelina.* So when Caleb Williams is brought before the magistrate for the alleged theft of Falkland's goods, the magistrate, one Mr. Forester, Falkland's brother-in-law, insists on imprisoning Williams against Falkland's wish to spare him. Falkland proclaims his faith in the law of honor over judicial law and the authority of his personal will over that of the magistrate's ruling: "I am sure things will never be as they ought, till honour and not law be the dictator of mankind. . . . If my calumniator were worthy of my resentment, I would chastise him with my own sword, and not that of the magistrate; but in the present case I smile at his malice and resolve to spare him" (182). According to the code of honor, Williams's status makes him unworthy of Falkland's reprisal. Falkland does not accept even the legal fiction of equality. Yet in the face of Forester's resolve to send Williams to jail, Falkland withdraws his opposition, acquiesces with the magistrate's pronouncement that "this is no time for us to settle the question between chivalry and the law," and bides his own time (182).

This contretemps between Falkland and Forester, between "chivalry and the law," produces the central narrative reversal in the novel. After Williams has broken out of jail, fallen in with a band of robbers, been misapprehended as an Irish mail thief, and escaped to London where he lives in disguise, he is finally dogged down by the thief-taker Gines. Taken into custody, Williams attempts to defend himself by making a formal disclosure against Falkland for murder. He is summarily dismissed by the magistrate: "A fine time of it indeed it would be, if, when gentlemen of six thousand a year take up their servants for robbing them, those servants could trump up such accusations as these, and get any magistrate or court of justice to listen to them!" (286). The magistrate's loyalty to the elite remains uncompromised by any greater allegiance that elite might harbor to the laws of honor than to the laws of the land. The familial, if uneasy, relation between Falkland and the magistrate Mr. Forester, his brother-in-law, articulates the intimate affiliation of the often competitive claims of status-authorized command and legal verdict. Falkland may scorn the law; nonetheless, the law never ceases to operate in his favor. Williams realizes that he has squandered his trump card: "Such was the success of this ultimate resort on my part, upon which I had built such undoubting confidence" (286). He is taken back to prison and awaits trial. The assizes are called; he goes to court, only to discover that not "a single individual of any description" is appearing against him. The recognizances are declared forfeited; he is set free (288–89).

Released from custody only to be immediately apprehended again by Gines, Williams is bundled off to a private tribunal before Falkland. This scene reverses the circumstance of all that precedes it, then reverses that reversal with a clarification of power and motive that only redoubles Falkland's hold on Williams. This reversed reversal follows a pattern of doubling used by Godwin to produce a collapse of distinctions and thus the evacuation of significance.

As it transpires, all the time up to now during which Williams had been trying to escape from Falkland, Falkland had been trying to protect him: "Did I not maintain you in prison? Did I not endeavour to prevent your being sent thither? Could you mistake the bigoted and obstinate conduct of Forester, in offering a hundred guineas for your apprehension, for mine?" (291). Falkland has overreached the law and had the charges against Williams dropped. Even Falkland's self-styled benevolence takes megalomaniacal shape as the exertion of his absolute will over the law and over the entire course of Williams's life. "I had my eye upon you in all your wanderings," Falkland tells Williams, "You have taken no material step through their whole course with which I have not been acquainted. I meditated to do you good" (291). Everything, as Williams has understood throughout, is ultimately in Falkland's power; but the significance of that agency is reversed in this scene. For one chaotic moment, Williams has no enemy. This produces severe psychological disorientation and an existential void. All of Williams's heroic feats of escape and endurance collapse into puny futility: "Was it for this that I had broken through so many locks and bolts, and the adamantine walls of my prison; that I had spent so many anxious days, and sleepless, spectre-haunted nights . . . that my existence had been enthralled to an ever-living torment?" (289). Falkland's persecution authorizes Williams's torment; without it, Williams's existence as a prisoner of hell on earth lacks cause or consequence.

But this moment during which Williams is bereft of his adversary is brief, interrupting the general history of his persecution only long enough to make a cruelly nihilistic joke of its first chapter. The all-seeing Falkland is aware that Williams had attempted to make a disclosure against him for his murder of Tyrrel. When Williams refuses to sign a document swearing that this charge is false, Falkland reverses the nature of his authority once again. This betrayal, he asserts, changes everything; no longer will he watch over Williams in order to protect him, but employing Gines as his agent, he will submit Williams to the full fury of his power and grind him "to atoms" (294). All of this, he vows, will take place outside the law, under his sole and absolute jurisdiction. "Do you think," Falkland asks Williams, "you are out of the reach of my power, because a court of justice has acquitted you?" (292). Once Falkland proclaims this campaign against Williams, things return to the pattern of pursuit that Williams had ever assumed. If anything has changed, it is only that Falkland's power, confirmed now in its lawlessness, seems even more absolute and, confirmed as the expression of omnipotent menace, even more terrific.

The odious Gines is Falkland's tool in this second chapter of Williams's pursuit and persecution. As thief and thief-taker, Gines embodies an instance of ethical doubling and instability best known from the popular incarnations of Jonathan Wild. In Godwin's novel this kind of doubled reversal of ethical orientation, as we have just seen, is most centrally performed by Falkland's role in Williams's trials and tribulations. That Falkland's doubled reversal of role is itself doubled in the figure of Gines reinforces the uncannily ubiquitous and dizzily mirroring patterns of social corruption that define what Williams curses as "the whole system of human existence" (260). Gines's favored instrument of persecution is the criminal biography of Williams that he covertly distributes within communities where Williams might attempt to build a creditable existence for himself. Both of these agents, Gines and the criminal biography, are products of a larger public network of juridical, penal, and popular print culture that Falkland appropriates privately. While Falkland refuses to be bound by the law and its institutions, he does not scruple to expropriate its instruments.

Itself conventionally constructed within ethical instabilities and their resultant reversals of authority, the criminal biography both celebrates and excoriates its protagonist, providing models for delinquent emulation, for moral affirmation, for popular celebrity, and for punitive apprehension. The novel underscores the cultural agency of popular criminal discourses by thematizing Williams's own production of them, and, more profoundly, the production of his character through them. During his London sojourn, Williams endeavors to support himself by writing for a magazine. Finding little market for poetry, on the advice of the publisher, he turns his hand to moral essays and short narratives or "tales" (268). Traversing a discursive divide that recalls the one strung between Mr. Spectator and Macheath in Boswell's *London Journals,* Williams masters moral essays in "the style of Addison's Spectators" and then moves on to tales based on "the histories of celebrated robbers" (268). The discussion in chapter 3 argues that in the *London Journals* the figures of Mr. Spectator and Macheath, despite their ethical polarity, mutually support Boswell's conceptualization and performance of his masculinity. In Godwin's novel, Williams's relation to these two popular discursive strands remains more distinct; indeed, his shift from one to the other describes, not Williams's psychic integration of both, but his abdication of the moral authority of the essay and self-relegation to the fatal guilt of the criminal. He leaves off writing Addisonian essays because he doubts his own "resources in the way of moral disquisition" and takes up criminal tales "by a fatality" he cannot understand (268). That Williams's fancy turns to these tales seems all too obviously a symptom of his identification with them: as a pursued criminal he, like the "memorable worthies" he narrates, is likely to end up "upon the gallows or the scaffold" (268).

Blind to the source of his fascination with these legendary criminals, Williams understands it, not in connection with his own circumstances and psyche, but as determined by the uncannily comprehensive net of persecution cast by Falkland that he experiences as a diabolical version of Providential design. The "fatality" of his fascination, as he understands it, lies in his retrospective awareness that it is on account of his criminal tales that Gines, whose brother is their publisher, identifies and apprehends Williams. But a greater fatality inheres in the identification Williams forges with the guilt of the criminals whose lives he narrates. Finally, Williams can only write his own story as the biography of a felon doomed to "endure the penalty of [his] crime" (336).[55]

Williams's narrative cannot appropriate the positive principles of radical dissent conventionally associated with discourses of criminality; for in his relations with Captain Raymond and his gang of thieves, Williams himself invalidates these principles.[56] Furthermore, his own experiences with his popular-culture doubles affirm the ultimately repressive uses to which such discourses are put, however emancipating and appealing they might first appear. Yet predictably enough, Williams's attitude toward criminals and their stories shifts with his own situation. During his first stint in jail, Williams recalls his boyhood fascination with stories of house- and prison-breakers such as Jack Sheppard and draws on his them for inspiration and justification of his own attempts (195). While in prison, Williams also befriends a classically educated and genteel highway robber named Brightwel, whose subsequent death he laments extravagantly (199). This sympathetic identification with criminals and their texts serves to bolster Williams's, and Godwin's, criticism of penal law and its institutions. Additionally, it accords well with Godwin's technique of showing how character is shaped by circumstance: himself a prisoner, Williams identifies sympathetically with other prisoners. But as circumstances shift, so does Williams's relationship with criminals and criminality; for like everything in the novel, this orientation is vulnerable to reversal.

After his escape, Williams is held captive by a gang of robbers led by one Captain Raymond, a figure Eric Hobsbawm might identify as a "social bandit." A victim here rather than a fellow sufferer, Williams resists recruitment into their ideology and into their ranks. While Captain Raymond remains in Williams's estimation elevated above his more common criminal cohort, his conventional apology for criminality as a realm of justice, equity, and democracy loses authority within the context of the actual practices of these criminals, who, Williams observes, were ever ready "to sacrifice the human species at large to their meanest interest or wildest caprice" (228).[57] In their self-authorization of absolute will, these thieves operate very much like that other elite absolutist, Falkland, and like all the criminal types examined in this study. In a lengthy debate on the authority of criminality, Williams further elaborates on this propensity for absolute self-interest not only to erode social relations but also finally to backfire and destroy its agent, just like "the man who should set himself up as a mark for a file of musqueteers to shoot at" (235). Williams convinces himself that he should "have no share in their occupation" (235–36).

But Williams's dissociation from a criminal role does not last. We have observed how Williams's existence is emptied when his persecutor is withdrawn; conversely, it is as a criminal whose life is circulated publicly through popular discourse that Williams achieves his fullest sense of self-affirmation. Like his relation to Falkland, Williams's relation to this public character of himself is at once thrilling and terrifying, sustaining and potentially annihilating. Indeed, Williams's relation to his criminal doubles mediates his relation to Falkland, who, with his false charge of theft, produces these fictional characters. At the close of the novel, Williams observes that Falkland's crime results from his fatal investment in discourses of gallantry and romance: "Thou imbibedst the poison of chivalry with thy earliest youth" (336–37). So can we observe Williams's fatal identification with the popular discourses that cast him as a criminal. Like Odysseus listening to the Sirens' song, Williams is enthralled by his own fame, by these stories of himself, even as he realizes that their mass distribution threatens to raise up an army of informers, "a million of men in arms against me" (279). Always, when hearing his own biography or seeing it in print, he is resistless against the charm of self-recognition. Overhearing, at a public house, patrons talk over the tale of "Kit Williams," he "began inwardly to exult" (245). When the landlady affirms her own sympathy for the now-legendary, glamorous thief "as handsome, likely a lad, as any in four counties round," Williams takes great pleasure in the "sincere and generous warmth with which she interested herself in [his] behalf" (246). In London, Williams hears his own biography hawked on the street: "Petrified as I was . . . I had the temerity to go up to the man and purchase one of his papers" (278). In Wales, Williams discovers in a copy of this biography the cause of his social rejection: "My eyes accidentally glanced upon a paper . . . which, by some association I was unable to explain, roused in me a strong sensation of suspicion and curiosity, I eagerly went towards it" (311).

Unlike Dick Turpin and other more media-savvy criminals, Williams finally is undone by publicity and the popular press. His fascination with criminal biography does bring with it a "fatality," not merely in the sense that this popular publicity supports first his criminal detention and then his social extermination, but more profoundly in the ways in which it locks him within an identification with the "MOST WONDERFUL AND SURPRISING HISTORY AND MIRACULOUS ADVENTURES OF CALEB WILLIAMS" (278). Identifying himself with the popular rogue Kit Williams from the first time he hears of him, Williams remains blindly enthralled with this persona whose guilty tale, "by some association I was unable to explain," draws him in, just as the tales of those legendary criminals "by a fatality, for which I did not exactly know how to account" captivate his imagination and just as he had first been drawn in to penetrate Falkland's secret through a fatal and obscure curiosity (268). Indeed, Falkland's secret—that he is the murderer of Tyrrel—is itself the inverted double of Williams's guilt—that he is the servant who stole from his master. Concealing the first produces the second.

The criminal lives of these "memorable worthies" that Williams rehashes for publication find their ending in the outcome of judicial process that condemns them to death. No such finality is available to Caleb Williams. For as we have seen, in his narrative's central reversal Falkland short-circuits judicial process, removing Williams from the maws of the penal code only to deliver him to the insatiable grinding of his own vengeance. Godwin's text explicitly denies Williams's "guilt" as a "criminal" within any juridical or evidentiary register; he is released by the judicial system and remains unimpeached by any evidence in the novel. Williams's "guilt" as a thief is Falkland's fabrication, one that, through his publication of the lie, produces the popular fictional doubles through which Williams mediates his own primary relation with Falkland as his "guilty servant."

Even though up until that fiction is inverted by Falkland's confession, Williams himself maintains an awareness of his own innocence, the foundational relation between Falkland and Williams reasserts itself absolutely in the novel's final reversal. The moment Falkland's rather than Williams's guilt is published, Williams condemns himself for his betrayal and loses all innocence. The relation of "guilty servant" defined by Falkland is no longer mediated by Williams's fictional doubles but is fully internalized in a guilty consciousness where his relation with Falkland, the "phantom of honor," may be pursued eternally. Williams is sentenced to a lifetime of haunting by the injured murderer: "Waking or sleeping, I still behold him. . . . I live the devoted victim of conscious reproach. Alas! I am the same Caleb Williams that so short a time ago boasted that, however great were the calamities I endured, I was still innocent" (336). Yet while Williams remains fatally invested in his own criminal character, the *fact* of his innocence evacuates from that character any ethical substance, positive or negative, just as surely as the fact of Falkland's guilt evacuates any authority from his character of chivalric honor. So finally, Caleb Williams is left not even with a criminal character, but with "no character."

Having explored how the social and political inequities of "things as they are" are maintained through discourses of masculine prestige and criminality that produce one another as self-annihilating doubles, Godwin ultimately empties both of ethical content. Thus, an understanding of "things as they are" must be validated outside the conventions of these discourses and initiated by a kind of ideological exorcism of their specters, the "phantom of honour" and the "character . . . no character" of the "still innocent" criminal.

Chapter 1. Historicizing Masculinity

1. The contemporary scholarly discussion of the history of manners was initiated when sociologist Norbert Elias's *Über den Prozeß der Zivilisation* (1939) was reprinted and published in English as *The Civilizing Process*, Vol. 1, *The History of Manners* (Oxford: Blackwell, 1969) and Vol. 2, *State Formation and Civilization* (Oxford: Blackwell, 1982). For discussions of the gentleman and the sociocultural milieu from which he emerges, see Jorge Arditi, *A Genealogy of Manners: Transformations of Social Relations in France and England from the Fourteenth to the Eighteenth Century* (Chicago: Univ. of Chicago Press, 1998); G. J. Barker-Benfield, *The Culture of Sensibility: Sex and Society in Eighteenth-Century Britain* (Chicago: Univ. of Chicago Press, 1992); John Barrell, "Introduction: Artificers and Gentleman," in *English Literature in History 1730–80: An Equal, Wide Survey*, series ed. Raymond Williams (London: Hutchinson, 1983), 17–50; Anna Bryson, *From Courtesy to Civility: Changing Codes of Conduct in Early Modern England* (Oxford: Oxford Univ. Press, 1998); Philip Carter, *Men and the Emergence of Polite Society, Britain 1660–1800*, Women and Men in History Series (Harlow, UK: Longman, 2001); Michael Curtin, "A Question of Manners: Status and Gender in Etiquette and Courtesy," *Journal of Modern History* 57 (1985): 395–423; Erin Mackie, *Market à la Mode: Fashion, Commodity, and Gender in "The Tatler" and "The Spectator"* (Baltimore: Johns Hopkins Univ. Press, 1997), esp. 1–29, 144–202; Shawn Lisa Maurer, *Proposing Men: Dialectics of Gender and Class in the Eighteenth-Century English Periodical* (Stanford: Stanford Univ. Press, 1998). For a popular, literary-cultural overview of the ideal of the gentleman from Chaucer through Kipling, see Philip Mason, *The English Gentleman: The Rise and Fall of an Ideal* (London: Andre Deutsch, 1982). Mason's account is especially compelling in its presentation of how the nineteenth-century public school gentleman served the administrative and military needs of the British Empire.

2. "We can speak of a gender order existing by the eighteenth century in which masculinity as a cultural form had been produced and in which we can define a hegemonic form of masculinity. This was the masculinity predominant in the lives of men of the gentry" (R. W. Connell, "The Big Picture: Masculinities in Recent World History," *Theory and Society* 22.5 (1993): 608. For a discussion of the ideological orientation of the "politeness" embodied by this modern gentleman, see Lawrence Klein, "Liberty, Manners, and

Politeness in Early Eighteenth-Century England," *Historical Journal* 32.3 (1989): 583–605. Michele Cohen has looked at how the definition of national language and national culture, especially in relation to France, intersects with the articulation of the modern polite gentleman in *Fashioning Masculinity: National Identity and Language in the Eighteenth Century* (New York: Routledge, 1996).

3. In contrast with the highwayman and the pirate, the rake has received much serious scholarly attention, some of it intersecting with the concerns I detail here and in chapter 2. The point remains that these figures are never examined together as elements in a shared cultural milieu and shared history.

4. A representative collection of these treatises on conduct and education has been compiled on microfilm by Michele Cohen from sources in the Bodleian library, see *Masculinity, 1560–1918: Men Defining Men*, Part 1: 1600–1800 (Marlborough, UK: Adam Matthew, 2000), 20 reels. Three of the most inclusive, influential, and available compilations of seventeenth- and early eighteenth-century criminal biographies are Captain Alexander Smith, *A Complete History of the Lives and Robberies of the Most Notorious Highwaymen, Footpads, Shoplifts, and Cheats* (London, 1714); rpt. and ed. Arthur Hayward (London: Routledge, 1926); Captain Charles Johnson, *A General History of the Lives and Adventures of the Most Famous Highwaymen, Murderers, and Street-Robbers* (London, 1734–35); and Daniel Defoe [attr.], *A General History of the Pyrates* [1724–28], ed. Manuel Schonhorn (Mineola, NY: Dover, 1999). For an exhaustive bibliography of criminal biography in this period, see Lincoln Faller, *Turned to Account: The Forms and Functions of Criminal Biography in Late Seventeenth- and Early Eighteenth-Century England* (Cambridge: Cambridge Univ. Press, 1987).

5. For scholarship on the history of manners and the gentleman, see note 1. Studies of crime and dissent include Eric Hobsbawm, *Bandits* [1969] (New York: New Press, 2000); Douglas Hay et al., *Albion's Fatal Tree: Crime and Society in Eighteenth-Century England* (London: Allen Lane, 1975); E. P. Thompson, *Whigs and Hunters: The Origins of the Black Act* (London: Allen Lane, 1975); Geoffrey Pearson, *Hooligan: A History of Respectable Fears* (London: Macmillan, 1983); Marcus Rediker, *Between the Devil and the Deep Blue Sea: Merchant Seamen, Pirates, and the Anglo-American Maritime World, 1700–1750* (Cambridge: Cambridge Univ. Press, 1987); Peter Linebaugh, *The London Hanged: Crime and Civil Society in the Eighteenth Century* (Cambridge: Cambridge Univ. Press, 1992); Peter Linebaugh and Marcus Rediker, *The Many-Headed Hydra: Sailors, Slaves, Commoners, and the Hidden History of the Revolutionary Atlantic* (Boston: Beacon Press, 2000).

6. See Thomas Laqueur, *Making Sex: Body and the Gender from the Greeks to Freud* (Cambridge: Harvard Univ. Press, 1990); Michael McKeon, "Historicizing Patriarchy: The Emergence of Gender Difference in England, 1660–1760," *Eighteenth-Century Studies* 28 (1995): 295–322; Randolph Trumbach, "The Birth of the Queen: Sodomy and the Emergence of Gender Equality in Modern Culture, 1660–1750," in *Hidden from History: Reclaiming the Gay and Lesbian Past*, ed. Martin Duberman et al. (Markham, ON: New American Library / Penguin, 1989), 129–40, and "Sodomitical Subcultures, Sodomitical Roles, and the Gender Revolution of the Eighteenth Century: The Recent Historiography," *'Tis Nature's Fault: Unauthorized Sexuality during the Enlightenment*, ed. Robert Purks Maccubin (Cambridge: Cambridge Univ. Press, 1987), 109–21; Alan Bray, *Homosexuality in Renaissance England*, Between Men—Between Women Series (New York: Columbia Univ.

Press, 1995), esp. chap. 4; Tim Hitchcock, *English Sexualities, 1700–1800*, Social History in Perspective Series (London: Macmillan, 1997). George Haggerty discusses homoerotic discourses in a literary study attentive primarily to modes of emotional attachment, *Men in Love: Masculinity and Sexuality in the Eighteenth Century*, Between Men—Between Women Series (New York: Columbia Univ. Press, 1999). In what I find the most satisfying of all treatments of masculinity in this period, Thomas King's *The Gendering of Men, 1600–1750: The English Phallus* (Madison: Univ. of Wisconsin Press, 2004) argues for a radical discontinuity between the "pederastic subjection" characteristic of earlier sexual-social relations and modern gendered "liberal subjectivities" (12). Modern gendered masculinity is achieved "by displacing the demonized publicity of aristocratic bodies onto a male body figured as outside privacy: the theatrical, effeminate, and finally queer male body" (6).

7. King, *Gendering of Men*, 181.

8. See note 5. Thompson examines changes in judicial and customary law that define notions of property and ownership and so of theft and criminality, see *Whigs and Hunters*, and "Custom, Law, and Common Right," in *Customs in Common* (London: Merlin Press, 1991), 97–184.

9. Lennard Davis, "Wicked Actions and Feigned Words: Criminals, Criminality, and the Early English Novel," Rethinking History: Time, Myth, and Writing, *Yale French Studies* 59: 106–18; Hal Gladfelder, *Criminality and Narrative in Eighteenth-Century England: Beyond the Law* (Baltimore: Johns Hopkins Univ. Press, 2001); Bryan Reynolds, *Becoming Criminal: Transversal Performance and Cultural Dissidence in Early Modern England* (Baltimore: Johns Hopkins Univ. Press, 2002). John Richetti explicates the ideological coordinates of pirate and travel fiction in "Travellers, Pirates, and Pilgrims," in *Popular Fiction Before Richardson* (Oxford: Clarendon Press, 1969), 60–118.

10. Faller, *Turned to Account*.

11. Donna T. Andrew, "The Code of Honour and Its Critics: The Opposition to Duelling in England, 1700–1850," *Social History* 5.3 (1980): 409–34; Robert B. Shoemaker, "The Taming of the Duel: Masculinity, Honour, and Ritual Violence in London, 1660–1800," *Historical Journal* 45.3 (2002): 525–45, and "Male Honour and the Decline of Public Violence in Eighteenth-Century London," *Social History* 26.2 (2001): 190–208; Susan Dwyer Amussen, "Punishment, Discipline, and Power: The Social Meanings of Violence in Early Modern England," *Journal of British Studies* 34.1 (1995): 1–34, and " 'The Part of a Christian Man': The Cultural Politics of Manhood in Early Modern England," *Political Culture and Cultural Politics in Early Modern England: Essays Presented to David Underdown*, ed. Susan D. Amussen and Mark A. Kishlansky (Manchester: Manchester Univ. Press, 1995), 213–33. Historian of crime J. A. Sharpe remarks: "Future research will doubtless reveal how other forms of criminality [than assault] involving men were tied into concepts of masculinity" (*Crime in Early Modern England 1550–1750*, 2nd ed., Themes in British Social History Series [London: Longman, 1999], 160).

12. See Connell, "The Big Picture."

13. John Tosh, "What Should Historians Do with Masculinity? Reflections on Nineteenth-Century Britain," in *Gender and History in Western Europe*, ed. Robert Shoemaker and Mary Vincent (London: Arnold Press, 1998), 73–74.

14. For discussions of the concept "hegemonic masculinity," see Connell "The Big

Picture"; Jeff Hearn, "From Hegemonic Masculinity to the Hegemony of Men," *Feminist Theory* 5.1 (2004): 49–72; R. W. Connell and James W. Messerschmidt, "Hegemonic Masculinity: Rethinking the Concept," *Gender and Society* 19.6 (2005): 829–59.

15. However, as Bryson, *From Courtesy to Civility*, has documented in her study on the transition from the culture of courtesy to the culture of civility, many of the traits embodied by the modern gentleman had been developing over the previous two centuries before they found their philosophical champion in the Third Earl of Shaftesbury and their polite popularization in Joseph Addison's and Richard Steele's *The Tatler* and *The Spectator* (46). Lawrence E. Klein has written extensively on Shaftesbury's treatment of the concept of sociability and on the national-political inflections of the new codes of civility and politeness in the early eighteenth century; see *Shaftesbury and the Culture of Politeness: Moral Discourse and Cultural Politics in Early Eighteenth-Century England* (Cambridge: Cambridge Univ. Press, 1994); "Liberty, Manners, and Politeness in Early Eighteenth-Century England"; and "The Figure of France: The Politics of Sociability in England, 1660–1715," *Yale French Studies* 92 (1997): 30–45.

16. McKeon, "Historicizing Patriarchy," 297. King, *Gendering of Men*, emphasizes the departure from the courtly, aristocratic body accompanying the emergence of modern gendered subjectivity.

17. McKeon, "Historicizing Patriarchy," 297–98. For the increasing hold that juridical discourses and their ideology of contractual relations have on the modern subject, see John P. Zomchick, *Family and the Law in Eighteenth-Century Fiction* (Cambridge: Cambridge Univ. Press, 1993).

18. McKeon, "Historicizing Patriarchy," 300. For a discussion of how men from the middle ranks of society developed institutions, especially the clubs, that resisted patron-client power relations and fostered horizontal class relations of mutuality and dependence, see John Brewer "Commercialization and Politics," in *The Birth of Consumer Society: The Commercialization of Eighteenth-Century England* (London: Europa, 1982), 197–64.

19. See note 6.

20. King, *Gendering of Men*, 16.

21. R. W. Connell, *Masculinities* (Berkeley: Univ. of California Press, 1995), 29.

22. King, *Gendering of Men*, views rakish behavior as part of an increasingly discredited economy of pederasty, discontinuous with "a modern economy of heterosexual, homosexual, and bisexual subjectivities" (5): "I have located the libertine, whose erotic practices were organized according to the aim of penetration rather than by desire for a particular gendered object, within the residual economy of pederasty" (238).

23. Trumbach, "Sodomitical Subcultures," 118. For the nature of defamation and the value placed on sexual control, see Amussen, " 'The Part of a Christian Man' " and "Punishment, Discipline, and Power"; and Elizabeth A. Foyster, *Manhood in Early Modern England: Honour, Sex, and Marriage*, Women and Men in History Series (London: Longman, 1999).

24. As I discuss in chapter 2, much contemporary criticism focuses almost exclusively on the rake's aesthetic-stylistic and erotic powers and overlooks his overtly violent, criminal behavior. See, for example, Harold Weber, "Rakes, Rogues, and the Empire of Misrule," *Huntington Library Quarterly* 47.1 (1984): 13–32, and *The Restoration Rake-Hero: Transfor-*

mations in *Sexual Understandings in Seventeenth-Century England* (Madison: Univ. of Wisconsin Press, 1986); James G. Turner, "The Properties of Libertinism," in *'Tis Nature's Fault*, 75–87, and "The Libertine Sublime: Love and Death in Restoration England," *Studies in Eighteenth-Century Culture* 19 (1989): 99–115. A notable exception to this general silence on the (nonsexual) criminality of the rake is Daniel Statt, "The Case of the Mohocks: Rake Violence in Augustan London," *Social History* 20.2 (1995): 179–99.

25. As my colleague Patrick Evans remarked, these invasions might themselves be viewed as attempts at the highway robbery of Britain itself.

26. See Jürgen Habermas, *The Structural Transformation of the Public Sphere: An Inquiry into a Category of Bourgeois Society,* trans. Thomas Burger with Frederick Lawrence (Cambridge: MIT Press, 1989); Peter Uwe Hohendahl, *The Institution of Criticism* (Ithaca, NY: Cornell Univ. Press, 1982); Terry Eagleton, *The Function of Criticism: From "The Spectator" to Post-Structuralism* (London: Verso, 1984); Peter Stallybrass and Allon White, "The Grotesque Body and the Smithfield Muse: Authorship in the Eighteenth Century," in *The Politics and Poetics of Transgression* (Ithaca, NY: Cornell Univ. Press, 1986), 80–124; Mackie, *Market à la Mode,* and "Being Too Positive about the Public Sphere," in *"The Spectator": Emerging Discourses,* ed. Donald J. Newman (Newark: Univ. of Delaware Press, 2005), 81–104.

27. King, *Gendering of Men*, 223. See Mackie, *Market à la Mode*.

28. See Nancy Fraser, "Rethinking the Public Sphere: A Contribution to the Critique of Actually Existing Democracy," in *The Phantom Public Sphere*, ed. Bruce Robbins for the Social Text Collective, Cultural Politics Series, vol. 5 (Minneapolis: Univ. of Minnesota Press, 1993), 1–32; Geoff Eley, "Nations, Publics, and Political Cultures: Placing Habermas in the Nineteenth Century," in *Habermas and the Public Sphere*, ed. Craig Calhoun (Cambridge: MIT Press, 1992), 289–320; Mackie, *Market à la Mode*.

29. Margaret Hunt, *The Middling Sort: Commerce, Gender, and the Family in England, 1680–1780* (Berkeley: Univ. of California Press, 1996), 67.

30. See James G. Turner, *Libertines and Radicals in Early Modern London: Sexuality, Politics, and Literary Culture, 1630–1685* (Cambridge: Cambridge Univ. Press, 2002), esp. 164–94.

31. Hunt, *Middling Sort*, 69.

32. Randoph Trumbach, *Sex and the Gender Revolution,* Vol. 1, *Heterosexuality and the Third Gender in Enlightenment London,* Chicago Series on Sexuality, History, and Society (Chicago: Univ. of Chicago Press, 1998), 69–72. See also Vern L. Bullough, "Prostitution and Reform in Eighteenth-Century England," in *'Tis Nature's Fault*, 61–74.

33. Terry Eagleton, *The Rape of Clarissa: Writing, Sexuality, and Class Struggle in Samuel Richardson* (Oxford: Basil Blackwell, 1982), 88–89; James G. Turner, "Lovelace and the Paradoxes of Libertinism," *Samuel Richardson: Tercentenary Essays,* ed. Margaret Anne Doody and Peter Sabor (Cambridge: Cambridge Univ. Press, 1989), 70–88.

34. Elaine McGirr, "Why Lovelace Must Die," *Novel: A Forum on Fiction* 37.1–2 (2003): 5.

35. Michael McKeon, "The Devolution of Absolutism," *The Secret History of Domesticity: Public, Private, and the Division of Knowledge* (Baltimore: Johns Hopkins Univ. Press, 2005, 3–48). The competition between this absolute *hierarchical* individualism and the absolute *sentimental* subject is examined in the discussion of France Burney's *Evelina* in chapter 5.

36. Isaac Kramnick, *Bolingbroke and His Circle: The Politics of Nostalgia in the Age of Walpole* (Cambridge: Harvard Univ. Press, 1968), 228; Michael Denning, "Beggars and Thieves," *Literature and History* 8.1 (1982): 53.

37. Daniel Defoe, *Colonel Jack*, ed. Samuel Monk, intro. David Roberts (Oxford: Oxford Univ. Press, 1989), and *The Compleat English Gentleman*, ed. Karl D. Bulbring (London: Ballantyne Press / David Nutt, 1890). Subsequent citations to these texts will be made parenthetically.

38. See Curtin, "Question of Manners"; Arditi, *Genealogy of Manners;* Stephen Greenblatt, "To Fashion a Gentleman: Spenser and the Destruction of the Bower of Bliss," in *Renaissance Self-Fashioning from More to Shakespeare* (Chicago: Univ. of Chicago Press, 1980), 162–65; J. G. A. Pocock, "Virtues, Rights, and Manners: A Model for Historians of Political Thought," in *Virtue, Commerce, and History: Essays on Political Thought and History, Chiefly in the Eighteenth Century* (Cambridge: Cambridge Univ. Press, 1985), 49.

39. Mason, *English Gentleman,* 10.

40. Some may find it tempting to read this as an ironic comment on all claims to inherited honors.

41. Michael McKeon, *The Origins of the English Novel, 1600–1740* (Baltimore: Johns Hopkins Univ. Press, 1987), 131–265.

42. Michael Shinagel, *Daniel Defoe and Middle-Class Gentility* (Cambridge: Harvard Univ. Press, 1968), 169, 162, 170.

43. I borrow the description "gentleman-thug" from David Roberts's Introduction to *Colonel Jack* (xxiii).

44. Shoemaker, "Taming of the Duel," 525.

45. Andrew, "Code of Honour and Its Critics," 422.

46. Andrew gives some sense of the scope and source of this code's influence: "It contained the rules by which men of gentle birth and fashion wee to live, and sometimes die. It prescribed proper behaviour for the beau monde and proper methods of punishment when its rules had been disobeyed. The duel served to settle infractions of the code of honour; it dispensed both judgment and execution in a single event. Central to this system was the recognition of the desire for honour, or social approbation, as the basic passion of human motivation" (ibid., 413). In his book on contemporary status regimes and the anxieties that support them, Alain de Botton emphasizes the persistent nature of the "vulnerability to the disdain of others" engendered and exploited by the code of honor, see Botton, *Status Anxiety* (London: Hamish Hamilton / Penguin, 2004), 117.

47. George Boulukos, "Daniel Defoe's *Colonel Jack*, Grateful Slaves, and Racial Difference," *ELH* 68 (2001), 615–31. See Sidney W. Mintz and Richard Price, *The Birth of African-American Culture: An Anthropological Perspective* [1976] (Boston: Beacon Press, 1992); Erin Mackie, "Cultural Cross-Dressing: The Colorful Case of the Caribbean Creole," in *The Clothes That Wear Us: Essays on Dressing and Transgressing in Eighteenth-Century Culture,* ed. Jessica Munns and Penny Richards (Newark: Univ. of Delaware Press, 1999), 250–70; Roxann Wheeler, *The Complexion of Race: Categories of Difference in Eighteenth-Century British Culture* (Philadelphia: Univ. of Pennsylvania Press, 2000).

48. Boulukos, "Daniel Defoe's *Colonel Jack*," 615.

49. David Blewitt, "Jacobite and Gentleman," *English Studies in Canada* 4.1 (1978): 15–24.

50. As I discuss in chapter 3, these two types, the Jacobite and the gentleman highwayman, are tied in the popular imagination through the criminal biographies of those most gallant and illustrious highwaymen, James Hind, Philip Stafford, and Claude Duval. Hind and Stafford were militant royalists, and Duval was a French footman brought over to England with the Restoration by his master, a member of the exiled court at St. Germain.

51. *The English Theophrastus, or, The Manners of the Age* (London: W. Turner, 1702). See J. W. Smeed, *The Theophrastan "Character": The History of a Literary Genre* (Oxford: Clarendon Press, 1985).

52. Deidre Lynch has traced the development of novelistic "developed characters" from earlier character writing in *The Economy of Character: Novels, Market Culture, and the Business of Inner Meaning* (Chicago: Univ. of Chicago Press, 1998), esp. 1–122.

53. See Mackie, *Market à la Mode* (for the use of character writing, esp. 148–50).

54. Lynch, *Economy of Character,* 38.

55. Ibid., 47–48.

56. Smeed, *Theophrastan "Character,"* 38.

57. Mackie, *Market à la Mode,* 148.

58. Bryson, *From Courtesy to Civility,* 243.

59. Mackie, *Market à la Mode,* 144–64.

60. Graham Holderness, "Bardolatry: or, The Cultural Materialist's Guide to Stratford-upon-Avon," in *The Shakespeare Myth,* ed. Graham Holderness, Cultural Politics Series (Manchester: Manchester Univ. Press; New York: St. Martin's 1988), 11.

61. As a figure in historical romance, Ainsworth's Dick Turpin comes closest to operating in the kind of naturalization of history with which Barthes is concerned.

62. Ellen Pollak, *The Poetics of Sexual Myth: Gender and Ideology in the Verse of Swift and Pope,* Women in Culture and Society Series (Chicago: Univ. of Chicago Press, 1985), 3–6.

63. John Bender, "The Novel as Modern Myth" ("Der Roman als modernen Mythos," *Merkur: Deutsche Zeitschrift fur Europaisches Denken* 58:12 [2004]: 1088–1100). Professor Bender kindly provided me with this essay in English.

64. Laura Brown, *Fables of Modernity: Literature and Culture in the English Eighteenth Century* (Ithaca, NY: Cornell Univ. Press, 2001), 1.

65. Faller, *Turned to Account,* 2–4.

66. Ibid., 20.

67. Thanks to my colleague Alex Evans for suggesting this notion of cultural palimpsests.

68. Richard Holmes, ed, *Defoe on Sheppard and Wild* (New York: HarperPerennial, 2004), x. This edition includes three of the earliest lives of these figures.
The History of the Remarkable Life of John Sheppard [corporate authorship; possibly in part by Daniel Defoe] (Applebee, 1724), 1–44; *A Narrative of all the Robberies and Escapes of John Sheppard* [attr. Defoe] (Applebee, 1724), 45–68; *The True and Genuine Account of the Life and Actions of the Late Jonathan Wild* [attr. Defoe] (Applebee, 1725), 69–118.

69. McKeon, *Origins of the English Novel,* 383–94.

70. Holmes, *Defoe on Sheppard and Wild*, 105.

71. Ibid., 97–105.

72. Ibid., 97.

73. Ibid., ix.

74. Ibid., 109.

75. Linebaugh, *London Hanged*, 39.

76. Ibid., 40–41.

77. Holmes, *Defoe on Sheppard and Wild*, xxi.

78. Kramnick, *Bolingbroke and His Circle*; Denning, "Beggars and Thieves."

79. Matthew Buckley, "Sensations of Celebrity: *Jack Sheppard* and the Mass Audience," *Victorian Studies* 44.3 (2002): 434.

80. Ibid., 427.

81. Keith Hollingsworth, *The Newgate Novel 1830–1847: Bulwer, Ainsworth, Dickens and Thackeray* (Detroit: Wayne State Univ. Press, 1963), 145; Buckley, "Sensations of Celebrity," 426.

82. Ainsworth highlights this adaptation with the chapter title, II.1, "The Idle Apprentice." See Buckley, "Sensations of Celebrity," 430–33.

83. William Harrison Ainsworth, *Jack Sheppard*, Historical Romances of William Harrison Ainsworth Victorian Edition (Philadelphia: George Barrie & Son [1900]), 486.

84. Buckley, "Sensations of Celebrity," 443–44.

85. See ibid., 449.

86. Ainsworth, *Jack Sheppard*, 5, 8.

87. Ibid., 83–84.

88. Ibid., 85.

Chapter 2. Always Making Excuses

1. Charles Lamb, "On the Artificial Comedy of the Last Century," *The Works of Charles and Mary Lamb*, ed. E. V. Lucas (London: Methuen; and New York: AMS Press, 1903), 2:142.

2. I discuss the historical and literary reception of the Restoration rake below. For the status of the other outlaw figures such as the highwayman and the pirate, see John Richetti, *Popular Fiction Before Richardson: Narrative Patterns 1700–1739* (Oxford: Oxford Univ. Press, 1969); Eric Hobsbawm, *Bandits*, Pageant of History Series (New York: Delacorte Press, 1969); Peter Linebaugh, *The London Hanged: Crime and Civil Society in the Eighteenth Century* (New York: Cambridge Univ. Press, 1992); Marcus Rediker, *Between the Devil and the Deep Blue Sea: Merchant Seamen, Pirates, and the Anglo-American Maritime World, 1700–1750* (New York: Cambridge Univ. Press, 1987); Hans Turley, "Piracy, Identity, and Desire in *Captain Singleton*," *Eighteenth-Century Studies* 31 (1997–98): 199–214, and *Rum, Sodomy, and the Lash: Piracy, Sexuality, and Masculine Identity* (New York: New York Univ. Press, 1999); Linebaugh and Rediker, *Many-Headed Hydra*; Erin Mackie, "Welcome the Outlaw: Pirates, Maroons, and Caribbean Countercultures," *Cultural Critique* 59 (2005): 24–62.

3. *To the Postboy, The Complete Poems of John Wilmot, Earl of Rochester*, ed. David M.

Vieth (New Haven: Yale Univ. Press, 1968), 130–31. Dueling, that historically tenacious, criminal, and violent performance of elite masculine status, worked through just such an extension of sovereign privilege through ritualized social violence. Social historian Andrew remarks: "The code of honour . . . allowed each man to act like a sovereign power vis-à-vis all other men of honour. By thus claiming the rights of independent sovereignty, the duellist defied and threatened the continuance of both the Law and the State" ("Code of Honour and Its Critics," 422).

4. I borrow, in admiration, the phrase "savage nobles" from James Grantham Turner, *Libertines and Radicals in Early Modern London*, 166.

5. Jonathan Swift, *A Tale of a Tub*, in *The Writings of Jonathan Swift*, ed. Robert A. Greenberg and William B. Piper, Norton Critical Edition (New York: Norton, 1973), Section II, 302–3.

6. Turner, *Libertines and Radicals*, 197; Gilbert Burnet, *Bishop Burnet's History of his own Time* (London, 1838), 1:69; Peter Stallybrass and Allon White, *The Politics and Poetics of Transgression* (Ithaca, NY: Cornell Univ. Press, 1986), 101.

7. These include, in chronological order, John Traugott, "The Rake's Progress from Court to Comedy: A Study in Comic Form," *Studies in English Literature 1500–1900* 6.3 (1966): 381–407; Robert Jordan, "The Extravagant Rake in Restoration Comedy," in *Restoration Literature: Critical Approaches,* ed. Harold Love (London: Methuen, 1972), 69–90; Maximilian E. Novak, "Margery Pinchwife's 'London Disease': Restoration Comedy and the Libertine Offensive of the 1670s," *Studies in the Literary Imagination* 10.1 (1977): 1–23; Robert Hume, "The Myth of the Rake in Restoration Comedy," *Studies in the Literary Imagination* 10.1 (1977): 25–55; Michael Neill, "Heroic Heads and Humble Tails: Sex, Politics, and the Restoration Comic Rake," *Eighteenth Century* 24.2 (1983): 115–39; Harold Weber, "Rakes, Rogues, and the Empire of Misrule," *Huntington Library Quarterly* 47.1 (1984): 13–32; James G. Turner, "The Properties of Libertinism," in *'Tis Nature's Fault,* 75–87; Harold Weber, *The Restoration Rake-Hero: Transformations in Sexual Understandings in Seventeenth-Century England* (Madison: Univ. of Wisconsin Press, 1986); James G. Turner, "The Libertine Sublime: Love and Death in Restoration England," *Studies in Eighteenth-Century Culture* 19 (1989): 99–115; Duane Colthorp, "Rivall Fopps, Rambling Rakes, Wild Women: Homosocial Desire and Courtly Crisis in Rochester's Poetry," *Eighteenth Century* 38.1 (1997): 23–42; Randolph Trumbach, "The Birth of the Queen: Sodomy and the Emergence of Gender Equality in Modern Culture, 1660–1750," in *Gender and History in Western Europe,* ed. Robert Shoemaker and Mary Vincent (London: Arnold, 1998), 161–73. For discussions of *libertinage* in French culture, see Elena Russo, "Sociability, Cartesianism and Nostalgia in Libertine Discourse," *Eighteenth-Century Studies* 30.4 (1997): 383–400; and Catherine Cusset, ed., "Libertinage and Modernity," Special Issue of *Yale French Studies* 94 (1998).

8. See, for example, Barker-Benfield, *Culture of Sensibility*; Bryson, *From Courtesy to Civility,* esp. chap. 7; Carter, *Men and the Emergence of Polite Society;* Michael Curtin, "A Question of Manners: Status and Gender in Etiquette and Courtesy," *Journal of Modern History* 57 (1985): 395–423; Martin Ingram, "Reformation of Manners in Early Modern England," in *The Experience of Authority in Early Modern England,* ed. Paul Griffiths, Adam Fox, and Steve Hurdle (London: Macmillan; New York: St. Martin's, 1996), 47–88; Law-

rence E. Klein, "Liberty, Manners, and Politeness in Early Eighteenth-Century England," *Historical Journal* 32.3 (1989): 583–605, and *Shaftesbury and the Culture of Politeness: Moral Discourses and Cultural Politics in Early Eighteenth-Century England* (Cambridge: Cambridge Univ. Press, 1994); Mackie, *Market à la Mode*, esp. 1–29, 144–202; Maurer, *Proposing Men;* Richard Sennett, *The Fall of Public Man* (Cambridge: Cambridge Univ. Press, 1976).

9. Bryson, *From Courtesy to Civility*, 243–45, 252–53.

10. Robert Shoemaker, "Male Honour and the Decline of Public Violence in Eighteenth-Century London," *Social History* 26.2 (2001): 192, 190.

11. Shoemaker, "Male Honour," and Sharpe, *Crime in Early Modern England*, 136–41.

12. Sharpe, *Crime in Early Modern England*, 139.

13. So Bryson comments: "The image of the gentleman as 'libertine' or 'rake,' which crystallized in the later seventeenth century . . . in its repudiation of much of the code of 'civility' presents a major obstacle to any linear theories of the civilization of manners" (*From Courtesy to Civility*, 243).

14. Lawrence Stone, *The Crisis of the Aristocracy 1558–1641* (Oxford: Clarendon Press, 1965), 223.

15. Bryson, *From Courtesy to Civility*, 245.

16. In the somewhat different context of seventeenth- and eighteenth-century France, Elena Russo refers to the nostalgia of libertine discourse: "By appearing to reject the discourse of politeness and *honnetete*, the libertine tries to deny the interactive notion of the self that politeness carries with it. . . . The libertine looks back at a time when the self was conceived as a substance or substratum, he looks back at the Cartesian equation of the self with autonomous will and reason. Libertinage appears thus as a reactive discourse, a discourse of nostalgia" (390). Much of what Russo says here holds true for the English rake; however, I want to emphasize the historical specificity of the nostalgia embodied by that rake whose dispossession by his immediate political and social history is widely noted. See, for example, Christopher Hill, "John Wilmot, Earl of Rochester (1647–80)," in *The Collected Essays of Christopher Hill*, Vol. 1, *Writing and Revolution in Seventeenth-Century England* (Brighton, UK: Harvester Press, 1985): "The aristocrats who retained their privileged position after 1660 had no significant role to play in the reconstructed social order. . . . It was this that left [Rochester] feeling betrayed, not just the inadequacy of human reason" (301); Stallybrass and White, "The defiant, transgressive devilry of the Restoration court seemed to betoken a crisis of nobility after the civil wars despite the control and political influence which it had maintained" (*Politics and Poetics of Transgression*, 100–101); and Michael Neill, "In effect the pensioner of his father's gallantry, Rochester, like most younger members of the Restoration establishment, lived in the shadow of the Cavalier past" ("Heroic Heads and Humble Tails," 116).

17. Aphra Behn's graphic depiction (*Oroonoko*, 1688) of her Royal Slave's self-mutilation, torture, and execution illustrates the almost insupportable tension between, on the one hand, physical violence as the sign of primitive brutality (as with the Indian chiefs and Oroonoko's executioners) and, on the other, as the badge of the stoic martial prowess of the noble prince.

18. John Dryden, *Selected Poetry and Prose of John Dryden*, ed. Earl Miner (New York: Modern Library, 1985), 205.

19. Carol Houlihan Flynn, *Samuel Richardson: A Man of Letters* (Princeton: Princeton Univ. Press, 1982), 113.

20. Samuel Richardson, *Clarissa*, ed. with an Introduction, Angus Ross (London: Penguin Books), 669–70. All subsequent citations will be made parenthetically to this edition except for those to the mass rape and trial fantasy in Letter 208, which this modern edition, following Richardson's first, omits.

21. Flynn, *Samuel Richardson*, 221.

22. Judith Wilt, "He Could Go No Farther: A Modest Proposal about Lovelace and Clarissa," *PMLA* 92 (1977): 19–32.

23. As Terry Eagleton observes, "Thoroughly narcissistic and regressive, Lovelace's 'rakishness,' for all its virile panache, is nothing less than a crippling incapacity for adult sexual relationship" (*The Rape of Clarissa: Writing, Sexuality, and Class Struggle in Samuel Richardson* [Oxford: Basil Blackwell, 1982], 63).

24. After arriving at this conclusion independently, I found that it is supported by Bryson (*From Courtesy to Civility*, 271).

25. Kathryn Norberg, "The Libertine Whore: Prostitution in French Pornography from Margot to Juliette," *The Invention of Pornography: Obscenity and the Origins of Modernity, 1500–1800*, ed. Lynn Hunt (New York: Zone Books, 1993), 228.

26. Oliver Goldsmith, *She Stoops to Conquer* (1773), ed. Tom Davis, New Mermaids Series (New York: W.W. Norton, 1979), 2.1.92.

27. Rita Goldberg, *Sex and Enlightenment: Women in Richardson and Diderot* (Cambridge: Cambridge Univ. Press, 1984), 112.

28. See J. A. Sharpe, who notes that the conventional gendering of "serious crime" as masculine has obscured attention to women's participation in crimes other than the characteristic ones of infanticide, prostitution, witchcraft, and scolding, *Crime in Early Modern England 1550–1750*, 2nd ed., Themes in British Social History, ed. John Stevenson (London and New York: Longman, 1999), 154–60. I do not mean to suggest that there were not scores of female criminals, but simply that their criminality would be culturally coded as masculine or at least as anti-feminine. For women as victims and perpetrators of crime, see Frank McLynn, *Crime and Punishment in Eighteenth-Century England* (London and New York: Routledge, 1989), 96–132.

29. Of course, some forms of criminality are much more strongly linked than others into models of masculinity; white collar crime, for example, does little to enhance the macho allure of its perpetrators.

30. But this link between masculinity and criminality, especially in the elite sphere, has not received much attention; noting its cultural-historical importance, Sharpe (*Crime in Early Modern England*, 160) calls for its further examination.

31. For the historical relation between the fop and the rake, see Trumbach, "Birth of the Queen." See also Carter, *Men and the Emergence of Polite Society*, chap. 4, and Susan Staves, "A Few Kind Words for the Fop," *SEL* 22.3 (1982): 413–28. To date, the most compelling discussion of the fop is found in King, *Gendering of Men*, 228–59.

32. King, *Gendering of Men*, 234.

33. Ibid., 238, 228.

34. In conversation with Young Bellair, Harriet remarks of Dorimant, "He's agreeable

and pleasant, I must own, but he does so much affect being so, he displeases me." When Bellair counters that everything Dorimant "does and says is so easy and natural," Harriet claims her greater insight: "Some men's verses seem so to the unskilful; but labour in the one and affectation in the other to the judicious plainly appear," (3.3.20–24) (George Etherege, *The Man of Mode, or, Sir Fopling Flutter* [1676], ed. John Barnard, New Mermaids Series [New York: W.W. Norton, 1979].)

35. King, *Gendering of Men*, 6.

36. In *Man of Mode*, Lady Woodvill uses this phrase to describe Dorimant's seductive allure (3.3.108–9). Lovelace also is frequently figured as a serpent-tongued Satan figure. For Richardson's attempts to get his readers to understand Lovelace as an "unamiable" character, see Flynn, *Samuel Richardson*, 229–30. Much of the revision of Clarissa in the second and third editions centered on providing more material that damned Lovelace.

37. Although dueling was illegal and widely condemned, "few people suffered serious legal penalties for dueling . . . those duelists who killed their antagonists and were prosecuted for murder were invariably pardoned or convicted of manslaughter and given token punishments" (Shoemaker, "Taming of the Duel," 537). See Daniel Statt's discussion of the Mohocks and the general immunity of propertied men from legal prosecution: "The rakes' offences posed no obvious threat to the established order of property and power. So long as they presented little threat to property, crimes of personal violence excited little zeal in eighteenth-century law-makers, and in that respect the law betrayed its fundamental bias toward serving those who had property to lose" ("Case of the Mohocks," 96).

38. For Lovelace's assumption, see Letter 208, omitted in Ross's edition but included in those that follow Richardson's third edition, such as Samuel Richardson, *The History of Clarissa Harlowe*, in *The Works of Samuel Richardson*, ed. Lesley Stephen (London: Henry Sotheran, 1883), 6:190.

39. John Harold Wilson, *Court Wits of the Restoration* (Princeton: Princeton Univ. Press, 1948), 46.

40. Neill, "Heroic Heads and Humble Tails," 133.

41. Statt ("Case of the Mohocks") provides a notable exception to this general silence on the (nonsexual) criminality of the rake.

42. Geoffrey Pearson, *Hooligan: A History of Respectable Fears* (London: Macmillan, 1983), 236.

43. Thus the lively anti-dueling campaigns engaged in the eighteenth century. See Andrew, "Code of Honour and Its Critics," and Shoemaker, "Taming of the Duel."

44. *Albion's Fatal Tree: Crime and Society in Eighteenth-Century England*, Douglas Hay, Peter Linebaugh, John G. Rule, E. P. Thompson, Cal Winslow (London: Penguin / Allen Lane, 1975), 14. As Linebaugh explains in the preface to *London Hanged*, the distinction, which neither can nor should be neatly maintained, between "social crime" and "crime without qualification" is that "the former receives popular support and the latter is merely deplored" (xix).

45. This is the case with the duel. A ritualized performance of violence, central to the maintenance of those modes of behavior (manners) that maintained categories of social power (honor, prestige), the duel presented a stumbling block to social reformers who would redefine the concept of honor in ways that would preserve the notion and the social

order it supported while discountenancing its violent demonstration. See Andrew, "Code of Honour and Its Critics."

46. Turner, *Libertines and Radicals*, 228.

47. Rochester, *The Disabled Debauchee*, in Vieth, 116–17.

48. Rochester, *A Ramble in St. James's Park*, in Vieth, 43. Hereafter cited parenthetically in the text.

49. Here I follow Marianne Thormahlen's reading of the poem in *Rochester: The Poems in Context* (Cambridge: Cambridge Univ. Press, 1993), 97–98.

50. Colthorp, "Rivall Fopps, Rambling Rakes, Wild Women," 38.

51. Letters from Sir Robert Howard to Rochester and from Rochester to his wife in 1672 record these financial difficulties, *The Letters of John Wilmot, Earl of Rochester*, ed. Jeremy Treglown (Oxford: Basil Blackwell, 1980), 78–81.

52. I discuss the Mohocks in the following section of this chapter. See Statt, "Case of the Mohocks," and Robert J. Allen, *The Clubs of Augustan London* (Hamden, CT; Arkon Books, 1967); Thornton Shirley Graves, "Some Pre-Mohock Clansmen," *Studies in Philology* 20 (1925): 395–421; Louis C. Jones, *The Clubs of the Georgian Rakes* (New York: Columbia University Press, 1942); Norman Pearson, *Society Sketches in the Eighteenth Century* (London: Edward Arnold, 1911). For seventeenth- and eighteenth-century dramatizations of such gangs, see Thomas Shadwell, *The Scowrers* (1690), in *The Complete Works of Thomas Shadwell*, ed. Montague Summers (London: Fortune Press, 1927), 5:83–148, and John Gay, *The Mohocks: A Tragi-Comical Farce* (1712), in *John Gay: Dramatic Works*, ed. John Fuller (Oxford: Clarendon Press, 1983), 1:77–100. In 1712, the Mohocks appear in a number of ephemeral and periodical papers, including *Who Plot Best; The Whigs or the Tories* (London: A. Baldwin, 1712); *The Town-Rakes: or, The Frolicks of the "Mohocks" or "Hawkubites"* (London: J. Wright, 1712); *The Spectator* 324, in *The Spectator*, ed. Donald F. Bond (Oxford: Oxford Univ. Press, 1965), 2:186–88.

53. Weber, *Restoration Rake-Hero*, 3.

54. As Statt observes, "One reason for the traditionally favourable view of libertinism has been a somewhat misleading tendency to lay a preponderance of stress on the sexual side of libertinism. This risks casting the libertine too much in the role of an enlightened and practicing exponent of a cultured and reflective hedonism" ("Case of the Mohocks," 181).

55. Attr. Richard Ames, *The Rake: or, The Libertine's Religion* (London: R. Taylor, 1693).

56. Ronald Paulson, *Hogarth* (New Brunswick: Rutgers Univ. Press, 1991–93), 2:21.

57. *The Tatler*, ed. Donald F. Bond (Oxford: Oxford Univ. Press, 1987).

58. Pierre Bourdieu, *Distinction: A Social Critique of the Judgement of Taste*, trans. Richard Nice (Cambridge: Harvard Univ. Press, 1984), 65–76,

59. Andrew, "Code of Honour and Its Critics," 418. Steele's satire on dueling appears in *Tatler* 25.

60. Steele, *Tatler* 27.

61. Statt, "Case of the Mohocks."

62. David Nokes, *John Gay: A Profession of Friendship* (Oxford: Oxford Univ. Press, 1995), 93–96.

63. See John Fuller's commentary in his edition of Gay (1:408). I concur with the

critics he cites there, who find much of the Mohocks' language reminiscent of Milton's *Paradise Lost,* although allusions as exact as this to Dryden may be missing. I think Gay's use of the mock-heroic here shows how conventionalized the heroic has become and so how generic parodies of it may be.

64. There are a number of popular histories of British rakes, such as E. Beresford Chancellor, *The Lives of the Rakes* (London: Philip Allan & Co., 1924), 6 vols., and, most recently, Fergus Linanne, *The Lives of the English Rakes* (London: Portrait, 2006). Elaine McGirr has drawn the best portrait of the eighteenth-century rake in literature, *Eighteenth-Century Characters: A Guide to the Literature of the Age* (New York: Palgrave Macmillan, 2007), 27–38.

65. Eagleton, *Rape of Clarissa,* 63.

66. Terry Castle, *Clarissa's Ciphers: Meaning and Disruption in Richardson's "Clarissa"* (Ithaca, NY: Cornell Univ. Press, 1982).

67. Eagleton, *Rape of Clarissa,* 88–89; Elaine McGirr, "Why Lovelace Must Die," in *Novel: A Forum on Fiction* 37.1–2 (2003): 5–23; Tita Chico, *Designing Women: The Dressing Room in Eighteenth-Century English Literature and Culture,* Bucknell Studies in Eighteenth-Century Literature and Culture (Lewisburg, PA: Bucknell Univ. Press, 2005), 165–66; James G. Turner, "Lovelace and the Paradoxes of Libertinism," *Samuel Richardson: Tercentenary Essays,* ed. Margaret Anne Doody and Peter Sabor (Cambridge: Cambridge Univ. Press, 1989), 70–88; Flynn, *Samuel Richardson,* 196–254; R. F. Brissenden, *Virtue in Distress: Studies in the Novel of Sentiment from Richardson to Sade* (London: Macmillan, 1974), 172–73; Jocelyn Harris, "Protean Lovelace," in *Passion and Virtue: Essays on the Novels of Samuel Richardson,* ed. David Blewett (Toronto: Univ. of Toronto Press, 2001), 92–113; William Warner, *Reading "Clarissa": The Struggles of Interpretation* (New Haven: Yale Univ. Press, 1979), 28–55; John P. Zomchick, *Family and the Law in Eighteenth-Century Fiction* (Cambridge: Cambridge Univ. Press, 1993), 81–104. For a summary of Clarissa criticism before 1983, see Sue Warrick Doederlein, "Clarissa in the Hands of the Critics," *Eighteenth-Century Studies* 16.4 (1983): 401–14.

68. Charles Hickman, Anna Howes's suitor, is the text's nice, polite young man. Yet neither he nor the reformed rake Belford stand as unequivocal paragons of masculine virtue; that position is reserved for Sir Charles Grandison in Richardson's next and last novel. Lovelace's loathing of the nouveau riche Harlowes updates the conventional hostility between the rake and the cit, the libertine elite and the dour merchant class.

69. See Turner, "Lovelace and the Paradoxes of Libertinism," 72.

70. See McGirr, "Lovelace Must Die"; Chico, *Designing Women;* Turner, "Lovelace and the Paradoxes of Libertinism"; and Eagleton, "Lovelace is a reactionary throwback, and old-style libertine or Restoration relic who resists a proper 'embourgeoisement'" (*Rape of Clarissa,* 89).

71. Angus Ross, Introduction, *Clarissa,* 17.

72. On the discourses and history of mental illness during this period, see Michel Foucault, *Madness and Civilization: A History of Insanity in the Age of Reason* [1961], trans. Richard Howard (New York: Vintage / Random House, 1973); Roy Porter, *Mind-Forg'd Manacles: A History of Madness in England from the Restoration to the Regency* (London: Athlone Press, 1986); John Mullan, "Hypochondria and Hysteria: Sensibility and the Physicians," in *Sen-*

timent and Sociability: The Language of Feeling in the Eighteenth Century (Oxford: Clarendon, 1988), 201–40; Allan Ingram, *The Madhouse of Language: Writing and Reading Madness in the Eighteenth Century* (London: Routledge, 1991).

73. Since in Belford Richardson does present something very much like Steele's reformed rake of *Tatler* 27, it does not seem that Richardson is discarding this possibility altogether; rather, he, like Frances Burney after him, presents the proposition that such narratives are anything but inevitable.

74. "His dominion is internal" (Goldberg, *Sex and Enlightenment*, 101).

75. Ibid., 102. The title of McGirr's essay is "Why Lovelace Must Die."

76. Often through the logic of post-structuralism, the psychosexual is related to the linguistic and rhetorical, as in Eagleton, Warner, and Castle. Doederlein's feminist evaluation of *Clarissa* criticism (Doederlein, "Clarissa in the Hands of the Critics") highlights the extent to which readings of that novel expose the critics' own relations to Lovelace's sexuality.

77. Other considerations of legal issues in the text include Sandra Macpherson, "Lovelace LTD," *ELH* 65 (1995): 99–121; Mary Vermillion, "Clarissa and the Marriage Act," *Eighteenth-Century Fiction* 9.4 (1997): 395–414; Beth Swan, "Raped by the System: An Account of *Clarissa* in the Light of Eighteenth-Century Law," *1650–1850: Ideas, Aesthetics, and Inquiries in the Early Modern Era*, ed. Kevin L. Cope (New York: AMS, 2001), 113–29; Beth Swan, "Clarissa Harlowe, Pleasant Rawlins, and Eighteenth-Century Discourse of Law," *The Eighteenth-Century Novel*, vol. 1, ed. Susan Spencer (New York: AMS, 2001), 71–93; Joan I. Schwarz, "Eighteenth-Century Abduction Law and *Clarissa*," in *Clarissa and Her Readers: New Essays for the "Clarissa" Project*, ed. Carol Houlihan Flynn and Edward Copeland (New York: AMS, 1999), 269–308.

78. Zomchick, *Family and the Law*, xi.

79. Ibid., 81.

80. Ibid., 82, 81, my emphasis.

81. Ross, Introduction to *Clarissa*, 16–17. I follow the numbering of Ross's edition, which omits Letter 208 yet retains its place in the sequence.

82. Flynn, *Samuel Richardson*, 220.

83. "Worse [to Richardson's sensibility] even than Restoration libertinism, however, is the flagrant criminality of the modern stage," writes Tom Keymer in *Richardson's "Clarissa" and the Eighteenth-Century Reader* (Cambridge: Cambridge Univ. Press, 1992), 148. And see McGirr, "Lovelace Must Die."

84. So Clarissa confirms that rape is a "crime thought too lightly of" by the law and by society more generally (1253).

85. Goldberg, *Sex and Enlightenment*, 99.

86. "For the rake is not merely any man of loose character, but a man of fashion" (Flynn, *Samuel Richardson*, 201).

87. Yet all these conventional apologies for the rake are, of course, shown to be the rake's own apologies, all part of his criminal self-authorization.

88. Macpherson, "Lovelace LTD," 109.

89. See Douglas Hay "Property, Authority, and the Criminal Law," in *Albion's Fatal Tree*, 17–64; and Linebaugh, *London Hanged*, xx–xxi and 75 (courtroom theatrics).

90. Lord Marplot is a character in Susan Centlivre's drama *The Busie Body* (1709).

91. Lovelace frequently adopts this defensive posture, as when he pleads to Lady Betty and Lady Charlotte as preemptive justification of any "future mischiefs" against the Harlowes that "they were the aggressors" (1035). As I have noted, Lovelace on trial only recapitulates the criminality that brings him there in the first place.

92. See Wilt, "He Could Go No Farther."

93. Letter 515 (1436–39).

94. Macpherson, "Lovelace LTD," 110–11, her emphases.

95. Zomchick, *Family and the Law*, argues that "the reader must accept poetic justice in lieu of civil sanctions" at the end of *Clarissa* (102).

96. Ibid., 102.

97. Jonathan Swift, "On Good Manners and Good Breeding," *The Prose Writings of Jonathan Swift*, ed. Herbert Davis and Louis Landa (Oxford: Basil Blackwell, 1957), 4:214.

Chapter 3. Romancing the Highwayman

1. The two collections I rely on most here are Captain Alexander Smith, *A Complete History of the Lives and Robberies of the Most Notorious Highwaymen, Footpads, Shoplifts, and Cheats* (London, 1714), rpt. and ed. Arthur Hayward (London: Routledge, 1926); and Captain Charles Johnson, *A General History of the Lives and Adventures of the Most Famous Highwaymen, Murderers, and Street-Robbers* (London, 1734–35).

2. John Gay, *The Beggar's Opera*, in *John Gay: Dramatic Works*, ed. John Fuller (Oxford: Clarendon, 1983), 2:67–146; William Harrison Ainsworth, *Rookwood: A Romance* [1834] (London: Routledge, 1898).

3. "The Life of Capt. Phillip Stafford," in Johnson, *A General History*, 77–85; "The Life of Capt. James Hind," ibid., 86–90; "Du Vall, A Notorious Highwayman," ibid., 144–52. In the text I follow the spelling "Duval" and cite passages from these lives parenthetically.

4. Ian Duncan, *Modern Romance and Transformations of the Novel: The Gothic, Scott, Dickens* (Cambridge: Cambridge Univ. Press, 1992).

5. See Keith Hollingsworth, *The Newgate Novel 1830–1847: Bulwer, Ainsworth, Dickens and Thackeray* (Detroit, MI: Wayne State Univ. Press), 105–6, and E. S. Turner, *Boys Will Be Boys* (London: Joseph Press, 1957).

6. James Sharpe, *Dick Turpin: The Myth of the English Highwayman* (London: Profile Books, 2005), 216.

7. Ibid., 210.

8. Faller, *Turned to Account*.

9. See McKeon, *Origins of the English Novel*, 96–100.

10. Lennard J. Davis, "Wicked Actions and Feigned Words: Criminals, Criminality, and the Early English Novel," *Yale French Studies* 59 (1980): 108; Bryan Reynolds, *Becoming Criminal: Transversal Performance and Cultural Dissidence in Early Modern England* (Baltimore: Johns Hopkins Univ. Press, 2002).

11. Davis, "Wicked Actions," 107.

12. McKeon, *Origins of the English Novel*, 98.

13. Ibid., 98.

14. The eighteenth-century "Gentleman Highwayman" James Maclane comes chronologically after both Macheath and Dick Turpin and will be considered in relation to Turpin in the final section of this chapter.

15. Sharpe, *Dick Turpin*, 49.

16. Eric Hobsbawm, *Bandits* (New York: New Press, 2000).

17. William Wycherley, *The Country Wife* [1675], ed. Thomas H. Fujimura, Regents Renaissance Drama Series (Lincoln: Univ. of Nebraska Press); George Etherege, *The Man of Mode* [1676], ed. John Barnard, New Mermaids Series (London: A & C Black; New York: W.W. Norton, 1979).

18. John Wilmot, Earl of Rochester, *The Disabled Debauchee, The Complete Poems of John Wilmot, Earl of Rochester*, ed. David M. Vieth (New Haven: Yale Univ. Press, 1968), 116–17.

19. Walter Pope, *The Memoires of Monsieur Du Vall* [1670], in *Restoration Prose Fiction, 1666–1700: An Anthology of Representative Pieces*, ed. Charles C. Mish (Lincoln: Univ. of Nebraska Press, 1970), 199–214,

20. Ibid., 209.

21. John Wilmot, Earl of Rochester, *Ramble in St. James's Park*, in Vieth, 40–46.

22. Kramnick, *Bolingbroke and His Circle*, 228; Denning, "Beggars and Thieves," 53.

23. See Patricia Meyer Spacks, "Young Men's Fancies: James Boswell, Henry Fielding," in *Imagining a Self: Autobiography and Novel in Eighteenth-Century England* (Cambridge: Harvard Univ. Press, 1976), 227–63; Felicity Nussbaum, "Manly Subjects: Boswell's Journals and *The Life of Johnson*," in *The Autobiographical Subject: Gender and Ideology in Eighteenth-Century England* (Baltimore: Johns Hopkins Univ. Press, 1989), 103–26; and Michael McKeon, "Writer as Hero: Novelistic Prefigurations and the Emergence of Literary Biography," *Contesting the Subject: Essays in the Postmodern Theory and Practice of Biography and Biographical Criticism*, ed. William H. Epstein (West Lafayette, IN: Purdue Univ. Press, 1991), 17–42.

24. Spacks, "Young Men's Fancies," 230.

25. Nussbaum, "Manly Subjects," 103–10.

26. David Weed, "Sexual Positions: Men of Pleasure, Economy, and Dignity in Boswell's *London Journal*," *Eighteenth-Century Studies* 31.2 (1997–98): 216.

27. Philip Carter, "James Boswell's Manliness," *English Masculinities, 1660–1800*, ed. Tim Hitchcock and Michele Cohen (New York and London: Longman, 1999), 111–30.

28. Weed, "Sexual Positions," 220.

29. For the cultural logic of *concordia discors* and oxymoron, see Terry Castle, *Masquerade and Civilization: The Carnivalesque in Eighteenth-Century English Culture and Fiction* (Stanford: Stanford Univ. Press, 1986), 5–7; and Margaret Doody, *The Daring Muse: Augustan Poetry Reconsidered* (London: Cambridge Univ. Press, 1985), 212–17. John Bender notes how paradox consumes distinction in *The Beggar's Opera*: "All categories cancel one another out. . . . Macheath is hero and highwayman, husband and adulterer, hanged and reprieved, great man and scoundrel—a pure paradox" (*Imagining the Penitentiary: Fiction and the Architecture of Mind in Eighteenth-Century England* [Chicago: Univ. of Chicago Press, 1987], 87).

30. William Empson, *Some Versions of Pastoral* (London: Chatto & Windus, 1935), 195.

31. *Boswell's London Journal: 1762–1763*, ed. Frederick Pottle, 2nd ed. (New Haven: Yale Univ. Press, 2004), 252. All references will be made parenthetically in the text.

32. Michael Friedman, "'He was just a Macheath': Boswell and *The Beggar's Opera*," *Age of Johnson* 4 (1991): 98.

33. Donald Newman, "James Boswell, Joseph Addison, and the Spectator in the Mirror," *James Boswell: Psychological Interpretations*, ed. Donald J. Newman (New York: St. Martin's, 1995), 1–32.

34. In addition to Friedman and Newman, for useful readings of Boswell's masculinist ambitions, see Carter, Nussbaum, Spacks, and Weed.

35. While Newman has examined Boswell's identification with the persona Mr. Spectator, quite strictly conceived, here I work with an understanding of *The Spectator's* influence that extends to include not merely the persona per se, but also both *The Tatler* and *The Spectator*.

36. William Eben Schultz, *Gay's "Beggar's Opera": Its Content, History, and Influence* (New Haven: Yale Univ. Press, 1923), 199.

37. McKeon writes of Boswell's "self-conscious conception of social behavior as role-playing" ("Writer as Hero," 28); Friedman notes the way Boswell "seeks literary avatars for preliterary problems" ("He was just a Macheath," 98); Newman examines Boswell's identification with Mr. Spectator as an example of the adoption of a "fictive personality" (*James Boswell*, 2).

38. Gordon Turnbull, "Boswell and Sympathy: The Trial and Execution of John Reid," *New Light on Boswell: Critical and Historical Essays on the Occasion of the Bicentenary of "The Life of Johnson,"* ed. Greg Clingham (Cambridge: Cambridge Univ. Press, 1991), 111.

39. Boswell's association of his own misdeeds with those of a criminal type renowned for his success with the ladies seems appropriate to his own preferred forms of bad behavior: illicit sexuality and disobedience to his father, staunch executor of criminal justice on the Scots bar.

40. See chapter 2.

41. McKeon, "Writer as Hero," looks at how Boswell achieves through literary self-description "the autonomy of subjectivity and that of self-sufficiency" in a composite character of "the man of economy" and "the man of letters" (30).

42. Margery Bailey, *Boswell's Column: Being his Seventy Contributions to "The London Magazine"* (London: William Kimber, 1951), xxiii; Lawrence Stone, *The Family, Sex, and Marriage in England 1500–1800* (New York: Harper & Row, 1977), 572–73. Later in his life Boswell wrote extensively on melancholy under the nom de plume "The Hypochondriack," see Bailey. For an analysis of Boswell's relation to his own depression, see George Haggerty, "Boswell's Symptoms: The Hypochondriack in and out of Context," in *James Boswell: Psychological Interpretations*, ed. Donald J. Newman (New York: St. Martin's), 111–26.

43. Friedman, "He was just a Macheath," 102.

44. For historical discussions of the staging and significance of the drama of the condemned at Tyburn, see Douglas Hay, "Property, Authority, and the Criminal Law," *Albion's Fatal Tree: Crime and Society in Eighteenth-Century England*, ed. Douglas Hay et al. (London: Allen Lane, 1975), 17–64; see also Linebaugh, *London Hanged*, xx–xxi, 75.

45. Turnbull, "Boswell and Sympathy," 111.

46. Boswell's "sober winter" here refers not to the depression he had been suffering but to the bout of gonorrhea that kept him indisposed earlier in the year.

47. Boswell's later identification with the criminals he defended, such as the sheep stealer John Reid, has been examined by Turnbull, who notes the oedipal overtones to such bonds of sympathy that often, as in the case of Reid, positioned Boswell in opposition to his father, who convicted Reid. Lewis, the condemned highwayman, might be viewed as an early member of this small constellation of criminals, failed rebels "against Scots religio-legist authority," with whom Boswell strongly, if guiltily, identifies throughout his life (Turnbull, "Boswell and Sympathy," 105). The anti-authoritarian and the anti-patriarchal character of Boswell's identification with the criminal is manifest as well in the blackguard episode. Boswell's rebellion is against both the internalized dictates of conformity to "religio-legist authority" and their external manifestation.

48. Castle, *Masquerade and Civilization*, 5–6.

49. John Gay, *The Mohocks*, in *John Gay: Dramatic Works*, 1:2.3.159–60.

50. See Turner, *Boys Will Be Boys*, 46.

51. Hollingsworth, *Newgate Novel*, 105–6. See also Lyn Pyket, "The Newgate Novel and Sensation Fiction, 1830–1868," in *Cambridge Companion to Crime Fiction*, ed. Martin Priestman (Cambridge: Cambridge Univ. Press, 2003): "Turpin has little plot function in *Rookwood*, but he adds considerably to its colourfulness and raciness, not to mention its romanticisation of the criminal" (26); Stephen James Carver, *The Life and Works of the Lancashire Novelist William Harrison Ainsworth, 1805–1882*, Studies in British Literature, vol. 75 (Lewiston, NY: Edwin Mellen Press, 2003): *Rookwood* is "the well from which the popular craze for penny dreadfuls of the highwaymen had sprung with its resurrection of the spirit of Dick Turpin" (8). James Sharpe, in *Dick Turpin*, confirms Ainsworth as the source for the modern romantic highwayman.

52. "James Maclane," in *The Complete Newgate Calendar*, ed. G. T. Crook (London: Navarre Society, 1926), 3:180–83; "James Maclean," *The Ordinary's Account, 12th September 1750*, The Proceedings of the Old Bailey, www.oldbaileyonline.org.html; *A Genuine Account of the Life and Actions of James Maclean* (London, 1750); *The Letters of Horace Walpole*, ed. Paget Toynbee (Oxford: Clarendon Press, 1903), 3:5–7, 1:xl; *Gentleman's Magazine*, November 1749, 522; *Supplement to the Letters of Horace Walpole*, ed. Paget Toynbee (Oxford: Clarendon Press, 1918–25), 3:132–35.

53. Julius E. Day and Arty Ash, *The Immortal Turpin: The Authentic Story of England's Most Notorious Highwayman* (London and New York: Staples Press, 1948), 11.

54. Ibid., 52–53.

55. Ibid., 66.

56. "Dick Turpin," in *Complete Newgate Calendar*, 3:91; *The Genuine History of the Life of Richard Turpin* (London: J. Standen, 1739).

57. "Dick Turpin," 91.

58. Ibid., 94.

59. Day and Ash, *Immortal Turpin*, 111.

60. "Dick Turpin," 96.

61. Day and Ash, *Immortal Turpin*, 126.

62. Ibid., 134.

63. Ibid., 65.

64. Ibid., 60.

65. This legendary and media-generated dexterous velocity forms an ample strand in the "mythical" Turpin produced by Ainsworth's *Rookwood*, where it is combined with more moral attributes, such as resolution and generosity: "His reckless daring, his resistless rapidity (for so suddenly did he change his ground, and renew his attacks in other quarters, that he seemed to be endowed with ubiquity), his bravery, his resolution, and, above all, his generosity, won for him a high reputation amongst his compatriots, and even elicited applauses from those upon whom he levied his contributions" (166).

66. Barrell, *English Literature in History, 1730–80*, 17–50.

67. This is reprinted as an introduction to the 1898 Routledge edition of *Rookwood* that I cite here.

68. Hollingsworth, *Newgate Novel*, 139. See the discussion of Wild and Sheppard in chapter 1 above.

69. Hollingsworth, *Newgate Novel*, 145–46.

70. The two of Scott's novels most relevant to the context of *Rookwood* as discussed here are *Waverley* (1814) and *Rob Roy* (1818).

71. Carver, *Life and Works*, 168.

72. *Blackadder III* (1987).

73. Hollingsworth, *Newgate Novel*, 99–100; Duncan, *Modern Romance*, 213; on Ainsworth's contemporary critical invisibility, see Carver, *Life and Works*, 9–12.

74. Duncan, *Modern Romance*, 7.

75. Ibid., 59.

76. Edward Bulwer Lytton, *Paul Clifford* (1830).

77. "James Maclane," 182–83.

78. *Letters*, 2 August 1750, 5.

79. *A Genuine Account of the Life and Actions of James Maclean*, iii-iv.

80. Ibid., iv.

81. *Letters*, 2 August 1750, 5–7.

82. Duncan, *Modern Romance*, 5.

83. This later became a hit, and a source of some negative criticism along the lines of that levied against Jack Sheppard, when *Rookwood* was adapted for the stage (Hollingsworth, *Newgate Novel*, 139–40).

84. Duncan, *Modern Romance*, 14.

85. Ibid., 21.

86. See Reynolds, *Becoming Criminal*, 23–63. Gamini Salgado comments on the commonplace identification of Romany and criminal cant and on the close association between gypsy and other underworld cultures in *The Elizabethan Underworld* (London: J. M. Dent & Sons; Totowa, NJ: Rowman and Littlefield, 1977), 156–57 and 159–62.

87. Duncan, *Modern Romance*, 87.

88. Carver, *Life and Works*, 11. Latrobe was the son of the famous Gothic revivalist architect and himself chief engineer to the Baltimore and Ohio railway.

89. Day and Ash, *Immortal Turpin*, 74–78. See Sharpe (note 6), 208–17.

90. Duncan, *Modern Romance*, 33.

91. Mark Twain, *The Adventures of Huckleberry Finn*, vol. 13 of *The Writings of Mark Twain* (New York: Harper & Row, 1912), 5. Subsequent citations will be given parenthetically.

Chapter 4. Welcome the Outlaw

1. See especially the two-volume *General History of the Pyrates* [1724], Captain Charles Johnson [attr. Daniel Defoe], ed. Manuel Schonhorn, 2nd ed. (New York: Dover, 1999). The attribution of this collection of pirate lives to Daniel Defoe was made by John Robert Moore in 1931 and has been challenged by P. N. Furbank and W. R. Owens, *The Canonisation of Daniel Defoe* (New Haven: Yale Univ. Press, 1988), 100–121.

2. Hans Turley, *Rum, Sodomy, and the Lash: Piracy, Sexuality, and Masculine Identity* (New York: New York Univ. Press, 1999).

3. King, *The Gendering of Men*, 228–59.

4. Randolph Trumbach, "Birth of the Queen," 161–73; "Sodomitical Subcultures"; and "Sodomitical Assaults, Gender Role, and Sexual Development in Eighteenth-Century London," *Journal of the History of Sexuality* 16: 1–2 (1988): 407–29.

5. Turley, *Rum, Sodomy, and the Lash*, 39, 61, 74–75, 115.

6. Ibid., 81–85, 109.

7. Daniel Defoe, *The Life, Adventures, and Pyracies, of the Famous Captain Singleton*, ed. Shiv K. Kumar (London: Oxford Univ. Press, 1973); Turley, *Rum, Sodomy, and the Lash*, 109–27.

8. *Rum, Sodomy, and the Lash*, 81–85.

9. Ibid., 78.

10. Defoe, *Captain Singleton*, 277.

11. Turley, *Rum, Sodomy, and the Lash*, 125, 127.

12. Defoe, *Captain Singleton*, 269.

13. Daniel Defoe, *The Life and Strange Surprizing Adventures of Robinson Crusoe*, ed. J. Donald Crowley (Oxford: Oxford Univ. Press, 1972), 202–24.

14. Peter Hulme, *Colonial Encounters: Europe and the Native Caribbean, 1492–1797* (London: Routledge, 1992), 175–224,

15. Stephen Gregg, "Male Friendship and Defoe's Captain Singleton: 'My every thing,'" *British Journal for Eighteenth-Century Studies* 27 (2004): 203–4.

16. John Wilmot, *A Ramble in St. James's Park*, in Veith, 40–46; see also *The Imperfect Enjoyment* (37–40). Restoration literature is replete with this anxiety, as expressed, for example, by Dorimant's vulnerability to Fopling in Etherege's *Man of Mode*. See above, chapter 2.

17. *The Guardian*, 14 June 2003.

18. See Sebastian Clarke, *Jah Music: The Evolution of the Popular Jamaican Song* (London: Heinnemann, 1980), 110–12, and Anita Waters, *Race, Class, and Political Symbols: Rastafarians and Reggae in Jamaican Politics* (New Brunswick, NJ: Transaction Books, 1985), 231–35. For the evolution of the connection between the JNP and JLP and the youth gangs in West Kingston, see Laurie Gunst, *Born Fi' Dead: A Journey through the Jamaican Posse*

Underworld (New York: Henry Holt, 1995), and Obika Gray, "Power and Identity among the Urban Poor of Jamaica," in *Globalization and Survival in the Black Diaspora: The New Urban Challenge,* ed. Charles Green, SUNY Series in Afro-American Studies (Albany: State Univ. of New York Press, 1997), 199–226.

19. An extensive, perhaps complete, transcript of the speech can be found in Peter Tosh, "One Love Equal Rights Integration Peace Concert," recorded by Karl Pitterson and transcribed by Carl Gayle, *Jah Ugliman* 1 (October 1978): 29–36. Here, I have followed the more standardized spelling in Clarke's citation, a much more widely available, if less complete, source (*Jah Music,* 112).

20. As the early eighteenth-century pirate Captain Bartholomew Roberts explains, "In an honest Service . . . there is thin Commons, low Wages, and hard Labour," whereas piracy offers "Plenty and Satiety, Pleasure and Ease, Liberty and Power" (*General History of the Pyrates,* 244).

21. Carolyn Cooper, *Noises in the Blood: Orality, Gender, and the "Vulgar" Body of Jamaican Popular Culture* (Durham, NC: Duke Univ. Press, 1995), 10–11.

22. Ibid., 10.

23. See the classic film starring Jimmy Cliff, which tells the story of Ivan Martin, the archetypal and original rude boy, *The Harder They Come* (1973) and the even more socio-culturally detailed novel based on the film, Michael Thelwell's *The Harder They Come: A Novel* (New York: Grove Press, 1988), esp. 141–49, 197–203. For the historical Ivan Martin and his cultural status as "the first media-created superstar" in Jamaican history, see Kevin J. Aylmer, "Towering Babble and Glimpses of Zion: Recent Depictions of Rastafarians in Cinema," in *Chanting Down Babylon: The Rastari Reader,* ed. Nathaniel Samuel Murrell, William David Spencer, and Adrian Anthony McFarlane (Philadelphia: Temple Univ. Press, 1998), 284–307. For a narrative depiction of Jamaican posses in London in the 1990s, see Victor Headley's trilogy: *Yardie* (London: Pan, 1992), *Excess* (London: Pan, 1993), and *Yush!* (London: X Press, 1994). The Wild West trope continues to color West Indian youth subculture, both in the thematics of its music (e.g., Terry Ganzie's early 1990s dancehall hit, "Welcome the Outlaw") and in the popular iconography and dominant media's representation of West Indian—"Yardie"—criminal elements: an article on gang violence that appeared in the Manchester *Guardian* for June 2, 1993, is headlined, "London drug killings 'like gunfights at the OK Corral.'" And an investigative article on glamorous gun-slinging drug dealers by Duncan Campbell and Joseph Harker quotes a London merchant: "They [the youth emulating these outlaws] don't mind that these people are wrecking young lives through drugs and violence, they see them like modern-day Wild West cowboys," (*Guardian,* 22 October 1993).

24. Daniel Defoe, *Review of the State of the English Nation* (New York: Facsimile Text Society / Columbia Univ. Press, 1938).

25. Defoe, *Captain Singleton,* 153.

26. Robert Ritchie, in his biography of Captain Kidd, whose career careened from pirate to privateer to pirate-taker and back again, ending in his execution, asserts: "By the end of the seventeenth century several types of piracy were discernible: officially sanctioned piracy, commercial piracy, and marauding. They were not mutually exclusive, and the ca-

reer of any given pirate might encompass all three" (*Captain Kidd and the War against the Pirates* [Cambridge: Harvard Univ. Press, 1986], 10).

27. Aphra Behn, *Oroonoko, or, The Royal Slave* (New York: W.W. Norton, 1973), 62.

28. John Gay, *Polly*, in *The Poetical Works of John Gay*, ed. G. C. Faber (New York: Russell & Russell, 1926), 533–91. See Robert G. Dryden, "John Gay's *Polly*: Unmasking Pirates and Fortune Hunters in the West Indies," *Eighteenth-Century Studies* 34 (2001): 539–57. At first I thought that "Morano" was simply a misspelling of *moreno*, a brown man, or Negro. But the problematic "a" where Spanish gives an "e" makes the name resonate as well with this word for hog, *marrano*, the etymological root often assumed for Maroon in the eighteenth century. See discussion below.

29. The characterization of the merchant navy and the sugar plantation as proto-industrial institutions is fairly common. Two of the best discussions of this are in Rediker, *Between the Devil and the Deep Blue Sea*, and Sidney Mintz, *Sweetness and Power: The Place of Sugar in Modern History* (New York: Viking, 1985), 53–61.

30. Linebaugh and Rediker, *Many-Headed Hydra*, 173.

31. Norman C. Stolzoff, *Wake the Town and Tell the People: Dancehall Culture in Jamaica* (Durham, NC: Duke Univ. Press, 2000), 166.

32. Ibid., 164.

33. Faye V. Harrison, "The Politics of Social Outlawry in Urban Jamaica," *Urban Anthropology* 17 (1988): 274.

34. Douglass Hall, *In Miserable Slavery: Thomas Thistlewood in Jamaica, 1750–86*, Warwick University Caribbean Studies (London: Macmillan, 1986), 14.

35. "The word became incorporated into the West Indian vernacular until it came to be the verb for piratical punishment, the deliberate abandonment of an expendable person upon a desert island," according to George Woodbury, *The Great Days of Piracy in the West Indies* (New York: W.W. Norton, 1951), 128.

36. David Cordingly also makes this point in *Under the Black Flag: The Romance and the Reality of Life among the Pirates* (New York: Harcourt Brace, 1995), 137–39.

37. R. K. Kent, "Palmares: An African State in Brazil," *Maroon Societies: Rebel Slave Communities in the Americas*, ed. Richard Price, 3rd ed. (Baltimore: Johns Hopkins Univ. Press, 1996), 170–90, and Sidney Mintz, *Caribbean Transformations* (New York: Columbia Univ. Press, 1989), 78.

38. Richard Price points out the similarities among treaties made between the colonial governments of Spain, Portugal, and England and the Maroon communities in the territories they were trying to hold (*Maroon Societies*, 3).

39. John Masefield, *On the Spanish Main* (London: Methuen, 1925), 22–95; Price, *Maroon Societies*, 14.

40. Cordingly, *Under the Black Flag*, 28–29.

41. Masefield, *On the Spanish Main*, 79–80, 95.

42. These two waves of piracy are documented in, respectively, A. O. Esquemelin [Exquemelin], *Bucaniers of America* (London: William Crooke, 1684), and *A General History of the Pyrates*. For twentieth-century narratives of the buccaneers, see Masefield, *On the Spanish Main*, 106–217; Cordingly, *Under the Black Flag*, 26–55; Woodbury, *Great Days of Piracy*,

27–69; and Philip Gosse, *The History of Piracy* (New York: Tudor Publishing, 1946), 141–75. The second wave of pirates was generated when sailors serving in the Royal Navy were no longer needed and privateers serving the English military against the French were released from their commissions. According to Linebaugh and Rediker, these pirates were quelled because of the threat they posed to the slave trade (*Many-Headed Hydra* 169–72).

43. For the early connections among Jamaican Maroons, Amerindians, and buccaneers evident in their practices of curing meat, see Bev Carey, *The Maroon Story: The Authentic and Original History of the Maroons in the History of Jamaica, 1490–1880* (St. Andrew, Jamaica: Agouti Press, 1997), 66–76.

44. Price, *Maroon Societies,* 1–2.

45. Bryan Edwards, *The History, Civil and Commercial, of the British West Indies,* 5th ed. (London: T. Miller, 1819), 1:523.

46. Cordingly, *Under the Black Flag,* 39; Woodbury, *Great Days of Piracy,* 29–30.

47. See Mintz, *Caribbean Transformations,* "for most of the islands during most of their post-Columbian history, labor had to be impressed, coerced, dragged, and driven to work— and most of the time, to simplify the problems of discipline, labor was enslaved" (45).

48. Esquemelin, *Bucaniers of America,* 1:20–22.

49. Mintz, *Caribbean Transformations,* 49.

50. Esquemelin, *Bucaniers of America,* 1:74.

51. Joan Dayan, "Vodoun, or the Voice of the Gods," *Sacred Possessions: Vodou, Santeria, Obeah, and the Caribbean,* ed. Margarite Fernandez Olmos and Lizabeth Paravisin-Gebert (New Brunswick, NJ: Rutgers Univ. Press, 1997), 33.

52. Conversely, indenture could be meted out as punishment to those convicted of piracy, as it was on April 26, 1721, to Thomas How and his cohorts, who were indentured with the Royal African Company for seven years (Woodbury, *Great Days of Piracy,* 39–41).

53. Morgan himself became one of the biggest landholders in Jamaica, where he served as lieutenant governor. Late in his life he was knighted for his services to England (Cordingly, *Under the Black Flag,* 42–55).

54. R. C. Dallas, *The History of the Maroons* [1803] (London: Frank Cass, 1968), 1:xxx–viii.

55. Orlando Patterson, "Slavery and Slave Revolts: A Socio-Historical Analysis of the First Maroon War, Jamaica, 1655–1740," *Social and Economic Studies* 19.3 (1970): 290.

56. Edward Ward, *A Trip to Jamaica,* 7th ed. (London: J. How, 1700), and Orlando Patterson, *Sociology of Slavery* (London: MacGibbon & Kee, 1967; Rutherford, NJ: Fairleigh Dickenson Univ. Press, 1969).

57. Patterson, "Slavery," 289.

58. Patterson, *Sociology,* 260–83. See also Michael Craton, *Testing the Chains: Resistance to Slavery in the British West Indies* (Ithaca, NY: Cornell Univ. Press, 1982); for the Maroons, see Dallas, *History of the Maroons;* Carey, *Maroon Story;* Barbara Kopytoff, "The Early Political Development of Jamaican Maroon Societies," *William and Mary Quarterly,* 3rd Series, 35.2 (1978): 287–307; and Mavis C. Campbell, *The Maroons of Jamaica, 1655–1796: A History of Resistance, Collaboration, and Betrayal* (Granby, MA: Bergin & Garvey, 1988).

59. It is typical of the treaties other Caribbean Maroons made with colonial governments; see Price (*Maroon Societies,* 3–4).

60. "The Maroons, in manners and mode of speaking, are the same with the negroes; however there is no good will between them" (*Marly, or, A Planter's Life in Jamaica*, anon. [Glasgow: Richard Griffin & Co., 1828], 87–88).

61. Hall, *In Miserable Slavery*, 110.

62. Patterson, "Slavery," 317.

63. Marlon Regis, "Buju Banton: Journey to the Inna Heights," *The Beat* 17.4 (1998): 42–43.

64. My understanding of the notion of contemporary cultural marronage was enriched by a talk given by the Haitian author Edwige Danticat at a conference on Maroons held at Miami Dade Community College on September 26, 1997.

65. Edward Kamau Brathwaite, *Contradictory Omens: Cultural Diversity and Integration in the Caribbean* (Mona, Jamaica: Savacou, 1974), 31.

66. The first two lines of argument are made by Rediker, *Between the Devil and the Deep Blue Sea*. Peter Linebaugh discusses the sailor as an early proletariat in *London Hanged* 123–38. Building on Rediker's arguments, Christopher Hill emphasizes the democratic nature of pirate society, *Liberty Against the Law: Some Seventeenth-Century Controversies* (London: Allen Lane / Penguin, 1996), 114–22. Eighteenth-century literary scholar John Richetti reads the pirate tales, part fiction, part journalism and court documentary, in the *General History of the Pyrates* as an articulation of "the revolutionary implications of crime, the blasphemous logical extension of the secular habit of mind" and explores the dramatization of "the utopian possibilities of piracy" in Captain Misson's tale, "Travelers, Pirates, and Pilgrims," in *Popular Fiction before Richardson: Narrative Patterns 1700–1739* (London: Oxford Univ. Press, 1969), 60–118. With a breezy skepticism, Lawrence Osborne has dismissed all such cultural-historical investigations of piracy, asserting that ships are not societies and that any liberatory aspects of piracy are utopian fantasies projected by an intellectual left looking desperately for historical validation; see "A Pirate's Progress: How the Maritime Rogue Became a Multicultural Hero," *Lingua Franca* (March 1998): 35–42.

B. R. Burg constructs a case for the sodomitical nature of pirate society in *Sodomy and the Perception of Evil: English Sea-Rovers in the Seventeenth-Century Caribbean* (New York: New York Univ. Press, 1983), which Cordingly (*Under the Black Flag*, 100–103) evaluates as unsubstantiated. As discussed above, Hans Turley has argued for a comparison between the criminally sexual sodomitical subject and the more variously and ambiguously transgressive piratical subject, emphasizing, for example, the "homoerotic" bond between Defoe's Captain Singleton and his friend Quaker William (see above, note 2). For an account of female pirates, see Jo Stanley, ed., *Bold in Her Breeches: Women Pirates Across the Ages* (London: Pandora / Harper Collins, 1995).

67. Linebaugh and Rediker, *Many-Headed Hydra*, 143–73.

68. In *Many-Headed Hydra*, published after this chapter was drafted, Linebaugh and Rediker make the same point: "Indeed, pirate ships themselves might be considered multiracial maroon communities, in which rebels used the high seas as others used the mountains and the jungles" (167, n. 30). They make the point in passing and do not offer a sustained analogy.

69. Tobias Smollett, *The Adventures of Roderick Random*, World Classics (Oxford: Oxford Univ. Press, 1980), 139.

70. James Boswell, *The Life of Johnson*, World Classics (Oxford: Oxford Univ. Press, 1980), 246–47.

71. Rediker, *Between the Devil and the Deep Blue Sea*, 209, 247.

72. Ibid., 8.

73. Ibid., 263–64.

74. *General History of Pyrates*, 211–12.

75. Rediker makes this point about ship societies (*Between the Devil and the Deep Blue Sea*, 161). All the parallels with slave societies are my own. For the conditions of West Indian slavery, see, e.g., Patterson, *Sociology*; Edward Kamau Brathwaite, *The Development of Creole Society in Jamaica* (Oxford: Clarendon Press, 1971); and Richard S. Dunn, *Sugar and Slaves: The Rise of the Planter Class in the English West Indies, 1624–1713* (New York: W.W. Norton, 1973).

76. Boswell, *Life of Samuel Johnson*, 927.

77. John Fielding, *A Brief Description of the Cities of London and Westminster* (London: J. Wilkie, 1776), xv. I was alerted to this text by Linebaugh's citation (*London Hanged*, 135).

78. Rediker, *Between the Devil and the Deep Blue Sea*, 159.

79. Ibid., 162.

80. Edward Barlow, a late seventeenth-century sailor (ibid., 213).

81. Henry Fielding, *The Journal of a Voyage to Lisbon*, World Classics (Oxford: Oxford Univ. Press, 1997), 153–54; qtd. in Linebaugh, *London Hanged*, 135.

82. Boswell, *Life of Samuel Johnson*, 927.

83. *The Four Years Voyages of Captain George Roberts*, [Daniel Defoe?], Foundations of the Novel Series (New York: Garland, 1972), 60.

84. Edward Long, *The History of Jamaica*, 3 vols. (London: T. Lowndes, 1774), 2:354, 383.

85. Linebaugh, *London Hanged*,135. No global characterization of the nature of the relations between white seamen (pirates or sailors) and African peoples can stand; the relations were various and local. Black and white sailors worked side by side; white sailors were instrumental in the transportation of slaves; Africans joined pirate crews; pirates owned, stole, and sold African slaves. Maroons also owned slaves, though nominally forbidden to do so. In John Gay's *Polly*, a number of the slaves run off from a local plantation and join Morano/Macheath's pirate crew. What can be said is that sailors generally had more contact with Africans and African Americans than did others. See W. Jeffrey Bolster, *Black Jacks: African Seamen in the Age of Sail* (Cambridge: Harvard Univ. Press, 1997); for blacks in the Royal Navy, see N. A. M. Rodger, *The Wooden World: An Anatomy of the Georgian Navy* (Annapolis, MD: Naval Institute Press, 1986), 159–61. For blacks as pirates, see Linebaugh and Rediker, *Many-Headed Hydra*, 164–67.

86. Paul Gilroy, *The Black Atlantic: Modernity and Double Consciousness* (Cambridge: Harvard Univ. Press, 1993), 13. See Adam Potkay's and Sandra Burr's Introduction, where they discuss the circum-Atlantic lives and identities of Ukawsaw Gronniosaw, Quobna Ottobah Cugoano, and Olaudah Equiano: "As protean as their professional identities were, their 'national' characters were still more fluid, for in their repeated sailings across the Atlantic they led lives that were neither simply African nor American, West Indian nor British, but in succession all of these, and ultimately all of these at once," *Black Atlantic*

Writers of the Eighteenth Century: Living the New Exodus in England and the Americas (New York: St. Martin's Press, 1995), 2.

87. Gilroy, *Black Atlantic*, 4, 12–17.

88. J. L. Dillard, *All-American English* (New York: Random House, 1975), and *Black English* (New York: Random House, 1972).

89. Richard D. E. Burton, *Afro-Creole: Power, Opposition, and Play in the Caribbean* (Ithaca, NY: Cornell Univ. Press, 1997), 16.

90. Dillard, *All-American English*, 42, 3–76; *Black English*, 73–185.

91. This is amply observed by visitors to the island. Lady Nugent records examples of Creole spoken by white women of high social standing: "The Creole language is not confined to the negroes. Many of the ladies . . . speak a sort of broken English" (*Lady Nugent's Journal of Her Residence in Jamaica from 1801–1805*, ed. Philip Wright [Kingston: Institute of Jamaica, 1966], 98). See also, e.g., Charles Leslie: "For a Boy, till the Age of Seven or Eight diverts himself with the Negroes, acquires their broken way of talking, their Manner of Behavior" (*A New History of Jamaica* [Dublin: Oliver Nelson, 1741], 27); and J. P. Moreton who records, for their comic value, a number of instances of white Creoles, especially women, speaking such "broken English," in *West India: Customs and Manners* (London: J. Parsons et al., 1793), 105, 116, 117.

92. Names listed in Stanley, *Bold in Her Breeches*, 163. However, rather than reading names such as *Most Holy Trinity* and *Blessing* as evidence of pirate's devotion to "noble principles," as does Stanley, I would suggest that this is just another instance of the blasphemy for which pirates were notorious.

93. Kopytoff, "Early Political Development of Jamaican Maroon Societies," 292.

94. Barbara Lalla and Jean D'Costa, *Language in Exile: Three Hundred Years of Jamaican Creole* (Tuscaloosa: Univ. of Alabama Press, 1990), 12.

95. So R. C. Dallas asserts that the "Maroons, in general, speak, like most of the other negroes in the island, a peculiar dialect of English, corrupted with African words; and certainly understand our language"(1.92); whereas Bryan Edwards (note 45) refers to the mixture of Spanish, English and African languages in Maroon speech.

96. Mervyn C. Alleyne, *Roots of Jamaican Culture* (London: Pluto Press, 1988), 120–31. See Katherine Dunham's account of her stay with the Maroons. She waits, almost in vain, for some evidence of the traditional Coromantee language, dance, and song preserved in Obi and Myal rituals (*Katherine Dunham's Journey to Accompong* [New York: Henry Holt, 1946], esp. 128–37 and 145–48). Dunham visited the Maroon town of Accompong as a graduate student in anthropology during the 1930s when, according to her account, the Colonel of the Maroons, in a mistaken bid for cultural parity, was suppressing those features of Maroon culture, especially in music, dance and religion, associated with African "barbarity." Alternately, one might surmise that these traditions were being purposively withheld from the eyes of a foreigner.

97. Lalla and D'Costa, *Language in Exile*, 14. Nor would the presence of African language among the Maroons, in itself, distinguish them linguistically from plantation societies where enslaved Africans continued to use their native tongues alongside the Creole they had to learn.

98. Burton, *Afro-Creole*, 132.

99. Ibid., 6–9, 74, and: "In other words, I see cultural opposition in the Caribbean as double-edged to the extent that an (Afro-)Creole culture cannot, by dint of its very creole-ness, get entirely outside the dominant system in order to *resist* it (in de Certeau's sense of the word) and so tends unconsciously to reproduce its underlying structures even as it consciously challenges its visible dominance" (8).

100. Ibid., 135–36.

101. Gilroy discusses the maintenance of the term "tradition" (at the heart of which we often find Africa) in similar terms: "This would involve keeping the term [tradition] as a way to speak about the apparently magical processes of connectedness that arise as much from the transformation of Africa by diaspora cultures as from the affiliation of diaspora cultures to Africa and the traces of Africa that those diaspora cultures enclose" (*Black Atlantic*, 199).

102. Ibid., 37.

103. Burton, *Afro-Creole*, 136.

104. Campbell, *Maroons of Jamaica*, 20, 132–33; Anita Waters, *Race, Class, and Political Symbols: Rastafarians and Reggae in Jamaican Politics* (New Brunswick, NJ: Transition Books, 1985), 95–98.

105. Waters, *Race, Class, and Political Symbols*, 115–289, passim.

106. Clarke, *Jah Music*, 111.

107. Thanks to my colleague Guinn Batten for our discussion of this point.

Chapter 5. Privacy and Ideology

1. Frances Burney, *Evelina, or, The History of a Young Lady's Entrance into the World*, ed. Edward A. Bloom and Lillian D. Bloom, World's Classics (Oxford: Oxford Univ. Press, 1982). References to the text will be given parenthetically.

2. Literary critic Barbara Zonitch has isolated some related concerns in her study of Burney's novels: "What are the social ramifications of the demise of aristocratic domination . . . ? What happens to women faced with a shifting patriarchal rule, who are thus confronted with the need not only for security but also for a new social identity?" (*Familiar Violence: Gender and Social Upheaval in the Novels of Frances Burney* [Newark: Univ. of Delaware Press, 1997], 15).

3. Burney had written and burned a version of this story, *The History of Caroline Evelyn*, before she wrote *Evelina*. See Margaret Anne Doody, *Frances Burney: The Life in the Works* (New Brunswick, NJ: Rutgers Univ. Press, 1988), 35–37.

4. Jennifer A. Wagner emphasizes Evelina's, and Burney's, devotion to the preservation of personal privacy against social intrusion in "Privacy and Anonymity in *Evelina*," *Modern Critical Interpretations: Fanny [sic] Burney's "Evelina,"* ed. Harold Bloom (New York: Chelsea House, 1988), 99–109.

5. "McCartney [*sic*] is an arresting figure, for he is implicated in many of the novel's motifs of family violence: incest, parricide, and suicide. In McCartney's case, we see how the possibility of parricide and incest bespeak the confusion of familial roles (particularly children's), the internalization of social violence in the family, and the threat to family continuity" (Zonitch, *Familiar Violence*, 45).

6. Susan Staves, "*Evelina;* or, Female Difficulties," *Modern Philology* 4.1 (1976): 368–69; on the use of farce, see Doody, *Frances Burney,* 47–50.

7. Zonitch, *Familiar Violence,* 32.

8. Michael McKeon, *The Secret History of Domesticity: Public, Private, and the Division of Knowledge* (Baltimore: Johns Hopkins Univ. Press, 2005), 673.

9. "In the space between outward injustice and inward self-justification flowers the interiorized absolute of the ethical subject" (McKeon, *Secret History,* 152).

10. On the concept of "the devolution of absolutism" see ibid., 3–48.

11. Nancy Armstrong has argued that such a feminine subjectivity is produced by the English novel. While I concur with her emphases on the historical priority of discursive production, on the ways in which this type of subjectivity emerges from a field of complementary gender relations that supercedes older hierarchical structures, and on the ethical authority of this inward arena of consciousness and feeling, I hesitate to see it as so purely a feminine arena; see Armstrong, *Desire and Domestic Fiction: A Political History of the Novel* (New York: Oxford Univ. Press, 1987).

12. Doody, *Frances Burney,* 57.

13. Doody uses the telling phrase "social buccaneer" without further comment. I emphasize the culturally foreign and marginally legitimate status of Captain Mirvan as a sailor. It is tempting to see in Captain Mirvan, as Kristina Straub has, a Smollettian "comic" figure akin to Commodore Trunnion in *Peregrine Pickle* (1751) (*Divided Fictions: Fanny Burney and Feminine Strategy* [Lexington: Univ. Press of Kentucky, 1987], 60). However, whereas Smollett seems to affiliate generous sensibility and benevolence with the rough-hewn manners of the commodore, Burney distinguishes these traits much more nicely.

14. Doody, *Frances Burney,* 52.

15. See above, chapter 3.

16. Doody, *Frances Burney,* 44.

17. Evelina is astounded when her grandmother falls for the flimsy story about Du Bois being held by a country magistrate on suspicion of treason: "When I heard the letter, I was quite amazed at its success. So improbable did it seem, that a foreigner should be taken before a country justice of peace, for a crime of so dangerous a nature" (141). Madame Duval remains blinded by her passions in this as in all the circumstances of her life: "With all her violence of temper, I see that she is easily frightened . . . and so little does she reflect upon circumstances or probability, that she is continually the dupe of her own—I ought not to say *ignorance,* but yet, I can think of no other word" (141).

18. For an argument that modern bourgeois consciousness is produced through juridical and novelistic discourses, see Zomchick, *Family and the Law,* esp. 10–11.

19. "Evelina's terrors seem more immediate and more real. The God who was a shield and bulwark to Richardson's heroines is outside her awareness" (Staves, "*Evelina;* or, Female Difficulties," 371).

20. The reference to a "time to come" during which Sir Belmont will suffer for his transgressions is one of the few instances in the text that may refer to divine judgment. But then again, the reference is ambiguous and may simply refer to some inevitable, if far distant, clarification of his relation to Evelina in this life.

21. As Gina Campbell notes, "although the reformation of rakes was a conventional

feminine temptation, it was notoriously dangerous"—even Sir Clement speciously promises to reform under Evelina's personal tuition ("How to Read Like a Gentleman: Burney's
Instructions to Her Critics in *Evelina*," *ELH* 57.3 [1990]: 572).

22. This narrative is exploited in Richardson's *Pamela* (1740), then explored and re-
jected in his *Clarissa* (1748) and *Sir Charles Grandison* (1753–54). It was debated on the
stage, most pointedly in Colley Cibber's *Love's Last Shift* (1696) and John Vanbrugh's sequel, *The Relapse* (1696).

23. McKeon, *Secret History*, 673–74.

24. Zonitch, *Familiar Violence*, 17, 36.

25. Mary V. Yates, "The Christian Rake in Sir Charles Grandison," *Studies in English
Literature, 1500–1900* 24.3 (1984): 558.

26. On the numerous editions and immense popularity of the novel, see Jocelyn Harris, Introduction, in Samuel Richardson, *The History of Sir Charles Grandison*, World's Classics (Oxford: Oxford Univ. Press, 1986), xii–xiv, and Sylvia Kasey Marks, *Sir Charles Grandison: The Compleat Conduct Book* (Lewisburg, PA: Bucknell Univ. Press, 1986), esp. 13–25.
On Grandison's influence in later fiction, see Gerard A. Barker, *Grandison's Heirs: The
Paragon's Progress in the Late Eighteenth-Century Novel* (Newark: Univ. of Delaware Press,
1985), and Gary Kelly, *The English Jacobin Novel* (Oxford: Clarendon Press, 1976), 192.

27. Marks, *Sir Charles Grandison*, 35–39.

28. James Boswell, *Life of Johnson*, ed. R. W. Chapman, World's Classics (Oxford: Oxford Univ. Press, 1980), 480.

29. Edward Hyde, Earl of Clarendon, *The History of the Rebellion and Civil Wars in
England*, ed. W. Dunn Macray (Oxford: Clarendon Press, 1969), 3:178–79.

30. Margaret Anne Doody, *A Natural Passion: A Study of the Novels of Samuel Richardson*
(Oxford: Oxford Univ. Press, 1974), 249–50.

31. Yates, "The Christian Rake," 554.

32. Ibid.

33. Ibid., 555.

34. Ibid., 548.

35. Barker, *Grandison's Heirs*, 36, 71.

36. Judith Lowder Newton, *Women, Power, and Subversion: Social Strategies in British
Fiction, 1778–1860* (Athens: Univ. of Georgia Press, 1981), 41.

37. See chapter 1 above, and Mackie, *Market à la Mode*, 144–46, 164–69, 187–89; King,
Gendering of Men, 220–27, 246–48, 257–59.

38. King, *Gendering of Men*, 223.

39. Newton, *Women, Power, and Subversion*, 41.

40. See Mackie, *Market à la Mode*, 186–202; King, *Gendering of Men*, 228–55; Kristina
Straub, "Colley Cibber's Fops: Actors and Homophobia," *Sexual Suspects: Eighteenth-Century Players and Sexual Ideology* (Princeton: Princeton Univ. Press, 1992): 47–68.

41. King, *Gendering of Men*, 228–30.

42. Zonitch discusses nostalgia at length in *Familiar Violence*, 17, 35–58.

43. William Godwin, *Caleb Williams, or, Things as They Are*, ed. Maurice Hindle (London: Penguin Books, 1988). All references to this text are made parenthetically.

44. Discussing the parallels between Godwin's Falkland and the seventeenth-century Royalist Lucius Carey, second Viscount Falkland, Gary Kelly notes the conventional analogies drawn by Godwin and his contemporaries "between the parties, doctrines, and personalities of the 1790s and those of the English Civil War" in *The English Jacobin Novel* (Oxford: Clarendon Press, 1976), 203. Ronald Paulson examines the revolutionary context of Gothic fiction in "Gothic Fiction and the French Revolution," *ELH* 48.3 (1981): 532–54.

45. Kelly, *English Jacobin Novel*, 192. Donald R. Wehrs notes how Falkland's rescue of Emily from Grimes echoes Grandison's rescue of Harriet Byron from Pollexfen in "Rhetoric, History, Rebellion: *Caleb Williams* and the Subversion of Eighteenth-Century Fiction," *SEL* 28.3 (1988): 501–4.

46. Godwin's treatment of the criminal gentleman through the Gothic and Revolutionary themes of "tyranny, prohibition, and transgression" produces an instance of that Gothic type, the "hero-villain," the "tormented tormentor" whose genealogy leads back to Milton's Satan and Richardson's Lovelace; see Kenneth W. Graham, *The Politics of Narrative: Ideology and Social Change in William Godwin's "Caleb Williams,"* AMS Studies in the Eighteenth Century, no. 16 (New York: AMS Press, 1990), 112–13.

47. Eric Rothstein, *Systems of Order and Inquiry in Later Eighteenth-Century Fiction* (Berkeley: Univ. of California Press, 1975), 211.

48. For the allusion to Lucius Carey, see Kelly, *English Jacobin Novel*, 201–3, and Rothstein, *Systems of Order*, 211–13. For the seventeenth-century Stuart orientation of Sir Thomas Grandison and his family, "all named in versions of Charles," see Morris Golden, "Public Context and Imagining Self in *Sir Charles Grandison*," in *Eighteenth Century: Theory and Interpretation* 29.1 (1988): 3–18. For Carey as a model for Sir Charles Grandison, see Doody, *Natural Passion*.

49. See David McCracken, "Godwin's *Caleb Williams*: A Fictional Rebuttal of Burke," *Studies in Burke and His Time* 37 (1969–70): 1442–52, and Kelly, *English Jacobin Novel*, 209.

50. William Godwin, *Enquiry Concerning Political Justice*, ed. Isaac Kramnick (New York: Penguin Books, 1985): "The Characters of Men Originate in their External Circumstances" is the title of 1.4.

51. Edmund Burke, *Reflections on the Revolution in France*, ed. J. C. D. Clark (Stanford: Stanford Univ. Press, 2001), 241.

52. To read Falkland's character as ethically "mixed" blunts this critique. Although, as literary critic Kenneth Graham says, "his inclinations are benevolent and yet his acts contradict his inclinations," Falkland's "contradictions" are not idiosyncratic, personally characterological, but symptomatic of his larger corporate identity; they are contradictions in the aristocratic ideology that shapes his character in perfectly necessary and consistent ways (Graham, *Politics of Narrative*, 199).

53. Robert J. Corber, "Representing the 'Unspeakable': William Godwin and the Politics of Homophobia," *Journal of the History of Sexuality* 1.1 (1990): 86–88.

54. King, *Gendering of Men*.

55. Jonathan H. Grossman remarks that Williams's "own life story sinks into the genre

that is framing it" (*The Art of Alibi: English Law Courts and the Novel* [Baltimore: Johns Hopkins Univ. Press, 2002], 45).

56. Hal Gladfelder looks at Caleb Williams's relationship with popular criminal discourses and at their articulation as principled dissent by Captain Raymond in *Criminality and Narrative in Eighteenth-Century England: Beyond the Law* (Baltimore: Johns Hopkins Univ. Press, 2001), xi, 1–5, 209–24.

57. See ibid., 210–11.

absolutism: and aristocracy, 2, 122; in Burney, 164; in criminal biography, 76; and fop, 176; and individual, 178; and individual sovereignty vs. outlaw, 11–12; and prestige, 120

Addison, Joseph, 10–11, 22, 87–88, 89, 91, 188; *The Spectator* (no. 128), 174, 175

aesthetics: and aristocracy, 10; in Boswell, 88, 89, 90–91, 93, 94, 96; and highwayman, 71; and Hind, 81; and rake, 35, 36; in Richardson, 61, 67

African culture, 127, 128, 131, 145–47

African diaspora, 26, 128, 131–32, 138

Ainsworth, William Harrison: crime/criminality in, 33, 73, 107, 109, 110, 111; criminal biography in, 110; highwayman in, 26, 71, 73–74, 97, 101, 102–4, 105–6; *Jack Sheppard*, 28, 32–34, 101–2; masculinity in, 67, 105, 110–11; nostalgia in, 73, 102–3; *Rookwood*, 12, 26, 67, 71, 73–74, 96–97, 100, 101, 102–4, 105–8, 113; working class in, 33, 34, 96

Applebee, John, 32

apprentices, 29, 30, 31, 32, 33, 34, 47, 48

Aretino, Pietro, *Postures*, 51

aristocracy: and absolutism, 2, 122; and aesthetics, 10; in Ainsworth, 33; in Burney, 151, 153, 154, 155, 163, 164, 168, 171, 176, 178; critique of, 13; in Defoe, 14; and gangs, 51; in Gay, 12; in Godwin, 27, 150, 179, 180, 183; and honor, 12; and ideals of refinement, 10; and masculinity, 10; and patriarchy, 9; and political settlement of 1689, 6; and rake, 38, 40, 41, 43, 45; and rank, 10; in Richardson, 61, 62, 64, 68, 70, 170; and Rochester, 49; sentiment against, 10; and sexuality, 2, 11

Auchenlick, Lord, 87

Austen, Jane, *Sense and Sensibility*, 159

authenticity: in Ainsworth, 107; of rake, 36, 49, 50, 51–52, 53, 54, 55, 62, 63; in Richardson, 62

authority, 1; in Ainsworth, 110; in Boswell, 73; in Burney, 177; and Charles I, 77; and Charles II, 41; in criminal biography, 75, 76, 77, 96; in Gay, 74, 83; in Godwin, 183, 184, 185, 189; and highwayman, 72, 97; and Hind, 81, 82, 83; and masculinity, 36; in Richardson, 62; in Rochester, 50; on ships and plantations, 142; and Stafford, 79–80, 82, 83; and subjectivity, 36–37

Baltimore, Lord, 42

Banton, Buju, 130, 138

Behn, Aphra, *Oroonoko*, 127–28, 202n17

Boswell, James: aesthetics in, 88, 89, 90–91, 93, 94, 96; and criminal biography, 73, 74, 96; criminality in, 16, 73, 85, 89, 90, 94–96; gentleman in, 73, 85, 90, 91, 94, 95–96; highwayman in, 22–23, 83, 84–85, 88, 89, 90, 91, 94; *The Life of Johnson*, 84; *London Journal*, 9, 16, 22–23, 73, 74, 84–96, 149, 150, 151, 155, 157, 188; Macheath in, 72, 73, 83, 84–88, 91, 92, 93, 94, 95, 96, 157; masculinity in, 84, 85, 86, 87, 88, 91, 94–96, 150, 151, 152, 155, 188; morality in, 16, 85, 88, 89, 90; self-fashioning of, 72, 149; and *The Spectator*, 85, 86–87, 88, 89, 91–92, 93, 94, 96; and *The Tatler*, 86, 88, 90, 94; theatre in, 86, 87, 90, 91, 92, 93, 94, 95

Bourdieu, Pierre, 53

bourgeoisie, 10, 83; in Burney, 153, 154, 162, 163; in Godwin, 180; in Richardson, 61, 62, 64

buccaneers, 131, 133, 134–36; social, 156, 157, 158

Buckingham, George Villiers, Duke of, 39
Burke, Edmund, *Reflections on the Revolution in
France*, 179, 182, 183
Burney, Frances: aristocracy in, 151, 153, 154, 155,
163, 164, 168, 171, 176, 178; bourgeoisie in,
153, 154, 162, 163; crime/criminality in, 27,
150, 151, 152, 153, 157, 158, 160, 161, 162, 163,
168; *Evelina*, 7, 12, 27, 149–68, 172–75, 176–
78, 179, 185; family in, 151, 152, 157, 162, 163;
gender in, 173, 174, 175, 176, 177–78; gentleman in, 27, 151, 171, 173, 177; highwayman in,
149–50, 151, 154, 157, 158, 160, 161, 163, 164;
law/judicial system in, 161–63, 164–65, 168,
172; manners in, 149, 152–54, 156, 159, 174,
175; masculinity in, 149, 150–51, 152, 153, 155,
156, 157, 158, 164, 175, 176, 177–78; morality in, 152, 155, 166, 172; paternalism in, 27,
175, 178; paternity in, 151, 152, 162, 165–66,
167–68; patriarchy in, 151, 153, 154, 156, 157,
162, 167, 175, 177, 178; prestige in, 149, 150,
153, 164, 175; rake in, 149, 151, 152, 154, 166,
167, 178; sensibility in, 149–50, 152, 153,
154, 162–64, 166–67, 168, 171; sentimental
discourse in, 27, 155, 165–66, 168, 172, 179;
sexuality in, 151, 152, 153, 154, 157, 158, 159,
171, 173, 175; women in, 151, 152, 153, 154, 156,
157, 158, 160, 162, 173–74, 175

Carey, Lucius, Viscount Falkland, 169, 170
Caribbean, 4, 121, 125, 132, 133, 135, 145–46
Cavalier, 12, 31, 73, 77–78, 79. *See also* royalists
character, 21, 22, 23, 35, 37, 84
Charles I, 5, 41, 67, 76, 77, 80, 82, 179
Charles II: authority of, 41; and Duval, 83, 96;
financial insecurity of, 50; and Hind, 82; and
libertine culture, 11; and morality, 38, 39;
restoration of, 5, 77; and Rochester, 48, 49,
50, 51; and sexuality, 42, 50
chivalry, 27, 179, 182, 183, 185, 190
civility, 7, 10, 39, 40, 98, 114, 116
Clarendon, Edward Hyde, Earl of, 169, 170
class: in Boswell, 90, 95; and crime, 46–48,
102; and gentleman, 6; and pirates, 116; and
prestige, 17; and rake, 37; in Richardson, 61;
and sexuality, 7; and social dominance, 7; in
West India, 124
colonialism: in Caribbean, 125; and labor, 142;
and Maroons, 122, 128, 136–38; and merchant

navy, 140; and pirates, 121, 128, 131; and Rastafarians, 122; resistance to, 129
conduct literature, 1, 13, 114, 154, 169
Courvoisier, B. F., 32, 102
crime/criminality: in Ainsworth, 33, 73, 107,
109, 110, 111; apology for, 59; in Boswell, 16,
73, 85, 89, 90, 94–96; in Burney, 27, 150,
151, 152, 153, 157, 158, 160, 161, 162, 163, 168;
and business, 28, 29; and Charles I, 77; and
class, 46–48, 102; in criminal biography, 75;
in Defoe, 13, 14, 15–16, 20; demotic, 47, 48;
and Duval, 84; exceptionalism of elite, 46–48,
51, 66; and gentleman, 2, 13, 150; in Godwin,
2, 23, 27–28, 150, 179–80, 181, 182, 183, 185,
187, 188–91; and heroic language, 48–49;
and highwayman, 73; and Hind, 80–82; in
Hogarth, 52–53; and ideology, 47; and labor, 3;
and law, 47; and Maclane, 105; and manners,
4; and masculinity, 4, 43, 49; and Mohocks,
56–57, 58–59; and picaresque novel, 25; and
pirates, 114; and prestige, 1, 2, 12, 49; and
rake, 26, 35, 36, 37, 39, 40, 41, 43, 45–46, 48,
51, 52–53, 56, 59; in Richardson, 46, 61, 62,
63, 64, 65, 66–67, 68–69, 70, 162, 170, 171;
and sensibility, 27; in sentimental discourse,
27; social, 48; and spiritual biography, 25; and
Stafford, 78, 79, 80, 82; and status hierarchies, 16; and Tosh, 127; in Twain, 112
criminal biography, 1–2, 3–4; in Ainsworth, 110;
authority in, 75, 76, 77, 96; and Boswell, 73,
74, 96; and Defoe, 15, 16, 21, 150; and Gay, 74,
96, 97; in Godwin, 181, 183, 187–88, 190; and
highwayman, 71, 72; individual and narrative
in, 74, 75–76; and morality, 96, 126; and
pirates, 122; in Twain, 112
Cromwell, Oliver, 5, 134
Cruickshank, George, *Jack Sheppard*, 28, 32–34
Cudjoe, Colonel, 132–33

Defoe, Daniel, 29–30, 114, 126; *Captain Singleton*, 117–20, 126; *Colonel Jack*, 10, 13, 15–16,
17–21, 149, 152, 185; *The Compleat English
Gentleman*, 10, 13, 14–15, 16, 20, 21; *Robinson
Crusoe*, 76, 118–19, 132–33
Digges, West, 87
dissent, 25, 27, 121, 122, 123, 127, 149, 188
domestic sphere, 33, 34, 174. *See also* family
Dorset, Charles Sedley, Earl of, 39

Drake, Francis, 133, 136

Dryden, John, 41–42, 58

duel, 204nn37, 45; in Burney, 154, 163, 164, 168, 176; in Defoe, 17, 18–19; in Godwin, 182; and Maclane, 105; in Richardson, 69–70; in Steele, 54

Duval, Claude, 72, 77, 82–83, 84, 96, 103, 112

effeminacy, 8, 45, 104, 175, 177. *See also* femininity; women

Eglington, Lord, 87, 93, 105

The English Theophrastus, or, the Manners of the Age, 21

Esquemelin, Alexander, *Bucaniers of America*, 135

Etherege, George, 51; *Man of Mode*, 44–45, 54

family: in Ainsworth, 33, 34; in Burney, 151, 152, 157, 162, 163; in Godwin, 186; mutuality in, 174; and patriarchy, 6; in Richardson, 169, 170–71

femininity, 8, 43, 116, 156, 175, 177. *See also* effeminacy; women

Fielding, Henry, 29, 30, 142–43

Fielding, John, 141

fop: Addison on, 175–76; and Burney, 27, 151, 176–77, 178; and gentleman, 9; and masculinity, 22; and pirates, 115; and prestige, 5; and rake, 37, 43–45, 48, 53, 116

gangs, 123, 125, 127, 128, 129, 147–48

Ganzie, Terry, 129

Garvey, Marcus, 138

Gay, John: aristocracy in, 12; *The Beggar's Opera*, 9, 12, 16, 22, 29, 30, 31–32, 58, 71, 72, 73, 74, 77, 83, 84–85, 86–87, 88, 91, 92, 93, 95, 96, 97, 126, 128, 157; and Boswell, 73, 84–85, 86–87, 88, 91, 92, 93, 95, 157; *The Mohocks*, 35, 36, 55, 56–57, 58, 59, 65, 88, 91, 95; *Polly*, 128; and Sheppard, 31, 32; and Wild, 29, 30, 32

gender: Addison on, 175; in Burney, 173, 174, 175, 176, 177–78; and gentleman, 3, 7; hierarchical model of, 16; and highwaymen, 3; and identity, 7–8; ideology of, 24; naturalized as sex, 7; and pirates, 3, 115, 116; and rake, 3, 55; in Richardson, 60, 61; and subjectivity, 7–8, 36, 37. *See also* sex/gender system

General History of Pyrates, "Of Captain Bartholomew Roberts," 140

gentility: in Burney, 152, 163; in Defoe, 15, 16, 19, 20, 21; in Godwin, 180, 189

gentleman: in Ainsworth, 73; in Boswell, 73, 85, 90, 91, 94, 95–96; in Burney, 27, 151, 171, 173, 177; characteristics of, 1, 6–7; and class, 6; and codes of conduct, 13; and crime/criminality, 2, 13, 150; in Defoe, 13, 15, 16, 17, 19–20, 21; and Duval, 83; and fop, 37, 45; gallant, 80; in Gay, 95; and gender, 3, 7; in Godwin, 2, 23, 27, 179–80, 181, 182; and hegemonic masculinity, 5; and highwayman, 23, 73; and Hind, 81; and law, 6; and manners, 7; masculinity of, 1, 44; and morality, 44; and myth, 23; and patriarchy, 23; and pirates, 23, 115; and rake, 9, 23, 37, 39, 43, 45, 54, 121; in Richardson, 62, 67, 169, 170, 182; self-discipline of, 1, 9; sexuality of, 8–9; social vs. moral meaning of, 13–14; and Stafford, 79, 80; status of, 7; in Steele, 169; subjectivity of, 7, 44; Turpin as, 98, 99, 101. *See also under* highwayman

George I, 20

Glorious Revolution, 1, 5, 6, 9, 10, 11, 38, 56

Godwin, William: *Caleb Williams*, 2, 23, 27, 149, 150, 179–91; *Enquiry Concerning Political Justice*, 179

Goldsmith, Oliver, *She Stoops to Conquer*, 43

gothic, the: in Ainsworth, 73, 74, 96, 103, 104, 108–9, 110–11; in Godwin, 2, 27, 179, 183

heterosexuality, 9, 11, 45, 115, 116, 117, 180, 181

highwayman: in Ainsworth, 26, 71, 73–74, 97, 101, 102–4, 105–6; and authority, 72, 97; in Boswell, 22–23, 83, 84–85, 88, 89, 90, 91, 94; in Burney, 149–50, 151, 154, 157, 158, 160, 161, 163, 164; Cavalier, 26, 77; celebrity, 65; in Defoe, 15, 16, 17, 19–20, 21; in Gay, 9, 12, 22, 31, 71, 72, 83, 97, 126, 128; gentleman, 4, 15, 16, 17, 19–20, 21, 72–73, 74, 77, 83, 85, 91, 97, 100, 101–8, 164; and gentleman, 1, 23, 73; in Godwin, 189; and hegemonic masculinity, 5; Hind as, 81; Maclane as, 105; and masculinity, 72, 73; and morality, 73; and myth, 23; and nostalgia, 11, 73, 101, 121; and pirates, 115; and prestige, 73; and print culture, 24; and sexuality, 77; social context of, 71, 72; Stafford as, 77–80; Turpin as, 99, 100, 101; in Twain, 111, 112; and Wild-Sheppard legend, 28–29

Hind, James, 25, 72, 77, 80–82, 83, 96

historical romance, 67, 72, 73, 96, 102, 103, 108
Hogarth, William, 31; *The Harlot's Progress*, 43; *Industry and Idleness* series, 32, 53; *The Rake's Progress*, 43, 52–53
homosexuality, 3, 115, 117, 118, 183
honor: and aristocracy, 12; in Defoe, 15–16, 17, 18, 19, 20; and duel, 18; in Godwin, 27, 150, 179, 180, 181, 182–83, 186; inherited, 6, 10, 14, 15, 17; masculine codes of, 8; and morality, 20; and rake, 45; in Richardson, 170–71; in Rochester, 49; as status, 16

individual, 54; absolute, 178; in Ainsworth, 73, 74; in Burney, 150, 155; in Richardson, 64; sovereign, 12–13, 37, 64, 155, 163, 164

Jacobites, 10, 11, 20, 21, 103
Jamaica, 123, 136–37, 143–44, 145, 147
James II, 6
Johnson, Charles, 77
Johnson, Samuel, 84, 87, 140, 141, 142, 169

labor, 2, 3, 34, 121; in Caribbean, 133, 135; and colonialism, 142; in merchant navy, 139, 140; on ships and plantations, 141. *See also* working class
Lamb, Charles, 38
Laqueur, Thomas, 7
law / judicial system: in Burney, 161–63, 164–65, 168, 172; complicity of outlaws with, 4, 114, 125, 126–27, 137; and crime, 47; in criminal biography, 75, 76; in Defoe, 13, 17–18; against dueling, 18; in Gay, 83; and gentleman, 6; in Godwin, 27, 179, 181, 185–86, 187, 189, 190–91; and Hind, 82; and Maclane, 105; and patriarchy, 6; in postcolonial world, 131; and rake, 38, 46, 54; in Richardson, 62, 63–70; and Stafford, 79–80
Lewis, Paul, 91, 92
Long, Edward, 142
Lyon, Elizabeth, 28

Macheath, figure of, 9, 31; in Boswell, 72, 73, 83, 84–88, 91, 92, 93, 94, 95, 96, 157; and Duval, 77, 83; and gallant highwayman, 12, 31–32, 71, 72–73, 77, 83
Maclane, James, 97, 101, 104–6
Manley, Michael, 123, 147

manners: ambiguity of term, 13; in Burney, 149, 152–54, 156, 159, 174, 175; changing trends in, 40; and crime/criminality, 4; in Defoe, 13, 21; and gentleman, 7; history of, 2; and morals, 13, 14; and pirates, 122; and prestige, 17, 27; and rake, 121; and reciprocity, 176; of Turpin, 98
Marley, Bob, 123, 138
Maroons: and African culture, 145, 146; and buccaneers, 134, 136; and colonialism, 128, 136–38; complicity with authorized powers by, 4, 122, 137, 147; cultural symbols of, 146; and gangs, 147; Haitian, 133; Jamaican, 133; and nostalgia, 122; origins of, 132–33; and pirates, 26, 121, 127–29, 133, 141, 147; resistance of, 144–45, 146; and slavery, 26, 132–33, 134, 135, 136–38, 141, 146; as subculture vs. counterculture, 130–31; as term, 134
marriage: Addison on, 175; in Burney, 157, 162, 166, 176, 177; in Defoe, 17; in Godwin, 180, 181; in Richardson, 42, 60
marronage, 127–28, 131, 138–39
Marshall, Bucky, 123
masculinity: in Ainsworth, 67, 105, 110–11; and aristocracy, 10; and authority, 36; in Boswell, 84, 85, 86, 87, 88, 91, 94–96, 150, 151, 152, 155, 188; in Burney, 149, 150–51, 152, 153, 155, 156, 157, 158, 164, 168, 175, 176, 177–78; and crime/criminality, 4, 43, 49; in Defoe, 152; and fop, 37, 45; in Gay, 83; of gentleman, 1, 44; in Godwin, 149, 179–80, 181, 183; hegemonic, 1, 5; and highwayman, 72, 73, 74; and Hind, 80; and myth, 23; and patriarchy, 24; performative, 87; and pirates, 114, 115, 116, 120; and politeness, 3; and prestige, 4, 121; and rake, 9, 36, 37, 41, 61, 121; in Richardson, 169, 170, 171; of rude boys, 124; and sexual difference, 2–3; and sexuality, 9, 120; and sociability, 3; and social relations, 8; social stereotypes of, 22; in *The Spectator*, 55; and subjectivity, 3, 8; in *The Tatler*, 55; of Turpin, 97, 99, 100; in Twain, 112; and violence, 4, 40
Massop, Claudie, 123
merchant navy, 26, 128, 139, 140, 147
Milton, John, 60, 61, 62, 63
mock-heroic, 49, 72, 85, 87, 90–91, 92, 94, 96
Mohocks, 47, 55–59, 88, 95, 157, 158
molly, 5, 8, 116–17

Monmouth, Duke of, 42

morality: in Ainsworth, 110; in Boswell, 16, 85, 88, 89, 90, 93; in Burney, 152, 155, 166, 172; and Charles II, 38, 39; and criminal biography, 96, 126; and criminal narratives, 25; in Defoe, 16, 20; in Gay, 83; and gentleman, 13–14, 44; in Godwin, 183, 187; and highwayman, 73; and Hind, 81; and honor, 20; and manners, 13, 14; and Maroons, 128; and pirates, 128; and prestige, 17; and rake, 41; in Richardson, 61, 62–63, 65, 170, 171, 172; and Stafford, 79–80

Morgan, Henry, 134–35

myth: and Ainsworth, 103, 111; in culture, 23–25; and highwayman, 71, 72, 74; and Maroons, 128; and outlaws, 38; and pirates, 114, 128, 131; and Turpin, 106

narcissism, 61, 63, 66, 116, 177

narrative, 74, 75–76, 79, 80, 81

nostalgia, 9–13; in Ainsworth, 73, 102–3; in Burney, 178; and highwayman, 11, 71, 73, 101, 121; and Maroons, 122; and pirate, 11, 12; and rake, 11, 12, 37, 41, 43, 55, 121; and Rastafarians, 122; in Richardson, 62; in Rochester, 49; and Stuarts, 38; and Wild-Sheppard legend, 28

Paine, Thomas, *The Rights of Man*, 179

paternalism, 27, 83, 170, 175, 178

paternity, 151, 152, 162, 165–66, 167–68

patriarchy: in Ainsworth, 74, 110–11; and aristocracy, 9; in Burney, 151, 153, 154, 156, 157, 162, 167, 175, 177, 178; and gentleman, 23; in Godwin, 182; and masculinity, 5, 24; and myth, 23; paternalistic, 24; and prestige, 2, 4–5; and rake, 9; reformulation of, 3, 9; in Richardson, 170, 171; and sentimental subject, 27; sexual difference, 7; shifting nature of, 5–6

patronage, 27, 150, 179, 180, 181, 183–84, 185

penal institutions, 27, 179, 186–87, 189

performativity/performance: and Boswell, 74, 87, 89; and fop, 44; and rake, 8, 35, 36, 44, 45, 53, 54, 59, 63; in Richardson, 62, 65, 67, 68–69

pirate(s): and absolute will, 121; and buccaneers, 134; in Burney, 157, 158; and capitalism, 147; of Caribbean, 4; and colonialism, 128, 131; and commerce, 126; complicity with authorized powers by, 4, 121, 127; and criminal biography, 2, 122; in Defoe, 126; democracy among, 139, 140–41; and Esquemelin, 135; and gangs, 147; in Gay, 128; and gender, 3; and gentleman, 1, 23, 115; and identity, 139; and labor history, 121; language of, 143; and Maroons, 26, 121, 127–29, 133, 141, 147; and marronage, 139; and masculinity, 5, 120; and merchant navy, 128, 139; and morality, 128; and myth, 23; and nostalgia, 11, 12; and personal sovereignty, 12; and print culture, 24; and rake, 120; and Rastafarians, 26, 121; and resistance and liberation discourses, 139; and Royal Navy, 26; and rude boys, 26, 121, 123–24, 125; and sexuality, 114–20; social context of, 71, 126; and subculture vs. counterculture, 129, 130–31; and violence, 120; and Wild-Sheppard legend, 28–29

plantation, 19, 26, 128, 133, 138, 141–43

politeness, 3, 10, 11, 17

Pope, Walter, 83

prestige: and absolutism, 120; in Ainsworth, 101, 110, 111; avenues to, 17; in Boswell, 155; in Burney, 149, 150, 153, 164, 175; and crime/criminality, 1, 2, 12, 49; in Defoe, 10, 13, 15, 19; and duel, 18; of Duval, 83, 84; of fop, 37; in Gay, 83; in Godwin, 27, 149, 150, 179–80, 181, 183; hierarchy of criminal, 101; and highwayman, 73; of Hind, 82; and manners, 27; and masculinity, 4, 121; and myth, 23; and patriarchy, 2, 4–5; of rake, 26, 35, 36, 37, 39, 43, 51, 53, 54, 55; and rank, 10; in Richardson, 61, 62, 66, 67, 68, 170; in Rochester, 49; of rude boys, 124; and sexuality, 10; of Stafford, 82; of Turpin, 100, 105; and Wild-Sheppard legend, 28

privateers, 4, 133–34

prostitution, 11, 43, 68, 90, 92, 94. *See also* women

rake: and absolute will, 121; and aesthetics, 35, 36; apology for, 26, 35–36, 43, 55, 56, 59, 60, 61; and aristocracy, 38, 40, 41, 43, 45; authenticity of, 36, 49, 50, 51–52, 53, 54, 55, 62, 63; authority of, 36; bisexuality of, 8; in Boswell, 96; in Burney, 149, 151, 152, 154, 166, 167, 178; character of, 35; and civility, 40; and class, 37; and crime/criminality, 26, 35, 36, 37, 39, 40, 41, 43, 45–46, 48, 51, 52–53, 56,

rake (continued)
59; and criminal biography, 2; and fop, 37,
43–45, 48, 116; in Gay, 35, 36; and gender, 3,
55; and gentleman, 1, 9, 23, 37, 39, 43, 45, 54,
121; and hegemonic masculinity, 5; heterosexuality of, 9, 45; and Hind, 81; in Hogarth,
52–53; and honor, 45; and hooligans, 51; and
imitation, 51–52; and individualism, 54, 64;
lack of feminine analogue for, 43; and law, 38,
46, 54; and manners, 121; and masculinity,
9, 36, 37, 41, 61, 121; and modern hooligans,
47; and Mohocks, 56; and morality, 41; and
myth, 23; and nostalgia, 11, 12, 37, 41, 43, 55,
121; as pathological, 63; and patriarchy, 9; and
performativity, 8, 35, 44, 45, 53, 54, 59, 63, 65;
and pirates, 114, 115–16, 117, 120; prestige of,
26, 35, 36, 37, 39, 43, 51, 53, 54, 55; and print
culture, 24; reformed, 9, 54, 58, 59, 63, 166,
167; and Restoration, 8, 43, 54; in Richardson,
21, 35, 41, 42, 43, 45, 46, 60–70, 166, 170, 171,
172; in Rochester, 45, 48–51; sentimental, 36,
54, 55, 58, 90, 172; and sexuality, 9, 11, 35, 45,
51, 116, 117, 120; social context of, 71; and social convention, 38; social performance of, 35,
36; sovereignty of, 68; and Stafford, 79; and
status, 35, 37; status of, 43, 55; in Steele, 9, 36,
52, 53–55, 56, 63, 165–66, 172; style of, 35, 36,
43–44, 45, 48, 53; subjectivity of, 35–36, 50, 55;
and violence, 40, 41, 56; and Wild-Sheppard
legend, 28–29
The Rake: or, The Libertine's Religion, 52
rank: and aristocracy, 10; in Burney, 154; in
Defoe, 10; and prestige, 10
rape: in Boswell, 94, 95; in Burney, 151, 160,
162; in Godwin, 180; in Richardson, 60, 65,
66, 67, 160, 162
Rastafarians, 128; and African culture, 145, 146,
147; and complicity with authorized powers,
4, 122; as counterculture, 131; misogyny of,
124; and nostalgia, 122; and pirates, 26, 121;
resistance of, 144–45; and rude boys, 127
Rebel, Tony, 130
religion, 162, 163, 164
Restoration court, 39, 40, 43
Restoration period, 11, 12, 38, 53, 54, 64, 72
Richardson, Samuel, 27, 179; Clarissa, 9, 11, 12,
21, 26, 35, 41, 42, 43, 45, 46, 60–70, 158, 160,
162, 171, 172, 180, 182, 185; crime/criminality

in, 46, 61, 62, 63, 64, 65, 66–67, 68–69, 70,
162, 170, 171; gentleman in, 62, 67, 169, 170,
182; morality in, 61, 62–63, 63, 65, 170, 171,
172; Pamela, 60, 170; rake in, 21, 35, 41, 42,
43, 45, 46, 60–70, 166, 170, 171, 172; sexuality
in, 63, 65, 66, 68, 172; Sir Charles Grandison,
12, 61, 62, 158, 169–72, 173, 176, 180, 182
Rochester, John Wilmot, Earl of: and apology,
35; The Disabled Debauchee, 48, 49, 56; and
Etherege, 44; independence in, 37; rake in,
48–51, 53, 60; A Ramble in St. James's Park,
49–51, 83, 120; self-authorization in, 21; self-
consciousness in, 11; skepticism of, 37
royalists, 12, 72, 77, 78, 79, 80. See also Cavalier
rude boys / rudies, 4, 26, 121, 123–25, 127, 128,
129–30
Russell, Lord William, 32, 102

sadism, 63, 65, 156, 157, 158, 159, 161
Scott, Sir Walter, 102, 103, 106, 107, 108
Seaga, Edward, 123, 147
sensibility, 7; in Burney, 149–50, 152, 153, 154,
162–64, 166–67, 168, 171; and criminality, 27;
in Richardson, 63
sentimental discourse: in Burney, 155, 165–66,
168, 172, 179; criminality in, 27; and Godwin,
179, 183; and Maclane, 105; in Richardson,
169, 179
sentimental subject, 12; authority of, 27; in Burney, 27; in Godwin, 27; in Richardson, 27
sex/gender system: and aristocracy, 2; hierarchical model of, 8; historical determination of,
7–8, 115; and pirates, 116; polarized difference
in, 3, 174. See also gender
sexual difference, 8; in Burney, 153, 175; and
complementary relations, 3, 45, 173; and masculinity, 2–3; models of, 16, 37; and patriarchy,
7; and pirates, 115; polarized, 45, 173; and rake,
9, 45; and reciprocal relations, 175
sexuality: and aristocracy, 11; in Boswell, 73, 90,
93; in Burney, 151, 152, 154, 157, 158, 159, 171,
173; and Charles II, 42, 50; and class, 7; and
Defoe, 118; in Dryden, 42; and Duval, 83; of
gentleman, 8–9; in Godwin, 180, 181, 183,
184; and highwayman, 77; and masculinity,
9, 120; and pirates, 114–20; and prestige, 10,
17; of rake, 8, 9, 11, 35, 45, 51, 116, 117, 120; in
Richardson, 63, 65, 66, 68, 172; in Rochester,

50–51; and rude boys, 124–25; in *The Spectator*, 10, 11; and Stafford, 78, 79; of Turpin, 100; and women, 24

Shaftesbury, Anthony Ashley-Cooper, Third Earl of, 10

Sharpe, Sam, 138

Sheppard, Jack, 28–29, 30–34, 101–2, 189

ships, world of, 139–40, 141–43, 156

slavery, 129; in Behn, 127–28; in Caribbean, 135; complicity with, 131; and Defoe, 132–33; as institution, 128; and language, 144; and Maroons, 26, 132–33, 134, 135, 136–38, 141, 146; and pirates, 131; and plantations, 141–43; resistance to, 129, 136–38

Smith, Alexander, 77

Smollett, Tobias, *The Adventures of Roderick Random*, 140

Spain, 133, 136

The Spectator: and Boswell, 85, 86–87, 88, 89, 91–92, 93, 94, 96; ethics of mutuality in, 10, 174; gentleman in, 169; masculinity in, 55; Mohocks in, 57–58, 59; rake in, 56; and Richardson, 170; social stereotypes in, 22

Stafford, Phillip, 72, 77–80, 81, 83, 96

status: in Burney, 153; among criminals, 16; in Defoe, 15, 19; of gentleman, 7; as historical accident, 14; honor as, 16; inherited, 14, 15, 54; of rake, 35, 37, 43, 55; in Richardson, 61; and social dominance, 7; in Steele, 53

Steele, Richard, 10–11, 172; and Boswell, 88, 90, 96; *Christian Hero*, 169; *The Conscious Lovers*, 169; and social stereotypes, 22; *Spectator*, 169; *Tatler*, 169; *Tatler* (no. 27), 9, 36, 52, 53–55, 56

stereotypes, 21–22, 23, 26, 73, 151, 152, 180

Stuart dynasty: and crime/criminality, 77; and Duval, 103; and Gay, 31; and highwayman, 72; nostalgia for, 9, 38; and rake, 37, 41; in Richardson, 11; and Stafford, 80

style: of fop, 43–44; of Hind, 81; of rake, 35, 36, 43–44, 45, 48, 53; in Richardson, 61–62, 67

subjectivity: and apologies for criminality, 59; and authenticity, 37; and authority, 36–37; in Boswell, 84, 86; in Burney, 154, 155; and culture, 23; feminine, 8, 27, 149, 151, 154, 155; and gender, 1, 7–8, 36, 37; of gentleman, 7, 44; internal, 23; male, 3; and masculinity, 3, 8; of rake, 35–36, 50, 55; in Richardson, 60, 62, 63; and social stereotypes, 26; in Steele, 62, 63

Swift, Jonathan, 70; *Polite Conversation*, 166–67; *A Tale of a Tub*, 38–39

The Tatler: and Boswell, 86, 88, 90, 94; gentleman in, 169; masculinity in, 55; Mohocks in, 59; rake in, 9, 36, 52, 53–55, 56; and Richardson, 170; social stereotypes in, 22

theatre: in Boswell, 86, 87, 90, 91, 92, 93, 94, 95; in Richardson, 67

theatricality: and crime/criminality, 65; and fop, 45; in Gay, 58, 59, 65; in Richardson, 65, 67, 68

Thistlewood, Thomas, 132, 137

Thornhill, John, 31

Tosh, Peter, 123, 125, 127, 147

Turpin, Dick, figure of, 74, 96–111, 112, 113, 190

Twain, Mark, *Huckleberry Finn*, 111–13

Villiers, William, Viscount Grandison, 169, 170

violence: in Burney, 149, 153, 156, 157, 158, 160, 161, 163, 165; in Defoe, 126; and duel, 18; in 18th century, 39–40; as elegance, 48; and gangs, 147–48; and hooligans, 47; and masculinity, 4, 40; and Mohocks, 56, 57; and pirates, 114, 117, 120; and rake, 40, 41, 56; of rude boys, 127; on ships and plantations, 141; upper-class, 47

Walpole, Horace, 31, 97, 104–5

West India, 4, 121, 124, 125, 128, 131

West Indies, 26

West Kingston, 4, 123, 127

Wild, Jonathan, 28–30, 187

will: absolute, 121, 189; individual, 73, 74; self-authorized, 172; sovereign, 18, 67, 178

women: in Boswell, 94; in Burney, 151, 152, 153, 154, 156, 157, 158, 160, 162, 173–74, 175; and Duval, 82, 83; in Gay, 83; and Maclane, 104, 105; as passive, 23–24; and Rastafarians, 124; in Richardson, 61, 62; and rude boys, 124–25; as sexually insatiable, 24; as spiritually idealized, 24; and subjectivity, 149, 151, 154. *See also* femininity; prostitution

working class: in Ainsworth, 33, 34, 96; and crime, 46, 47; and Sheppard, 101–2; and Sheppard-Wild legends, 28, 29, 30, 31. *See also* labor

Wycherley, 51

yardies. *See* rude boys / rudies